LOVING SPORTS

SPORTS

WHEN THEY
DON'T
LOVE YOU BACK

LOVING SPORTS

WHEN THEY DON'T LOVE YOU BACK

Dilemmas of the Modern Fan

**Jessica Luther and
Kavitha A. Davidson**

University of Texas Press, Austin

Requests for permission to reproduce material from this work should be sent to:
  Permissions
  University of Texas Press
  P.O. Box 7819
  Austin, TX 78713-7819
  utpress.utexas.edu/rp-form

♾ The paper used in this book meets the minimum requirements of ANSI/NISO
Z39.48-1992 (R1997) (Permanence of Paper).

Library of Congress Cataloging-in-Publication Data

Names: Luther, Jessica, author. | Davidson, Kavitha A., author.
Title: Loving sports when they don't love you back : dilemmas of the modern
fan / Jessica Luther and Kavitha A. Davidson.
Description: First edition. | Austin : University of Texas Press, 2020. | Includes
bibliographical references and index.
Identifiers: LCCN 2020005318 (print) | LCCN 2020005319 (ebook)
  ISBN 978-1-4773-1313-8 (cloth)
  ISBN 978-1-4773-2216-1 (library ebook)
  ISBN 978-1-4773-2217-8 (non-library ebook)
Subjects: LCSH: Sports spectators—United States—Attitudes. | Sports—Moral and
ethical aspects—United States. | Sports—Social aspects—United States. | Sports—
Economic aspects—United States.
Classification: LCC GV715 .L87 2020 (print) |LCC GV715 (ebook) | DDC
306.4/83—dc23
LC record available at https://lccn.loc.gov/2020005318
LC ebook record available at https://lccn.loc.gov/2020005319

doi:10.7560/313138

*Dedicated to every fan who loves sports
and just wants them to do and be better.*

CONTENTS

INTRODUCTION

We know why you are here, reading this right now: you love sports like we do, but like us, you often feel like sports don't love you back. But—and here's the real hurt—you don't know how to quit them. You are, instead, searching constantly for that middle space that allows you to quiet your conscience and indulge your fandom.

Sports are big business, and with that comes the dirtiness of any major moneymaking thing that holds cultural significance. You know that college athletes are exploited for their labor, but you also really love the roller coaster of March Madness. You are aware that violent hits to the head on the football field mean the players are sacrificing their bodies and brains—and sometimes they carry that violence off the field into their personal lives. Still, you love tailgating and a good, hard tackle is, well, a good, hard tackle. You get that the mascot of your team is a racist caricature of a Native person, but you've loved this team your whole life—long before you became aware of the mascot's problems. You understand why athletes are using their platforms to advocate for change within and beyond sports. But couldn't they just play the game you came here to see and give you a break from the ills of the world for a couple hours?

Welcome to our club for sports fans who care too much. It's exhausting here, but we can't leave. We don't want to.

Being a sports fan is often tiring. Part of what makes sports so wonderful is that you get to participate in a huge, emotional journey during every match and throughout a season, year after year. You can choose a side, root for a player or a team, feel the highs and lows of their heroics, cry with joy or sadness at the wins and losses.

Still—and we're going to be frank about this—the world of sports has long been an exclusionary space, barring athletes of color and/ or women and/or LGBTQ+ athletes from competing. If these athletes do find a way into this exclusive part of our culture, they face harassment and often suffer from a lack of resources. Any attempt they make to force sports to be more inclusive is branded negatively as bringing politics into games, casting blame upon those who are excluded for drawing attention to how the system was created and is maintained unfairly—rather than turning the spotlight on those who built the system and thrive within its strictures.

This exclusion bleeds over into fandom. There are certain people in our culture who are expected to be interested in sports, if not authorities on all things sports-related. Others, not so much. Take, for example, the woman fan who not only has to constantly swear on some holy book to the disbelievers (mainly men) that she actually cares about sports but who also is quizzed about her knowledge to prove it. The flip side of this is the man who cares not at all about sports. Jessica's husband doesn't follow sports (other than checking in to understand what she is watching or reporting on). He begs off the sports talk with other men, telling them to talk to his wife instead. Similarly, whenever Kavitha is at a bar watching sports, men who don't know that she's a sportswriter are often surprised to hear her comment on the game—surprised not just that she's knowledgeable, but that she's even interested in the first place. And if a patron asks the bartender something about sports, they immediately defer to Kavitha—much to the surprise of the guy asking the question.

Beyond that and perhaps more crucially, plenty of sports fans who are Black or brown and/or women and/or LGBTQ+ and/or from other marginal groups have played sports in Pee Wee leagues as children, or on high school teams, or on intramural or recreational teams—and they've experienced discrimination or bigotry as an athlete. When these fans watch collegiate or professional or international sports, they see the same forces at work, just with more prestige, money, and media behind it all. They also see the injustices present throughout our society reflected back in the sports they care about: players yelling homophobic slurs at opposing players on the pitch, male athletes being marketed exhaustively and paid a hundred times more than women athletes, white "owners" (a loaded term if there ever was one given the racial makeup of America's most profitable sports leagues) exploiting the labor and bodies of Black players.

Fans love sports, but it's unclear if sports love them back. *You* love sports, but do sports love you back? This is the ultimate truth about the long history and the current state of sports and politics. As Kavitha once wrote for espnW: "When you think about it really, the division between sports and politics has long been eroded. The separation is what takes effort to uphold—and it's mostly done by people whose right to exist in this space isn't questioned."

The "stick to sports" mantra has been repeated time and again by fans who view sports as a form of pure escapism, which is understandable. But the reality for many fans—and players—is that sticking to sports has never really been an option—particularly for people whose mere participation in competition can be seen as a radical act in itself.

This also belies history. Jesse Owens won four gold medals at the 1936 Summer Olympics in Berlin and upended Hitler's plans to use the Games as a showcase for the supremacy of the Nazi agenda and the Aryan race. John Carlos and Tommie Smith raised their fists on the medal podium at the 1968 Summer Olympics in Mexico City, creating one of the most indelible images in sports and in civil rights history. And the legendary matchup of the underdogs versus titans at the 1980 Winter Games in Lake Placid between the US men's hockey team and Russia (the "Miracle on Ice") became a proxy battle during the Cold War.

And so, when the International Olympic Committee (IOC) specifically banned protests—including kneeling and hand gestures—ahead of the Tokyo Summer Olympics, it did so with the intent of upholding sports as an arena of unity with little acknowledgment of how sports has sowed division. The US women's soccer star Megan Rapinoe's response to this directive: "We will not be silenced."[1]

————

The chapters in this book represent "separate moral dilemmas that get at different features of people's sensitivities, whether it's race, gender, class—and trying to minimalize it so you can stay consistent with your team's sport," says Dr. Susan K. Whitbourne, a developmental psychologist and professor at the University of Massachusetts–Amherst who is an expert on the psychology of sports fandom. "In the broadest sense, this is cognitive dissonance writ large. You've got competing sets of attitudes, values and behavior. And in the worst case scenario," she offers, "everything is in conflict, and individual team members are engaging in bad behavior that you cannot condone and then you try to somehow come up with a way to rationalize it. People are willing to suspend disbelief to allow their identification as a fan to continue unsullied."[2]

To be sure, cognitive dissonance isn't unique to sports—it's something music and film fans struggle with, too. "It's just more intense in sports because of all the other things about fandom," Whitbourne contends—things like pride in our communities, or early memories of our first game with our grandparents, or the emotional highs and lows of a back-and-forth game. Because sports allegiances are largely built early in life, they're not only harder to break but also more ingrained in who we are and where we come from.

"It depends on where the core of your identity is coming from. And for sports, it's huge," she says.

> And it's partly, I think, because the fandom does develop at a time that people are . . . starting to form their sense of identity. I tend to think that some of this—and I'm using the word carefully —is "inherited," not genetically, obviously, but you absorb it from your family. I know that the origins of a lot of fandom is that it's associated with family events, family culture. And so then that becomes kind of a defining set of events within your family at a time when you're growing up.

And the traits we inherit from our families can be good or bad, positive or negative, healthy or unhealthy. These traits can include positive, healthy attitudes toward fandom (such as rooting for the home team) or negative, unhealthy attitudes toward fundamental aspects of sports in the modern age (begrudging women's participation in traditionally male sports, for example, or expressing outright prejudice toward LGBTQ+ athletes). Thus, the way we tolerate sports is akin to the way we tolerate family members—because sports are, as Whitbourne tells us, so closely linked to family. In some cases, our teams even feel like family.

Moreover, the inherent nature of watching sports—the ebbs and flows of a game and of a season—contributes to this difficulty. "The difference between sports and everything else is that the outcome," as Whitbourne says, "is not predetermined in a game. And so that unpredictability arouses the emotions more, and means that the outcome will bring you up or bring you down that much more." "For some sports fans, [winning versus losing] actually is the difference between a happy and an unhappy day, week, month, year, [or] decade."

Similarly, the thought process of denial is hard-wired into sports fans—even before any moral considerations come into play. Whitbourne explains it this way: "I think sports fans are pretty good at denial. I mean, in a way, you kind of practice it because it's very adaptive, because then you can always look for a million excuses as to why your team lost rather than you having to confront it. So you're kind of rewarded for using denial because it's so much a part of being a sports fan."

———

This book is about embracing that such denial exists and figuring out what to do with it. It's about the intersections between sports and politics, sports and culture, sports and our own identities, sports and the ills of our world. We want to sit in those intersections, interrogate the status quos, and question how we—all of us, whether you are a casual or die-hard sports fan—should respond. Where and how do we draw the lines, especially as a fan who often feels unloved by our beloved sports?

Each chapter in this book tackles (get it?) a different issue within sports. Not every issue and not every sport is represented in these pages; we are human, and there is only so much time in a day. But we hope you can pull from these pages different ways to think more critically and deeply about these games we all spend so much time watching and about which we care so much. Many of the issues we discuss in tennis can be applied to, say, golf, and the dilemmas football fans face when it comes to brain injury are also felt by fans of boxing and hockey. Every town with a publicly funded stadium has felt the political and economic pressures that come with building that facility. And every fan has a bone to pick with their owner.

Also, we admit that this book is not full of solutions. Sorry! If we had the answers to the major systemic problems we discuss in these pages—racism, sexism, homophobia, class inequities, among many others—that would be a hell of a get. Truth be told, there is no single solution for how to be a sports fan because there *is* no single sports fan. We all contribute different identities and experiences to fandom. Each of us meets these moral dilemmas in distinct ways. Sometimes we ignore them, and sometimes we leave them behind. Often we may find ourselves somewhere in between.

Finally, we want to acknowledge that this book was drafted in the years leading up to the COVID-19 pandemic and it went to print while much of the world was still on lockdown in an attempt to stop the virus's spread. We are not sure what the world, much less sports, will look like in the next few weeks, months, and even years. We believe that makes this book more important than ever.

It was not lost on us that the pandemic touching sports is precisely what made this real to a lot of people in the United States. Businesses didn't start to close, cities didn't start shutting down, this didn't register nationally, until the NBA decided to suspend play after Utah Jazz center Rudy Gobert tested positive for COVID-19. And as the pandemic has unfolded, there have been discussions about inequity in healthcare as baseball players debated getting elective Tommy John surgery at a time when many couldn't access basic medical care; Stephen Curry used his Instagram account to do a live interview with Dr. Anthony Fauci, the director of the National Institute of Allergy and Infectious Diseases; Megan Rapinoe and Sue Bird's quarantine videos were a needed relief for those of us stuck at home; and sports equipment companies like Bauer, New Balance, and Formula 1's Mercedes retrofitted their factories to produce personal protective equipment for frontline workers.

If you step back to take the 30,000-foot view, the COVID-19 crisis has amplified the idea that sports are not just sports and can never be.

Perhaps some details in this book will change when sports re-emerge post-pandemic, but the systemic issues we address here are not going away. If anything, we are worried that in a fervor to get back to sports in whatever way we can, people will be less critical of the teams, leagues, institutions, and organizations that bring sports to them. What will that mean for under-resourced or marginalized athletes, for women's sports, for how sports get covered and who covers it, for pro-labor stances, or for the anger against politics in sports? In short, what will it mean for those who already feel that sports do not love them back?

We hope this book starts conversations. We hope it inspires you to reassess how to think about sports. More than anything, we hope it helps you figure out *how* or even *if* you can love sports when sports don't love you back.

CHAPTER 1

WATCHING FOOTBALL WHEN WE KNOW (EVEN A LITTLE) ABOUT BRAIN TRAUMA

On December 10, 2017, the NFL's Houston Texans hosted the San Francisco 49ers. In the second quarter, 49ers linebacker Elvis Dumervil brought opposing quarterback Tom Savage down hard. Savage's head bounced off the ground. The TV cameras then caught Savage rolling onto his left side, his arms held perpendicular to his body, both of them shaking. This involuntary arm spasming is known as the "fencing response," which happens immediately after a brain injury and is a telltale sign of a concussion.[1] There were reports that he even spit up blood.[2] Savage was checked by the medical team, and then—who knows why—returned to the game for a three-and-out series during which he threw two incompletions. When the Texans' next offensive series came up, he fought to go back on the field but was denied.[3]

It's hard to understand why this NFL moment mattered more than others. It wasn't the time Carolina Panthers quarterback Cam Newton took four helmet-to-helmet hits in a September 2016 game against the Broncos. It wasn't when the Dolphins' Matt Moore took a hard helmet hit into his jaw in January 2017. That was the kind of hit that takes your breath away as a spectator and one from which it took Moore minutes to get up off the field. He quickly returned to play, and the team was later chastised (though not punished) by the NFL for missing the fact that Moore had been bleeding from his mouth. It wasn't even when the same Tom Savage—a week before Moore's hit and eleven months before he seized on the field—got clocked on a quarterback sneak. Savage was pulled off the field and was immediately met by the athletic trainer. After being evaluated in the locker room (you know where this is going), he returned for one play, where he took the snap and then a knee to end the half. Savage was reevaluated at halftime and pulled from any further action in that game.

It must have been the visible seizure in December 2017 that did it. Whatever it was, this time mattered. The NFL announced only a couple weeks later that the league was updating its concussion protocol, including a new rule that players like Savage who have a seizure or similar response to a hit must leave the game and cannot return.[4]

It's a wonder that there needed to be an actual protocol in place to know that a seizure on the field is not, in fact, okay. As *Sports Illustrated* pointed out in 2016, in the section of the NFL game operation manual that describes the concussion protocol, "the words 'clear visual evidence' appear in bold."[5] The referee saw it (he was standing right there and ran over to check on Savage). We all saw it.

We all see it every week on the football field, in fact. If you think about it at all, you realize that we see it in so many places: on the soccer pitch, in the big surfing waves, during BMX or snowboarding events, at cheerleading competitions, in hockey games, in the boxing ring, and on the lacrosse field.[6] Cyclists sustain the most concussions, hands down.[7]

We know these head injuries are objectively bad. We understand that football, especially at the professional level, is dangerous to athletes' brains. We know that collisions cause concussions and are a part of sports, especially popular contact sports (football, boxing, hockey), and anyone can see that what happened to Savage is bad. But how bad? What can we do to protect players both on and off the field? And if we can't protect them well enough, then what should we do?

————

There are two ways we often talk about traumatic brain injuries (TBIs): concussions and Chronic Traumatic Encephalopathy (CTE). These are really only two parts of a larger spectrum.

"CTE is a neurodegenerative disease that probably is at one far end of 'here's the worst stuff that can happen to you,'" says Patrick Hruby, a sportswriter who has covered brain trauma for so long and in such depth that it's safe to call him an expert on this topic. "But on the other end, it could be like, maybe you get a concussion, then you recover, [and] you're okay. But it also knocks you out of school for a semester. And your grades plummet and you deal with some depression."[8]

Concussions are mild TBIs. Imagine your head is an egg, the brain the yolk. No helmet will save you from brain damage because that's not the point of a helmet. "They're great at preventing skull fractures," Hruby says, but they can't protect that yolk from getting swirled. "I could put a steel cube around an egg shell, and you wouldn't be able to punch the shell and break it," he says, "but the yolk still shakes when it moves."

Sometimes there are obvious symptoms, such as the fencing response, vomiting, and headaches, or perhaps the person is dazed, their movements are clumsy, they feel dizzy, they are sensitive to light or noise, or they pass out. Sometimes the symptoms take a while to present and can persist. Things like fatigue, confusion, difficulty remembering, or difficulty concentrating may cause significant problems in the short term or long term. On top of that, there can be damage without any outward indicators. Subconcussive hits can happen from repeated hits to the head, but it's hard to know that they are happening or even their long-term impact because they don't produce concussions or concussion-like symptoms.[9]

All of this together (concussive and subconcussive hits) can lead to CTE, which Boston University's Chronic Traumatic Encephalopathy Center believes "is caused by repetitive brain trauma." That's not to say that if you suffer repetitive brain trauma that you will get CTE. It's a possibility, and a bad one. "The symptoms of CTE," the CTE Center says, "include memory loss, confusion, impaired judgment, impulse control problems, aggression, depression, anxiety, suicidality, parkinsonism, and, eventually, progressive dementia."[10] You often don't start showing signs until well after you've suffered the TBIs, and there is currently no way to diagnose CTE while you are alive. It takes a postmortem study of the brain to do that.

It's worth noting the use of the word "believe" in the CTE Center's description of what causes CTE. Despite all the scrutiny around brain trauma in sports since the early 2000s, there is still so much we don't know. In July 2017, the *New York Times* published a beautiful, scary piece about a study by Dr. Ann McKee, director of BU's CTE Center. McKee had examined the brains of 202 football players. "Of the 202 players, 111 of them played in the N.F.L.—and 110 of those were found to have" CTE. "The brains here are from players who died as young as 23 and as old as 89. And they are from every position on the field—quarterbacks, running backs and linebackers, and even a place-kicker and a punter." This is damning, but it's also hard to contextualize because many of the brains that end up on McKee's table are from players whose families thought their loved ones showed symptoms of CTE while alive. If only those who seem to have CTE are donating brains, then the brains studied are likely to have CTE.[11]

The answer is that we need more science. But sports organizations fear just that: if science proves that the sports these organizations oversee are directly responsible for brain degeneration, then they could be held legally liable. For example, the NFL has historically been at odds with scientists.[12] In 2012, the league donated $30 million to the National Institutes of Health as "an unrestricted gift." In the press release, the league stated that this money could very well fund research into CTE, concussions, "and the understanding of the potential relationship between traumatic brain injury and late-life neurodegenerative disorders, especially Alzheimer's disease."[13] Four years later, a congressional committee found that the NFL attempted to influence how the money was spent in order "to steer funding away from one of its critics."[14]

The science is happening, though—and well beyond Boston University. Dawn Comstock is a professor in the Department of Epidemiology at the Colorado School of Public Health. She has run the National High School Sports-Related Injury Surveillance System for more than a decade. It is modeled after the one the National Collegiate Athletic Association (NCAA) runs on the collegiate level. It tallies weekly reports from athletic trainers across the country, which

> include any injury sustained by an athlete during the week and include the athlete's age, height, weight and what position he/she plays, as well as the severity of the injury, where it occurred on the athlete's body and the final diagnosis. Trainers also take note of the location of the injury event, the amount of time the student has to rest and whether the injury occurred during practice or competition, which is taken into account along with the total number of practices and competitions during the week.[15]

From this system, Comstock and her colleagues gather data about concussions: which athletes get them, their symptoms, how they are managed after suffering a concussion, and how long their recovery takes.

Part of the ongoing struggle to understand the frequency and severity of concussions and other TBIs is that we have no nationwide way to monitor and study them.[16] This is why, Comstock says, discussions about concussions often fall within the sports realm. Between her high school surveillance system and the NCAA's collegiate one, there is data to look at, pore over, compare and contrast, and study. "We should be just as concerned with the health of the high school student that slipped and fell on an icy sidewalk or who was in a car crash as we should be about the football player or the ice hockey player. Unfortunately, almost all of the national attention on concussions over the last decade has been centered on sports."[17]

What we have learned since public scrutiny has been focused on concussions is that the more aware people are of brain trauma, then the more likely they are to report it. "We probably don't have that many more kids getting concussions today than we did in 2005," Comstock says, "but those kids who are getting a concussion today are much more likely to come to the attention of medical providers."

Overall, Comstock thinks things are getting better: "Even though concussion rates have gone up, we've seen a much broader array of symptoms being reported, which indicates that people are much more knowledgeable about what constitutes concussion signs and symptoms, and we've seen more appropriate clinical care of the student athletes with regards to when they're allowed to return to play."

One area that needs more work is the gendered differences in concussion reporting and recovery. Comstock says that "in every single study, consistently females have higher concussion rates than males." But she cautions that if anyone tries to tell you that they know why this is true, then they are lying to you. "It probably falls into a combination of two different factors. It could truly be biophysiological, meaning that there's something about the female body compared to the male body that means that females really are at increased risk." But Comstock says even those biophysiological reasons could be traced more to the strength of any given individual's neck muscles. What else could explain it? "Undoubtedly there are also sociocultural issues going on. There's a ton of really good research out there that says that women are just more willing to talk about their physical health than men are." Even when girls and boys have the same knowledge of concussions and an equal understanding of symptoms, girls report more often. In short, we live in a culture where girls are more likely to self-report.

"So if girls are more willing to report than boys, maybe boys are getting just as many concussions or," Comstock says, "heck, maybe they're getting more, but we don't capture those because they don't get reported and they don't get diagnosed." In the end, there's no easy, obvious answer to the gender difference. "It's probably a combination of both biophysiological and sociocultural answers," Comstock says.

What does this mean then when it comes to CTE, the truly scary degenerate brain disease? Football is mainly played by boys and men, and it is a powerful vacuum that sucks up a lot of fans' attention, conversation, and resources when it comes to this topic.[18] As sports journalist Lindsay Gibbs has reported: "there have only been two peer-reviewed journal articles on chronic traumatic encephalopathy that addressed female CTE, and both came in the early 1990s—and both women's brains were included in the studies by accident. Most of the studies about CTE are focused solely on male football and hockey players."[19]

Female athletes report more concussions than their male counterparts and are suffering severe brain trauma, too. US women's soccer legend and goalkeeper Briana Scurry's career ended in 2010 when she took a knee to her temple during a professional game. The hit resulted in a TBI and debilitating physical and mental symptoms that were relieved only through surgery a few years later.[20] In 2019, another US soccer legend, Brandi Chastain (famous for her sports-bra celebration at the end of the 1999 Women's World Cup), Chastain's former teammate Michelle Akers, and eighteen other top-tier female soccer players participated in a long-term study to try to determine if headers and collisions in the sport have detrimental cognitive effects. They are unsure if their memory loss and migraine headaches are a consequence of playing soccer.[21]

Additionally, to help fill in the gender gap when it comes to CTE research, a brain bank focused on women was announced in late 2017. "PINK Concussions and the National PTSD Brain Bank will work together to actively recruit women over the age of 18 to donate their brains to TBI and PTSD research," Gibbs reported in the same article. She notes that when Chastain announced in 2016 that she would donate her brain to Boston University after her death, "only seven of the 307 brains at the [associated Concussion Legacy Foundation] were from women."

In early February 2018, just before the start of the Winter Olympics in Pyeongchang, South Korea, three female Olympians announced they would be donating their brains to the Concussion Legacy Foundation so that their brains could aid in concussion and CTE research.[22] Canadian ice hockey rock star and six-time Olympian Hayley Wickenheiser, US Olympic bobsledder Elana Meyers

Taylor, and US ice hockey legend and four-time Olympian Angela Ruggiero are the latest group of women to make this pledge.

It's a start.

———

US figure skater Ashley Wagner (who retired in 2019) told ESPN in 2017 that she had suffered five concussions up to that point in her career. The worst one was "from a really bad fall in which I fell onto my back and my neck snapped and my head hit the ice. My body started to shut down on me entirely. It was bad enough that I would suffer from full-on body tremors, I could barely walk, I couldn't even speak through them. I would have heart palpitations." It affected her short-term memory, and she now struggles to remember choreography both mentally and physically. Wagner says the reason people in figure skating remain quiet about head injuries is that they don't want to derail their quest to make it to the Olympics, often the singular focus of these athletes. Ignorance is better than having to quit.[23]

Dave Mirra, a famous BMX rider, died by suicide in early 2016, and a few months later CTE was found in his brain. In the wake of this news, many riders started to wonder about their own brains and the possibility of degeneration given the extent of injury (one star said he had more than a hundred concussions in his career!).[24] But knowing is hard. "I go back and forth between wanting to know and not wanting to know [if I have CTE]," Jay Fraga, a former BMXer, told the *Guardian*. "I already feel lousy; what's it going to do to my emotional state to confirm the worst-case scenario?"[25]

For both players and their families, not wanting to know is a common response. Deana Simonetto, a sociologist and assistant professor in the criminology department at Wilfrid Laurier University, did her graduate work on the wives of Canadian Football League (CFL) players. Simonetto found that in talking to players, wives, and coaches, "there's still a sense of fear and anticipation for the research."[26] In part this is because there is still so much to learn and there isn't as much of a consensus around it as we imagine, especially not in Canada.

The University of Toronto has its own brain lab. It's run by Dr.

Charles Tator, a professor of neurosurgery at UT's Faculty of Medicine and director of the Canadian Concussion Centre. According to a piece in *The Walrus* about Tator and his lab: "Compared to the Boston researchers, Tator's team has found fewer incidents of CTE in the brains it has examined. In fact, says Tator, 'We've seen examples of people who've had multiple concussions but who don't have any evidence of the disease. Like, none.'"[27]

The CFL's version of football is slightly different than the American version played in the NFL. A hybrid of football and rugby, it has a slightly larger field than its American cousin. The CFL plays with three downs instead of four, and so teams rely more heavily on the passing game to move the ball downfield more quickly. There is more distance between the linemen at the line of scrimmage in CFL games, and so the linemen tend to be smaller than their NFL counterparts.

Coupling Tator's lab's research and these differences in the style of play, some claim that the CFL's is the safer version of football. That could help explain why the Toronto lab's findings are different than what Ann McKee's crew at Boston University has seen. It's also convenient reasoning; this may be why the CFL, unlike the NFL, still won't admit to any link between the game and long-term brain damage. (Also, the CFL has a lot less money and perhaps would not survive the legal fallout from such an admission.)[28] Still, it's the CFL and not the NFL that made changes in 2017, according to the *New York Times*, barring "players from deliberately slamming into one another during regular-season practices, and while they still wear helmets, they no longer wear shoulder pads and other protective gear in practices." The *Times* says this is "aimed at reducing injuries like concussions."[29]

Yet, here's the overall takeaway: even scientists at top research labs don't yet agree on the causality between football—of all sports!—and CTE. In that *Walrus* piece about the CFL, another scientist who works with Tator is quoted: "We speculate that concussions cause CTE. But I'm not 100 percent sure that's the case. We lack proper controls to make that link." This is why the Boston University team uses the word "believe" in their FAQs on CTE.

What does this mean, then, for CFL players (and NFL players

and, really, any athlete) trying to navigate all of this? Patrick Hruby notes that fans who want to dismiss all of this by saying that these players are making a choice wherein they know the risks they are taking have to answer the currently unanswerable question: "What is the risk?" Hruby says: "We need a 50-year study to figure out how risky this really is, and then on the other hand, we'll say, 'Well, these guys know the risk.'" Simonetto says that players and their families tend to stake out a middle ground when talking about this. They will acknowledge that they are worried but then add: "We're watching the research."

It's important in all of this to remember that a lot of these athletes are making choices about things that even scientists don't know a ton about and disagree on. That's not to say that they are ignorant of the possibilities of their choices, but it is a call to empathy. When choosing to play football (or any professional sport), "it's how they make money for their family, to support the family," Simonetto notes. She is emphatic on this point: "This is work. This is a job." It is their livelihood.

And the job is not secure. One injury and time off for healing could significantly lower a player's chances that he gets to keep his roster spot. On top of this, the average playing time for most CFL and NFL players is a couple of years, and CFL players earn significantly less money. They want to play for as long as they can to maximize the financial benefits of everything they have worked toward. They want to do the best job they can. And they are making decisions about that and their health amid a steady stream of changing and increasing information about concussions and CTE.

There is one more aspect to this: to give up football would be to give up their communities and careers. Football "gives them a lot of their social contacts for their entire life. And there's a lot of camaraderie," Simonetto says. "They're very proud of being part of this group." It is often (though not necessarily) something they love. Simonetto says that when she interviewed CFL players, "they would talk about football being the most fun when they played in high school and college. And then it became about work."

Joel Anderson, a former ESPN senior writer and host of the *Slate* podcast "Slow Burn," grew up in Missouri City, Texas, just outside Houston. He was a fan of the NFL's Houston Oilers (remember them?) and the USFL's Houston Gamblers (you don't remember them, most likely). And he lived in a football household. "My father, who though you'd never know, because he is 5-foot-6 and like 150 pounds, was an all-state running back in Arkansas in the 1960s." Anderson started playing football as a kid and went on to play all the way into his first year of college at Texas Christian University in Fort Worth, where he was teammates with future all-pro running back LaDainian Tomlinson. He left the game then and turned his attention to journalism.

Anderson thinks back on playing football when he was young: "It was something that I loved; the competition aspect of it, the physical aspect of it. It is something that made my dad happy. It is something that I could enjoy with him. To this day, that is probably one of the things that we bond over the most, our love of football."[30] Anderson is well aware of the ongoing discussion around sports and brain trauma, specifically in football, a sport he still deeply loves. And he worries about what his past in football could mean for the future of his mental well-being. "I can't tell sometimes. Do I just have a bad memory? Am I having trouble remembering this because I am just having trouble remembering this, or is there something else to this?" He notes that he has nothing else to compare his own experience with. Maybe he is forgetful. Maybe it is an underlying symptom.

He compares it all to a coming storm: "I'm not going to say it's a cloud that hangs over me, but it's like a far away weather system that I've heard about, that may hit town at the end of the week. And I'm like, 'Oh wow, that rainstorm might come and hit me over here. But, I think I am okay.'" Anderson doesn't regret playing. "A lot of my best experiences came on a football field," he says. "I miss it. I do."

———

Starting in 2014, the satirical website *The Onion* has ended each Super Bowl by re-upping its post titled "Super Bowl Confetti Made Entirely from Shredded Concussion Studies."[31] The post is nothing more than that title and the picture of someone's arm holding up the championship Vince Lombardi Trophy, confetti falling all around. We don't need any other context to get the joke. Each year, this post feels fresh; you have to check the date when you click on the link—it's as relevant now as the first time it posted. It reflects a cruel, biting humor that reminds us of our own callousness in what we consume.

We know playing football is objectively bad for the body and the brain. And even though football might be one of the worst sports in this regard, other sports need better protocols, too. As a society, we need a better, more broad understanding of brain trauma. We know all this. But who cares?

Former players care.

In 2011, seventy-five retired NFL players filed a lawsuit against the NFL, charging that their former league not only failed to handle players' concussions correctly but purposefully hid evidence about the long-term effects of concussions from employees.[32] Two years later the league settled. By that point, more than 4,500 former players were involved in the litigation. Per the settlement terms, $765 million would be allocated to any of the roughly 18,000 retired players who suffered concussion-related injuries by compensating them, paying for medical care, and underwriting research. Individuals would receive a limit of money based on their diagnoses: $5 million for Alzheimer's, $4 million to families whose loved ones were diagnosed with CTE postmortem, or $3 million if they suffer from dementia.[33]

But this isn't as great as it sounds. Not only do former players say this is not enough money to cover all the players who suffered long-term effects of brain trauma while employees of the league; the compensation for players with CTE goes only to those who were diagnosed between January 2006 and April 2015. As Hruby wrote in 2016, "All subsequent diagnoses . . . will not be compensated. Not a penny, no matter what neuropathologists find in their brain tissue." And for players living with "the life-altering mood and behavior disorders associated with the CTE—including depression, explosive anger, and impulsive behavior," they "will not be compensated, either."[34]

And so the players continue to tell their stories, advocating for themselves and one another. Low payout amounts have sent some back to court as they appeal those payouts or money they say is being withheld. One lawyer who represented more than a thousand players in the original lawsuit told *USA Today* in 2018: "These players didn't know what they were getting into. The settlement is not what we thought it was."[35]

In 2019, a federal judge tightened rules for the claims process that appeared to favor the NFL, as it would make it even more difficult to qualify for medical reimbursements. But in December of that year, a federal judge appointed a mediator to resolve claims from about seventy families whose loved ones died before 2006. The concussion settlement and arguments over its implementation are ongoing and most likely will continue for a long time.

And it isn't only football players seeking financial support from former leagues. Hockey players have been waving red flags, too. In 2013, ten former NHLers pursued a class-action lawsuit stating that their former league was negligent when it came to head injuries. In 2016, NHL commissioner Gary Bettman, in response to an inquiry from a United States senator about the issue of CTE in hockey, wrote that "the relationship between concussions and the asserted clinical symptoms of C.T.E. remains unknown," refusing to say if a link exists. Still, two years later, in late 2018, the NHL settled the class-action suit, which had ballooned to include 146 plaintiffs and another 172 who retained counsel. The settlement awarded about $22,000 to each player (all 318 of them), promised to fund neuropsychological testing, and will reimburse up to $75,000 in medical fees for each player. It will cost the NHL about $19 million.[36]

As with the NFL, this settlement was only the beginning. The family of the late hockey enforcer Todd Ewen is suing the NHL after a doctor with the Canadian Concussion Centre misdiagnosed Ewen as not having CTE and then went on, while employed by the NHL, to use Ewen's misdiagnosis to argue against a link between hockey and CTE.[37]

––––

Okay, fine—those are the professionals. They are making complicated decisions for a host of reasons, decisions they are not always happy about later in life. But it becomes dire when we turn to youth sports. "There's a lot of things we don't let little kids do in society that we let adults do," Hruby notes.

Not only do children lack the knowledge that comes with living and learning; they are still developing rapidly, both physically and mentally. And the consequences of letting them play sports where they repeatedly suffer head injuries—many of them subconcussive and asymptomatic—are still largely unknown but potentially frightening. Boston University has found, according to the *New York Times*, that "athletes who began playing tackle football before the age of 12 had more behavioral and cognitive problems later in life than those who started playing after they turned 12."[38] Parents are beginning to seriously question if it is worth taking that risk, and some are finding it is not. Participation in youth football has been falling for more than a decade.[39]

There's also the moral question of combining sports (especially football) and school. Our educational system exists, Hruby says, for two main reasons: to "nurture young people's brains" and "to protect those same young people." To do this, "we have all sorts of safety measures on campuses we don't have in normal society. We have drug-free zones, gun-free zones." Maybe we need football-free zones.

Take, for example, a game in October 2017 at a Canadian high school. A football coach forfeited the game when too many of his players got concussions and had to go to the hospital. "Marcel Metti, the coach of the École L'Odyssée Olympiens, said nine of his players suffered blows to the head during Friday's game in Moncton against Sackville's Tantramar Titans. He said all players were taken to a hospital as a precaution. Four players showed serious symptoms of concussion, such as nausea and vomiting."[40] What does it mean, Hruby asks, that schools are "sponsoring an activity that has a not insignificant risk of brain damage, that literally damages the organ with which you would be trying to fulfill that primary mission as a school"?

There are ways to change this—if we are willing.

Kimberly Archie, who lives in Sherman Oaks, California, is an expert in brain injuries, an activist for safety in youth sports, founder of the National Cheer Safety Foundation, and a mom who lost her son when he was only twenty-four years old. He had been acting erratically in the lead-up to his motorcycle crash. He had played football as a kid, and Archie thought maybe there was something wrong with his brain. She was right. He had CTE. "He never had a concussion. He never had any major injuries," Archie says. "He only had overuse injuries. He had knee problems and back problems. That's how I knew he had brain problems. How stupid would I be to think he's got overuse everywhere, but his brain's just pristine."[41]

She wants people to stop encouraging kids to play tackle football. Flag football is fine. Hruby agrees: "There's no reason to expose little kids to that risk at all. None." And with flag, he continues, "they get all the benefits of football still, like the exercise, the team work, the camaraderie." Beyond that, Hruby suggests that kids at the high school level "play shorter seasons, have more time between games for recovery, and don't play football year-round. Go back to how it was in the 1950s, have an eight-game high school season, and you don't touch a football again."

Archie also has an idea to tax professional football games to fund "a federal agency like OSHA that overseas these clowns." She wants "the NFL [to] put a dollar voluntarily on every ticket sold. [Then] they could set up a fund that they would get the credit for, but not necessarily would have control [over]. I want them to set up an agency through advocates and fund it with this dollar," she says. "Our goal is to get, at the state level and at the federal level, like the tax on soda or cigarettes, [a] tax [on] pro tickets to create the Sport Health and Safety Administration." She wants to take sports out of "the regulation and standards-making business."

The goal is not to get rid of sports. Sports are important for a huge variety of reasons, both physically and mentally. Comstock says her work is about safety, not eradication: "I definitely do not want anybody to ever take any of my research out of context to say, 'See, kids shouldn't play sports' or 'See, sports are too dangerous for girls.'" She continues: "No. The positive health benefits of being physically active still far outweigh the really small likelihood that anyone is going to sustain a serious sports-related injury."

Comstock summarizes this issue using clear language: "We don't want anyone to be afraid to play. We want more people to be physically active more often, and sports are a great way to incorporate physical activity as part of a healthy lifestyle. We just want to have researchers, parents, coaches, policy makers, we want everybody to work together to make sports as safe as possible."

CHAPTER 2

FORGIVING THE
DOPER YOU LOVE

On a warm night in August 2004, the city of Austin, Texas, celebrated Lance Armstrong's sixth consecutive Tour de France victory. The setting was important. Austin was Armstrong's hometown, and it was also the home base for his charity, the Lance Armstrong Foundation, which helped cancer victims—a cause close to Armstrong's heart as a cancer survivor himself.

Approximately 40,000 people, most draped in yellow to honor the famed yellow jersey of the Tour winner, packed the downtown streets. The local paper set the scene: "Banners along the parade route proclaimed 'In Lance We Trust' and 'Welcome Home Lance.' Messages in chalk, some in yellow, were scrawled on the pavement echoing similar support: '7?,' 'Viva La Lance,' 'Austin Proud' and 'Live Strong'—Armstrong's motto for life. Yellow wristbands, headbands, high-tops and T-shirts were the fashion statement of the night. Traffic lights all along the route flashed yellow. The University of Texas Tower's windows were lighted to form a giant 'L.'"[1]

The festivities included a parade for Armstrong, in which he biked alongside the mayor and a US congressman. Armstrong's then-girlfriend, the singer-songwriter Sheryl Crow, and others played for the enormous crowd on a stage in front of the capitol building. The governor, Rick Perry, told them: "He is a living legend —and a great Texan!" Armstrong himself said: "I'm the happiest man here today because I am home." He would go on the next year to win his seventh and final Tour. By 2013, his hometown was not so happy to honor him any longer.[2]

In 2010, a handful of Armstrong's teammates admitted they had used banned performance-enhancing substances (commonly known as performance-enhancing drugs, or PEDs), and they implicated Armstrong not only as a fellow doper but as the ringleader and a pusher. In the summer of 2012, the US Anti-Doping Agency (USADA) filed antidoping charges against Armstrong, and in October that year USADA published a 1,000-page report detailing how Armstrong's team, the US Postal Service (USPS) Pro Cycling Team, "ran the most sophisticated, professionalized and successful doping program that sport has ever seen." Eleven teammates told USADA what they knew about Armstrong while Armstrong refused to cooperate. The CEO of USADA wrote the following in a press release at the time: "The evidence also includes direct documentary evidence including financial payments, emails, scientific data and laboratory test results that further prove the use, possession and distribution of performance enhancing drugs by Lance Armstrong and confirm the disappointing truth about the deceptive activities of the USPS Team, a team that received tens of millions of American taxpayer dollars in funding." The International Cycling Union then stripped Armstrong of his seven Tour de France titles and imposed on him a lifetime ban from the sport.[3]

A few months later in January 2013, Armstrong agreed to sit for a nationally televised interview with Oprah Winfrey during which he confessed to using performance-enhancing banned substances. He said he took erythropoietin (EPO, which stimulates the production of red blood cells), testosterone, and human growth hormone (HGH) and that he used blood transfusions during his seven Tour victories.[4]

The residents of Austin, once overflowing in their love for

Armstrong, turned away from him. Michael Hall, a writer at *Texas Monthly*, watched the Oprah interview at a local Austin bike shop with roughly sixty to seventy cyclists. "These were people who had ridden with Lance, who had admired him, who had become fans because of him," Hall wrote. "They had loved Lance. Not anymore." Hall described the anger in the room, the way people yelled back at the screen, derided Armstrong, and mocked his words.[5]

One of the cyclists told Hall: "I'm angry because I got fooled. I wanted to believe, like everyone else, that he could do it clean. Now he's just saving his ass." The anger was not necessarily about the doping itself. It never really is.

For years during his historic run, Armstrong let people believe he accomplished an extraordinary sporting feat without the help of banned substances—that his body alone, under the rules of the sport, was enough. He sued anyone who said otherwise. He repeatedly and consistently denied that he broke the rules. He won over millions of fans who believed in an idealized version of sports: no doping, clear rules, pure bodies, fair competition.

Winfrey asked Armstrong during the interview if he thought of himself as a cheater. "I kept hearing I'm a drug cheat, I'm a cheat, I'm a cheater," he responded. "I went in and just looked up the definition of cheat and the definition of cheat is to gain an advantage on a rival or foe that they don't have. I didn't view it that way. I viewed it as a level playing field." Everyone at the top of the sport at that time, he said, was doping. There was no other way to win—and he wanted so badly to win.

Isn't that the point of sports, after all?

Armstrong's confession, and his lack of remorse, showed fans instead what no one wants to admit: the rules of sports are arbitrary, athletes are willing to push their bodies in lots of ways in order to win, and competition is rarely (if ever) fair for all involved. Instead of fans, we were fools who chose to dream in the first place.

———

Sports are made up. That seems an obvious thing to say, but it's where we have to start in order to understand the furor and fervor over doping. The skeleton of any sport is its rules, and there is no rule in sports that cannot be altered or finessed. And so, what counts as breaking the rules—cheating—is just as subjective and easy to change.

Weeks before the 2012 Summer Olympics kicked off in London, sports journalist Joshua Rothman addressed a question on the fundamental conundrum at the center of doping in sports: Why is it even a rule that you can't enhance performance by using drugs? "Though pretty much everyone in sports agrees that doping is wrong, there's little deeper agreement about *why*. Everyone acknowledges that, according to today's rules, doping is wrong because it's cheating. What's not so obvious is whether doping is inherently wrong— whether there's something fundamentally unsportsmanlike about using drugs to enhance your performance."[6]

The history of antidoping was born of two things: doping was cheating, and it was potentially dangerous. In 1928, the international governing body for track and field banned "stimulants," which it deemed "cheating." According to two scholars of early antidoping efforts, Matthew P. Llewellyn and John Gleaves, "throughout the 1930s, authoritarian regimes had expended state funds to experiment with stimulants to enhance military and (to a lesser extent) sporting performance. Perceptions of clandestine government-funded doping programs, coupled with prevailing fears over the 'moral' sanctity of amateur sports, heightened the IOC's [International Olympic Committee] interest in the topic." Doping went against the idea of amateurism, an ideal the IOC held dear. IOC vice-president Henri de Baillet-Latour wrote at the time that "amateur sport is meant to improve the soul and the body, therefore no stone must be left unturned as long as the use of doping has not been stamped out. Doping ruins the health and very likely implies an early death."

And so, by the late 1930s, the International Olympic Committee put together a commission, which adopted wording put forward by Avery Brundage, an American who would become IOC president in 1952: "The use of drugs or artificial stimulants of any kind cannot be too strongly denounced and anyone receiving or administering dope or artificial stimulants should be excluded from participation in sport of the O.G. [Olympic Games]." According to Llewellyn and

Gleaves: "This language would continue as part of Rule 26 until 1975, when it was transferred from an amateur eligibility rule to part of the IOC's new medical code with separate by-laws created by the IOC's Medical Commission."[7]

This backstory helps explain our attachment to the idea of the pure, unadulterated, dope-free athlete. Dr. Thomas Hunt is an associate professor in the Department of Kinesiology and Health Education at the University of Texas at Austin and author of *Drug Games: The International Olympic Committee and the Politics of Doping, 1960–2008*. Hunt contends that the reason we care so much about whether athletes dope is because we have an "idea of purity when we think of sports in a way that's different than most of the rest of areas of life." We see drugs and certain medical interventions as offering an advantage without the same discipline of training, the sweat of practice, and the improvement earned through sore muscles that nondopers achieve without enhancements. This idea dovetails, he says, with how "we hope and we expect our athletes to be moral exemplars that are better than us." How they perform—or really how they *win*—is not just a physical pursuit but a righteous one.[8]

In 2008, Norman Fost, a professor at the University of Wisconsin School of Medicine and Public Health, suggested that the word "doping" be thrown aside altogether because "it is intentionally pejorative and misleading" and that using it "contributes to the demonisation and mass hysteria that have dominated this topic." Instead, Fost would like something more specific and neutral. When talking about policies that restrict access to performance-enhancing drugs or punish athletes who use them, Fost suggests a different approach. Instead of framing policies as a measure against doping, people should use something like the "globalisation of policies opposing performance enhancing technologies."[9] This is probably too wordy to catch on, but the point is that Fost actively rejects the moralizing that Hunt says happens around unsanctioned performance enhancement.

Fost did not choose the word "technologies" lightly in his alternative definition. We need to seek a more expansive idea of what "enhancement" means if we are going to be making decisions about which enhancements are considered against the rules. Why does it begin and end with drugs? In June 2012, as Lance Armstrong was in the midst of his fall from grace, Fost wrote an op-ed for *USA Today*, calling for the end of "steroid witch trials." He addressed what is, for him, the core issue in how we think about the globalization of policies opposing performance-enhancing technologies. He pointed to Armstrong's use of EPO to do so: "According to the moralists and the rule-makers, it's OK to train at altitude to stimulate EPO production, or to sleep in a hypobaric chamber, which simulates altitude," he wrote. "But achieving the identical result using the same hormone by injection, or by infusing one's own banked red blood cells, can cost you all of your medals and a prison term if you lie about it."[10]

The thing about doping in sports, when we really think about it, is that it makes no sense at all. There is no internal logic to which enhancements are okay and which ones go too far. The line between doing whatever it takes to be the best and going too far to the point of cheating is a thin one that is hard to pin down for those who make the rules.

If an athlete is independently wealthy or sponsored by a major corporation, and so has access to the best coaches, nutritionists, doctors, and training facilities, then that is okay and not an unfair advantage that must be neutralized; we envy the access and praise the use of resources. There are no disqualifications for swimmers based on arm length or rules prohibiting volleyball players who are too tall in order to equalize the competition; in fact, if one's wingspan happens to be extra long or their height extraordinary, we celebrate that anomalous form.

We all wanted so badly to believe that Lance Armstrong just had a different body than the rest of us and that his winning was somehow fair. This is how the *New York Times* wrote about him in 2008: "Lance Armstrong [is] known for having an unusually high maximum heart rate. And that, said Edward F. Coyle, an exercise physiologist who has studied Mr. Armstrong, was to his advantage because his heart also was extremely efficient." We saw in his body the possibility of his amazing "clean" titles. For many fans (certainly not all), we refused to see anything else.[11]

There's a particular irony to the intense scrutiny of drug doping in cycling, though. As Aaron Gordon, a former reporter at Vice Sports who now writes for Motherboard, says: "It's a sport that literally is a product of human ingenuity in building a machine to enhance human performance. All the things they have allowed bikes to become, [and they] spend 20 to 30 thousand dollars on top of the line equipment. Yet we cannot use human ingenuity to enhance our oxygen capacity when using those machines?"

In a 2014 piece for the *New York Times*, Alex Hutchinson, a runner and author, looked at "the apparent arbitrariness of the distinction between good and bad pills." We let athletes have creatine (a muscle builder), caffeine, and Tylenol—all known performance enhancers. But we ban a whole host of other things. Hutchinson pointed out that the code adopted by the World Anti-Doping Agency (WADA), which was created in 1998 and now sets the rules for doping for Olympic sports, "rests on three pillars, any two of which are sufficient to merit a ban: First, if use of a substance may enhance performance; second, if it carries potential health risks; and third, if it violates the 'spirit of sport.'"

It's that last one—the "spirit of sport"—that is the problem. WADA's code defines it as "the essence of Olympism, the pursuit of human excellence through the dedicated perfection of each person's natural talents." Gordon notes that WADA lists several characteristics to explain this essence. "One is 'respect for rules and laws,'" Gordon writes, "which, given that the Anti-Doping Code is a set of rules and laws, is a bit circular." Hutchinson's take is that the "spirit of sport says that we play by the rules." And once there is a formulated list of banned drugs, which we create "so that athletes can compete without endangering their health," if you break the rules, no matter how arbitrary they are, you are a cheater.[12]

This is not to say that the worry over health risks is not a legitimate reason to ban substances. It seems commonsensical that messing around with drugs could cause physical damage to one's body. The Mayo Clinic has a page on its website dedicated to outlining the risks of performance-enhancing drugs, and reading through it should scare off most people.[13]

This is all particularly acute when thinking about the dangers to young people. A 2009 two-page flier (titled "Dangers of Doping: Get the Facts") that WADA put together to target teenagers points out that while plenty of drugs on their prohibited list are available from a pharmacist, "medications are for people with specific health issues—not for healthy athletes." It specifically notes that blood doping increases the "risk of heart failure, stroke, kidney damage and high blood pressure." It lists all the possible negative outcomes of taking steroids, stimulants, and HGH. For EPO, it asks: "EPO (erythropoietin) may help with the way your body uses oxygen, *BUT* . . . why risk it when it may lead to death?"[14]

Still, despite the very real risks, doping has a long history. It is, one might say, part and parcel of sport itself. *Sports Illustrated* has a timeline chronicling the use of drugs in sport. It begins: "1886: Twenty-four-year-old Welsh cyclist Arthur Linton dies during a race from Bordeaux to Paris; though the cause of death is reported as typhoid fever, he is believed to have taken trimethyl, a stimulant." Jack Moore wrote for Vice Sports in 2014 that "the first scientifically proven incident of doping occurred at an Austrian horse race in 1910. It wasn't until the mid-20th century that widespread use of drugs made their way into sports." Moore contends that World War II was a catalyst for this because "soldiers who were introduced to amphetamines as a way to deal with combat brought their new knowledge (and addictions) back to the clubhouse." *Sports Illustrated* published a piece in 1960 titled "Our Drug-Happy Athletes" exposing "the use of amphetamines ('pep pills'), tranquilizers, cocaine and other drugs in elite sports." Then came the famous decades of PED use by East German female athletes in the 1970s, a slew of weightlifters disqualified in the early 1980s, and the infamous stripping of Canadian sprinter Ben Johnson's gold medal in the 100 meters at the 1988 Summer Olympics in Seoul after he tested positive for steroids.[15]

Johnson, like Armstrong, contends that doping was widespread in his sport. "As a youngster like me, that's what I was told by my coach, that everybody on my level was doing it," Johnson said in 2013, "so for me to be on a level playing field, I would have to join in, so to speak, so I said, 'Why not?'" He called himself "a small part of a problem" and noted that "just because an athlete didn't test positive doesn't mean they're clean."[16]

When Armstrong said he had to dope because everyone else was, he had a point. According to subsequent reporting, "During the 7-year window when he won every Tour de France (1999–2005), 87% of the top-10 finishers (61 of 70) were confirmed dopers or suspected of doping. Of those, 48 (69%) were confirmed, with 39 having been suspended at some point in their career."[17] Cyclists continue to fail drug tests. Before the 2017 Tour, "Andre Cardoso, a seasoned pro who was to have raced in support of 2007 and 2009 champion Alberto Contador in his quest for another Tour title, tested positive for EPO," the Associated Press reported.[18] That news came literally days after a new study found that EPO doesn't have the effect everyone thought it did. "We found that while [EPO] increased performance in a laboratory setting on high intensity tests, the differences largely disappeared in endurance tests, and were undetectable in a real-world cycling race," said Jules Heuberger, who helped lead the study at the Centre for Human Drug Research in the Netherlands.[19] Well, then. Does that mean EPO should become legal? Or will cyclists just stop doing it now? Or should we cease caring if it doesn't offer a true advantage?

When WADA was given the chance to come down hard on institutional fraud, it fell short. In 2015, WADA released a 323-page report detailing the myriad ways Russia created and ran a state-sponsored doping scheme that included destroying samples, intimidating workers into covering up positive tests, and swapping out the urine of athletes who were doping with clean urine. Months later, Grigory Rodchenkov, the former Moscow lab director, told the *New York Times* that "dozens of Russian athletes at the 2014 Winter Olympics in Sochi, including at least 15 medal winners, were part of a state-run doping program, meticulously planned for years to ensure dominance at the Games."[20]

The International Olympic Committee ended up banning Russia from the 2018 Winter Olympics—kind of. Russian officials couldn't attend the games, the flag and anthem were banned, and athletes deemed clean were allowed to compete but not under the name "Russia." Three days after the games ended, the IOC reinstated the Russian team.

Then, after Russia agreed to hand over testing results but instead manipulated and deleted data, WADA banned Russia in December 2019 from international competition for four years—kind of. As with the 2018 Olympics, for the 2020 and 2022 Games, Russian officials, the flag and anthem, and the team name "Russia" are banned. Russia is also not allowed to host international competitions during the ban. Still, as in 2018, loopholes abound. According to the *New York Times:* "Even some officials from . . . WADA said the punishment was too lax because it left open the possibility that hundreds of Russian athletes, including some who may have been complicit in the doping cover-up, will appear in Tokyo [Summer Olympics in 2020]." And Russia will still host part of the Euro soccer competition in 2020 because it's a continental competition, not an international one.[21] (Both competitions were delayed for a year due to the COVID-19 pandemic but retain the 2020 moniker despite being scheduled for 2021.)

Plenty of people were upset with the sanctions. Han Xiao, chairman of the Athletes' Advisory Council of the United States Olympic & Paralympic Committee, told the *New York Times* that "doping is already hard enough to prove with athletes who aren't coming from countries with systemic doping programs." Bruce Baumgartner, president of USA Wrestling, pointed out that "the perception of this being a stiff punishment, it's just that: a perception. It's not the reality."[22]

And if experts can't make sense of this and don't know how to manage it, what are sports fans supposed to make of it?

———

And then, of course, there's baseball. There is really no way to discuss PEDs in sports without talking about baseball during the 1990s and the fallout from the so-called steroids era ever since. The unraveling began in 2004, when, in a series of articles for the *San Francisco Chronicle*, Mark Fainaru-Wada and Lance Williams exposed the Bay Area Laboratory Collective, known as BALCO. According to an editorial at the paper in December 2004, "BALCO, a Burlingame drug lab, marketed itself as a nutrition and health supplement supplier but also distributed illegal designer steroids developed to evade drug tests, according to testimony." This led to a federal inquiry wherein huge names were implicated. "Yankees' slugger Jason Giambi, testifying with immunity from prosecution, said he obtained several different steroids from Greg Anderson—who just happens to be the strength trainer for Giants superstar Barry Bonds."

Trevor Graham, who coached Olympic 100-meter champion Justin Gatlin, was the whistleblower. Gatlin would eventually be suspended for four years after he tested positive for excessive testosterone, returning to the Olympic stage in 2016. C. J. Hunter, former husband of track superstar Marion Jones, told investigators that Graham had given Jones banned substances. Jones—who won three gold and two bronze medals in the 2000 Olympics—would eventually confess to using drugs, and the International Olympic Committee stripped her of her medals.[23]

The public outcry was sufficient enough that the following year, in 2005, a congressional committee held a hearing on the issue that lasted more than eleven hours. Congress convened this hearing with the notion that doping (especially in Major League Baseball) potentially harms children who are influenced by professional players and so, mimicking their heroes' choices, risk using steroids. Mark McGwire, who set baseball's single-season home-run record in 1998, refused to admit he had used banned substances; sluggers Sammy Sosa and Rafael Palmeiro outright denied it. Jose Canseco was there to confirm that he had used steroids and that he knew that McGwire and Palmeiro had, too.[24]

BALCO's association with Jason Giambi and Barry Bonds led the commissioner of baseball at the time, Bud Selig, to appoint former US senator George Mitchell to investigate the use of PEDs in the major leagues. In December 2007, after twenty months of investigation, Mitchell released a report based on "hundreds of interviews and thousands of documents" finding that "for more than a decade there has been widespread illegal use of anabolic steroids and other performance enhancing substances by players in Major League Baseball, in violation of federal law and baseball policy." The players implicated "range from players whose major league careers were brief to potential members of the Baseball Hall of Fame. They include both pitchers and position players, and their backgrounds are as diverse as those of all major league players." In total, eighty-nine players were named in the Mitchell report.

In 2010, McGwire finally admitted he had used steroids for nearly a decade, including in 1998 when he broke the home-run record. He maintained that he would have broken that record without the drugs. He told Bob Costas: "I believe I was given this gift. The only reason I took steroids was for health purposes."[25]

Barry Bonds, who broke McGwire's record three seasons later, was convicted for obstruction of justice in 2011 in federal court in connection with the BALCO investigation. A federal appeals court overturned the verdict, and the US Department of Justice chose not to fight the appeal. No jury ever determined that he had lied when he denied taking banned substances.

Keith Law, a baseball reporter at The Athletic and the author of *Smart Baseball: The Story Behind the Old Stats That Are Ruining the Game, the New Ones That Are Running It, and the Right Way to Think About Baseball* (2017), says that the saga of doping in baseball that played out in the first two decades of the twenty-first century was about "MLB want[ing] to send a clear public message that they took doping seriously." Also, though, the entire saga was about a sport that has a specific history and position in this country. It is, after all, "America's Pastime." Law says we care so much about doping in this sport because "baseball treats its history like a religious text, that these numbers [statistics] are sacred. We assume they were all clean, all the historical records, and then we treat them as if they're inviolable. If anyone's going to beat them they have to do it in this very carefully defined, clear fashion." And Law finds this frustrating, in large part because it is predicated on what he believes is a wrong idea: that baseball has always been clean.[26]

Law is also honest about the role money plays. "There's too much of a financial incentive for people to not be trying," he says. He aims this message both at individual players thinking about their careers and at teams thinking about the health of their players. "Where you look at the amount of money you're spending on these players, the amount of time we're losing to injury. If I told you I had this magic pill that a pitcher could take and he'd come back from Tommy John surgery a month earlier, every team in baseball would want their guys to take it."

Law thinks baseball is currently in a good place when it comes to antidoping efforts. Penalties are harsh, and there are postseason bans if a player is caught doping. Law knows that the system isn't perfect and that some players who continue to take banned substances will slip through. But "I don't think there's that much doping, and I don't think this sport has ever been clean. I don't think any sport has ever been perfectly clean." "My personal opinion/ suggestion," Law offers in regard to what comes next, "has been that Major League Baseball could certainly pay to have a set of doctors. 20 approved doctors around the country who you can go talk to, who can confirm this diagnosis, or who would supervise you if you're using a drug that's on the banned list, but are trying to use it for legitimate, medical purposes." That's intrusive for the players and to their privacy, no doubt, but it is a transparent move—and MLB is all about transparency now. "They don't want to get hauled before Congress, again," he quips.

———

Why do we care so deeply about doping in some sports but not others? Cycling, baseball, and track and field seem to attract most of the attention, and fans generally possess righteous ideas about the need for purity in those sports. It was a big deal for a moment in professional tennis, but that was only because the player in trouble was Maria Sharapova, one of the most famous female athletes in the world.[27]

What about, say, the most popular sport in America—professional football? Bigger and more muscular players make for a more entertaining game. They also make for a more dangerous one, with serious injury being a daily reality. In 2015, former National Football League quarterback Brady Quinn made waves when he said this: "I think the usage of HGH or performance-enhancing drugs or supplements is greater now than it's ever been because the money is bigger now than it's ever been, and the punishment isn't really that bad if you think about it." Professional soccer faces the same quandary: It's not that players aren't caught using PEDs; they are. It's just not big news when it happens.[28]

The BALCO scandal that led to congressional inquiry, investigative reports, and endless chatter about baseball had no real corollary in football—despite the fact that many NFL players were implicated. Dana Stubblefield, who was a defensive lineman for the San Francisco 49ers, pleaded guilty to making false statements to a federal agent when he lied and said he hadn't taken steroids or EPO. He had been suspended three games by the league in 2004 for taking PEDs. At least seven NFL players appeared before the grand jury that looked into the BALCO case. One of them, Bill Romanowski, admitted in 2005 that he used steroids and HGH supplied by the head of BALCO. Romanowski was a notoriously mean, brutal player. During a practice in 2003, he ended the football career of teammate Marcus Williams when he punched and broke Williams's eye socket.[29]

If anything, then, it would seem even *more* pressing to make sure players aren't using PEDs in a sport where PED use could not only endanger the health of the doper but also the athletes he is competing against. This is especially true when considering the long-term effects on the brains and bodies of the NFL players (see our discussion of brain trauma in chapter 1). There seem to be much less indignation and moralizing over ruining purity and competition in professional football.

Outcomes and punishments can seem random. Some athletes get crushed under the wheels of antidoping efforts, while others escape that fate. Recently, many athletes who failed tests argued that they did so not because they were doping but because they had kissed other people who had used a banned substance (on the theory that the kiss transferred enough dope into their system to register on a test). In July 2017, Gil Roberts, a 400-meter runner who won a gold medal in the 2016 Rio Summer Games as a member of the US men's relay team, was cleared of wrongdoing despite a positive test earlier that year indicating "a small amount of the well-known banned masking agent probenecid in his system," according to NBC Sports. Roberts's girlfriend had picked up medication in India for a sinus infection. "The arbiter decision document stated that Roberts and his girlfriend kissed between the time she took the medication and when Roberts provided a urine sample, including when Roberts told his girlfriend that he was leaving the room to be tested." The arbiter believed him.[30]

But then there are cases such as Eric Thompson, a high jumper from the city of Herrin in southern Illinois. While celebrating his graduation from Herrin High School in 2007, he took a bump of cocaine. Competing two days later in a scheduled track meet, he placed second at the Junior Outdoor Track & Field Championships. He was immediately drug-tested—his first ever. He failed the test, so USADA (which had jurisdiction over the amateur athletes) suspended him from competition for two years. (However, he was still eligible to attend the University of Arkansas, which he did on an athletic scholarship.)

Thompson appealed USADA's ruling, and Aaron Gordon chronicled his fight against the antidoping agency in a 2017 article for Vice Sports. Gordon writes of the appeal hearing:

> Over the next several hours, lawyers questioned Thompson and his father; Lakatos [his high school track coach], Booth [his coach at Arkansas], and a toxicology expert were also questioned over the phone. The expert testified that cocaine could only provide a performance-enhancing effect if ingested minutes before a meet. There was no debate over the idea that Thompson's cocaine use had no positive effect on his jumps. USADA's lawyers accepted it as fact.

Rather than a hearing about enhancing performance, Gordon writes, it focused on Thompson the person to determine if "he was at 'significant fault' for taking a banned substance."[31]

Gordon reports the repercussions: "'What I couldn't get over,' Thompson recalls now on his porch, 'was how small of a decision that I made will change the rest of my life.' He thought this kind of thing happened to other people. Bad people. People who hurt others or cheat or steal." Thompson did ultimately win the appeal, and his punishment was reduced to one year. But then he went home for spring break and missed a random but mandatory drug test from the NCAA. Because he was on probation for failing the USADA drug test, the missed test was registered officially as a positive result, which led to a two-year ban from collegiate competition. Thompson left school, bounced around, and eventually decided to do what people in his hometown do: he took a job working in the mines.

———

Finally, the subjective nature of determining fundamental questions—What is doping? and Who is a cheater?—does a material harm to a specific cohort of athletes: those whose gender identity does not square nicely with the culturally determined binary categories of "male" and "female." This most often means female athletes with naturally high testosterone levels, intersex athletes ("someone with a combination of sex characteristics that puts you somewhere outside the binary 'male' and 'female' boxes"), or transgender athletes ("people whose gender identity and/or gender expression differs from what is typically associated with the sex they were assigned at birth"). Sports organizations demand hormonal therapy or surgery or incredibly invasive practices (such as measuring the size of a woman's clitoris to determine if it is within a supposed "normal" size range) in order to make sure that the inclusion of these athletes is "fair."[32]

So much of the institutional panic surrounding these athletes has to do with testosterone levels and, for some competitors, managing testosterone levels with medicine in order to maintain personal health. Most of the discussion is based on wrong ideas about what natural testosterone does, our incomplete knowledge of the results of using synthetic testosterone, and deep-rooted cultural desires to police female bodies or bodies that are not gender-normative.

Dr. Katrina Karkazis, an anthropologist and bioethicist who is an expert on gender, sexuality, and the body, and coauthor of *Testosterone: An Unauthorized Biography*, says that in order to fix what's broken around this discussion we need to be much more specific when talking about testosterone, or T. "What you need to do to win the Tour de France is not the same thing that you need to do to get a gold medal in shot putting. They're both athletic endeavors, and they both require strength," Karkazis says. How, then, does testosterone benefit both sets of athletes in their athletic pursuits? "When people say 'T improves athleticism or performance,' you can't just say that," Karkazis says. "You have to say *how*. People have tried then to say 'Okay, it builds muscle.' Well, okay, yes, it does."

But then Karkazis points out that we know this from studies where people are given "huge doses of testosterone, well beyond anything that you'd naturally find in anybody, in men, and then they figured out that they built anabolic muscle from that." The doses were "well beyond what you'd even give a man with low T, well beyond what you'd even give a trans [transgender] person. Way beyond." It turns out that like every issue associated with doping, it's much more complicated than it appears.[33]

But this raises questions about female athletes with naturally high T levels and the connection—if any—to performance. And if there *is* a connection, why is naturally high T an enhancement that is bad, whereas tall bodies in basketball are seen as okay?

We can connect all of these things—testosterone, hormones, drugs, bodies outside of the binary—and we make the automatic conclusion that these athletes are cheaters. Karkazis says she is particularly bothered by equating "someone [who] is trying to compete in the sport for which they have been honest and they're trying to comply with rules, versus somebody who is purposely and knowingly obfuscating rules." Linking trans or intersex athletes with dopers implies that trans or intersex athletes—by simply existing in their bodies!—are breaking the rules.

The most famous case of an athlete being punished merely for having a body that didn't conform to the gender binary demands is that of Caster Semenya, a dominant middle-distance runner from South Africa. Since the first time she won a major race, Semenya has faced incredible scrutiny over her body, racist attacks from white opponents, forced medical intervention from the International Association of Athletics Federation (IAAF, her sport's governing body), and IAAF rule changes geared specifically to keep her from competition. All this because Semenya's body generates an amount of natural testosterone that the IAAF has arbitrarily decided is too high for a woman. And the underlying implication is that she is somehow cheating her way to winning—a wholly unfair description for a woman competing as she is.[34]

Another underlying issue (one not unique to sports but one that does come to the fore with doping) is the way people of color are policed by white authorities. Like most discussions about the subjective parts of sports, especially the punitive ones, no discussion is complete without at least a mention of how race and racism factor into who is seen as breaking the rules, who is punished, and who is demonized.

The fact that Semenya is a Black woman from the Global South whose womanhood is being determined mainly by a group of white people from the Global North certainly plays a role in her targeting. In 2018, the African National Congress, which was the ruling party in South Africa at the time, had this to say about the IAAF's targeting of Semenya:

> The regulations are a painful reminder of our past where an unjust government specifically legislated laws for certain activists in society to stifle their fight against an unjust system. The IAAF uses the same tactic to exclude those who have defined the past decade as champions and treasures of their home countries. We call on government to challenge this grossly unfair, unjust and blatant racist attempt by the IAAF to the court of arbitration for sport.[35]

For Karkazis, when talking about these athletes, we need to come at this from a different direction. The starting point should be: "Trans [and intersex] people are deeply discriminated against in society, and as a society we feel we value diversity and inclusion." Or perhaps: "How can we shoehorn them into this system where fairness is really fairness for gender normative bodies and not fairness for them?" In order to do this, she says, "we're going to [need to] educate athletes about what transgender is, [what] bodily variability [is], that testosterone is not jet fuel for athletes."

Beyond this perceptive observation, we must remember that

sports are made-up competitions, that rules change, and that doping and cheating are subject to arbitrary standards. Is it really worth the anguish to continue to pretend otherwise?

———

Long story short: athletes will always seek out performance enhancements to gain an edge. Cheating isn't going anywhere (see the 2017 Houston Astros). Neither is doping, and the ability to detect banned performance-enhancing technologies is getting much more difficult. A less sophisticated example involves cyclists doping using poop. Yes, you read that correctly: poop. There's a theory "that elite cyclists have a certain microbiome living in their intestines that may allow them to perform better," and anyone can place that certain microbiome into the gut via a fecal transplant. Is that cheating? We'll see.[36]

Dr. Thomas Hunt, the professor from Austin we introduced above, says that "we're on the verge of a genetic revolution in terms of understanding the human body, and so DNA manipulation may be possible in the future for [enhancing] athletic performance." There is a growing number of articles about gene manipulation, what gene doping could look like, and whether or not it is a bad idea.[37]

This may be too complex to speculate on right now, but when looking toward the future of doping policy it seems most people could agree it's okay to ban enhancements known to harm the health of athletes. Hunt thinks this is when fans should care about this issue. It's a compelling argument. If we start from that basic proposition (people are doping in order to win, break records, and be competitive), then "that may lead to different discussions about doping if [what] we're really concerned about is . . . focusing on protecting health rather than this antiquated conception of purity." This means that in deciding what is good for sports, we would have to de-center the competitive drive and the thirst for victory and replace it with the well-being of athletes. This is what Karkazis was suggesting, too. That's quite a shift.

One way this could happen: USADA and WADA start to seriously consider athletes' input in policy decision-making. Athletes have little say in the agencies' decisions about which drugs are banned, or even any concerns competitors may have over the entire process. In fact, athletes have no meaningful mechanism to appeal WADA's decisions regarding what substances are placed on the schedule of prohibited drugs.[38] Another idea is to mimic what happened in the sport of powerlifting. Dr. Jan Todd was the world's strongest woman during the 1970s. (YouTube clips of *The Tonight Show Starring Johnny Carson* feature her deadlifting enormous weights.) Today she runs the H. J. Lutcher Stark Center for Physical Culture and Sports at the University of Texas, which she started with her late husband, Dr. Terry Todd (he was also a powerlifter). She has written extensively about sports and ethics. She says she and her husband coined the term "the Parallel Federation Solution" to describe how powerlifting has responded to issues of doping (powerlifting is not weightlifting, which is an Olympic sport and therefore subject to rules set by the International Olympic Committee and WADA).[39]

The Parallel Federation Solution is, in its most basic form, the creation of different federations within a sport, each one with different requirements when it comes to performance enhancement. Jan Todd contends that this comes out of the fact that doping is arbitrary, "because who are we to say to people you can take thousands of milligrams of vitamins, you can eat all the liver you want, you can use massage, you can use ice baths, you can take Creatine, you can do all kinds of things, but that testosterone tablet, or whatever it is, is something you can't do?" Put simply, in some federations some things are allowed, and some are not. Some test for certain drugs, but others do not. Some allow certain technological enhancements, but others do not. The athlete gets to decide which one to compete in.

"In 1983 we formed what was then known as the American Drug Free Powerlifting Association," Todd recalls. Later there was the International Powerlifting Federation (IPF), the United States Powerlifting Federation (USPF), and the American Powerlifting Federation (APF), "which actually had written into its rules there will never be any drug testing in this organization." "So USPF is doing urinalysis testing with the IPF. The ADFPA, the drug-free group, didn't have much money. They were relying at that time mostly on lie detectors, not a good way to go," she says. "But the APF was attracting the most attention because the drug users were lifting the biggest weights." All of this caused three different sets of records, making it harder to determine who was the strongest of them all.

Over decades this framework of multiple parallel federations has grown in the sport of powerlifting. "Where we are right now, there are more than 30 different powerlifting federations in just the United States. There's about 10 different kinds of world federations." Jan Todd refers to this fracturing as "a postmodern approach to sport." And, she points out, despite all the places people can choose to powerlift these days, "what they call the 'raw movement' is the biggest thing now in powerlifting." On their own, people are choosing to compete in federations with less allowable performance enhancement.

Athletes are also coming together to create communities that celebrate sports that are free of PEDs. For example, the Clean Sport Collective (CSC), which comprises "athletes, brands, events, clubs, fans and public," has created a series of pledges that professional, amateur, and student athletes, as well as coaches, agents, health care providers, trainers, fans, brands, events, and sports clubs, can sign to demonstrate their commitment to "clean sport." Professional athletes can even pledge to donate $25,000 to CSC if they test positive. Coaches, agents, brands, and health care providers can promise not to work "with athletes who have tested positive for performance enhancing drugs." Fans can pledge to advocate "for athletes and entities who are committed to competition in the absence of performance enhancing drugs." Two multinational manufacturers of athletic shoes (Brooks and Saucony) have signed on, as have athletes like Olympians Kara Goucher, Gwen Jorgensen, and Alysia Montaño.[40]

Needless to say, it's unlikely that we'll see a Dirty Sport Collective anytime soon.

———

Austin's most notorious athlete, who is now described in articles as "the banned cyclist Lance Armstrong," hasn't given up on the sport or his role as America's preeminent cycling ambassador. In 2017, during the Tour de France, Armstrong was everywhere. He hosted a popular podcast ("Stages") to provide his analysis at the end of each stage of the Tour, and he wrote an accompanying blog for *Outside* magazine. These gigs earned him a profile in the *New York Times* written by Juliet Macur. The headline of the piece referred to him as the Tour's "Most Infamous Rider," and Macur described the podcast like this:

> In some ways . . . it's the same old Armstrong: He has not arrived on his knees, begging for acceptance or forgiveness from a sport he sent into turmoil, especially here in the United States, where he brought cycling into the mainstream. He curses and criticizes and challenges old enemies, like the longtime Tour director Christian Prudhomme, and he isn't afraid to say things that other commentators might be too timid to say.[41]

This coincided with his participation in a satirical mockumentary for HBO titled *Tour de Pharmacy* that made fun of the extent of doping in cycling. Initially, Armstrong appears on screen anonymously, his body in total shadow and his voice modified. He is identified only as "Former Professional Cyclist" and his first words are: "I mean, before anyone even got on a bike, you knew they were all on drugs."

All these years later, in some way we still care about this athlete. Perhaps it is a morbid fascination with fallen heroes. Or maybe it's our never ending thirst for stories of redemption in sports. It could also be that we don't care about doping as much as our public moral posturing would suggest. Likely it's some combination of all three.

Armstrong will never again enjoy another parade in his honor. His mere appearance on any stage will not be met with thunderous applause from thousands of cheering neighbors. And sightings of those yellow Live Strong bracelets are now extremely rare. But when reflecting on Armstrong's record, at the least we can acknowledge that in violating the rules of the game he had a lot of company. On top of that, those doping rules are all made up anyway. And, in the end, he won. Isn't that, after all, the point of sport?

CHAPTER 3

CHEERING FOR A TEAM
WITH A RACIST MASCOT

Hey hey! Ho ho! That racist name has got to go!

On Sunday, September 17, 2017, Washington, DC's National Football League team played an away game against the Los Angeles Rams. Outside the stadium a dedicated group of protesters gathered to draw attention to the Washington team's name: the Redskins.[1] Not only is the name a slur, but the image associated with the team is a man's free-floating head with a striking nose and jawline, black hair adorned with feathers, his skin a deep red color. The team wears this image on their helmets and uniforms, and fans show up to games in redface and wear generic headdresses that are sold at stores like Party City, often with the thin excuse that they are "honoring" Native people or upholding some "tradition."[2]

The protesters who gathered outside the Los Angeles Coliseum see no honor in these traditions. The rally was organized by the American Indian Movement Southern California. AIMSoCal's Facebook page for the event described the purpose: "Join grassroots efforts as we rally against the use of our identity and culture as a mascot and to end the use of a racial slur by the Washington Team."[3]

The group displayed many signs, including a large banner: "Native Americans Are People Not Mascots!"

One of the protesters was Temryss Lane, a former professional soccer player and an on-air analyst for multiple outlets. Lane's father is from the Golden Eagle Clan of the Lummi Nation, who live on the western coast of Washington State near Bellingham, just south of the border with Canada. "I grew up between the Rez and the town," she says.[4] She attended UCLA, where she earned a master's degree in American Indian Studies. She is also a Nike N7 Ambassador, working with the company to create more opportunities for sport and physical activity among Native American and Aboriginal youth in North America.[5]

She was one of about fifty people who showed up that day. "It was men and women and children, some non-native supporters that were a part of the Standing Rock movement," she reported, referring to the recent Indigenous-led campaign to stop the Dakota Access Pipeline near the Standing Rock Sioux Reservation in North Dakota.[6]

"We were confronting people," Lane remembers. "Saying [things] like, 'You know you're wearing a racist shirt? You know that that's the symbol for genocide.'" One video on the Facebook event page shows a couple of the protesters talking to some Washington fans. The fans, decked out in the team's jersey, are standing at a street crossing, trapped with nowhere to go as they wait for the light to turn. "It's racism and oppression," a protester says. The Washington fan says that's just an opinion. The protester responds: "An opinion? That's history."

Later, as columns of football fans silently shuffled by the group, they chanted "Walk of shame! Change the name!" Lane says that "most people didn't know what to do so they laughed, or they smiled." But there were some angry fans who flipped them off or cursed at them. One woman said to Lane: "You are my mascot!" Lane describes her response: "I would do my damnedest to look at people in their eyes and say, 'Sir, I'm not your mascot. *I'm not your mascot.* That's racist.' To children who would go by, Lane would say: "Ask your mom about the American genocide. Ask your mom what genocide is." She remembers some of the parents covering their children's ears.

Ah, yes. The covering of ears. For many—too many—sports fans across the decades, this has been the response to the protests of Native people to Native mascotry.[7] It's time to remove your hands from your ears and really listen.

————

The protester who retorted "that's history" is correct, and knowing that history is essential to understanding why these mascots are so hurtful. It goes back to the beginning (at least what white folks think of as the "beginning"). When European colonists arrived in the Americas, they carried diseases that wiped out Native peoples in numbers so large they are hard to fully comprehend. One scholar described the ravage of European disease in the Americas as "one of the greatest demographic disasters in history."[8] Those who survived were attacked, their land was taken, and many were enslaved. This was followed by centuries of different hells suffered at the hands of European settlers, US citizens, and the federal government itself, from forced removal and relocation to slaughter and war. One version of American history—one that is rarely taught—is the long and ongoing struggle for sovereign nations of Native people, as well as the US government entering into treaties with Native nations and then breaking them, often to further oppress tribes who were promised some autonomy and authority. Native people were kept so far from political power in the United States that federal law prohibited them from voting until 1924, and some states restricted that right until as late as 1957.

Efforts to erase Native peoples—either literally through murder or through assimilating them into the dominant white culture—are threaded throughout the history of the United States. In the nineteenth century, as white Americans pushed west and grabbed land, the government looked the other way, actively encouraged, or participated in the extermination of Native peoples. For example, in 1851, the governor of California said "a war of extermination will continue to be waged . . . until the Indian race becomes extinct." A year later, a US senator who would later become the governor of California stated that Natives "will be exterminated" because "the interest of the white man demands their extinction."[9]

In regard to the Washington NFL team, there are specific, critical historical points to address.

In 1755, Spencer Phips, the lieutenant governor of the Massachusetts Bay Province, acting on behalf of the Crown, issued bounties for captured Indians as well as money to anyone who turned in the scalps of murdered Natives.[10] In 2014, Baxter Holmes, of Cherokee and Choctaw lineage, wrote that his mother told him a story passed down in their family that "these bloody scalps were known as 'r*dskins.'"[11]

A September 24, 1863, ad in the *Daily Republican* newspaper in Winona, Minnesota, read: "The State reward for dead Indians has been increased to $200 for every r*d-skin sent to Purgatory. This sum is more than the dead bodies of all the Indians east of the Red River are worth."[12] An 1897 article appeared in the *Los Angeles Herald* titled "Value of an Indian Scalp: Minnesota Paid Its Pioneers a Bounty for Every R*dskin Killed." Referring to the 1860s, the article states that "the state treasury once paid out cash as bounties for Sioux Indian scalps."[13] It's harder to see the honor in the epithet used when it exists alongside promises of payments for Native scalps. It certainly makes clear which tradition was being upheld by using it.

Assimilation was often violent, too. Toward the end of the nineteenth century, Native children were forcibly taken from their families and placed in government boarding schools that focused on erasing Native culture through education. Captain Richard Henry Pratt, who founded the first such Indian boarding school, Carlisle, put it bluntly: "Kill the Indian and Save the Man." The schools were full of diseases, officials used brutal punishments to keep children in line, and students were often unable to return home. Many died before they could do so and were buried on site.

In 1895, members of the US military arrested nineteen Hopi men and sent them to Alcatraz, a military post at the time, for a year because the men refused to send their children to boarding school. An article in the San Francisco *Call* stated: "Nineteen murderous-looking Apache Indians were landed at Alcatraz island yesterday morning" and went on to describe the "crafty r*dskins" who refused to live according to the "civilized ways of the white men."[14]

The "taming" of the West was a large and long effort often met, expectedly, by hostility from the Native people being removed and/or killed. Therefore, the people who lived in the Plains, specifically the Sioux (which includes the Lakota, Nakota, and Dakota), became the face of the popular idea of the "savage Indian," and their imagery still plays an overwhelming role in our cultural imagination about Native people. You're thinking of the Sioux if you think of the Battle of Little Bighorn or Buffalo Bill's Wild West Show or of any generic Native mascot.

This history of enslavement, death, murder, broken treaties, displacement, and forced assimilation led to the popular myth of the "vanishing Indian," as if there were few Native people still living. The survivors became idealized symbols of the past, frozen in time. The historian Colin Calloway writes that by 1900, "in the eyes of most Americans, Indians were doomed for extinction."[15] It is finally here, at this moment, that sports intersects with this story.

Not only did "media coverage in the late nineteenth and early twentieth centuries quickly adapt . . . the language of the Indian Wars to their coverage of sports," but the blank slate offered up by the idea of the vanishing Indian—the one trapped in the past as the "savage" warrior on the Plains—gave white Americans something that dovetailed perfectly with sport. "Indianness," the scholar C. Richard King writes, "offered athletes, coaches, bands, boosters, and reporters a ready language of masculinity, a means to translate and transcribe fierceness, bravery, and honor while affirming the core attributes associated with whiteness and America, including freedom, independence, sacrifice, and strength."[16] Teams, fans, and reporters could make use of the Indian however they wanted, no matter how generic or stereotypical the rendering, because it was about what he represented in pop culture, not who he actually was or what his life or his history was like. As King puts it: "Fans and the [Washington NFL team] franchise alike have felt entitled to use Indians and Indianness as they have seen fit."[17]

This is the immediate backdrop to the first use of Native mascots by professional sports teams in the United States. The Boston Braves, the baseball team now in Atlanta, first used that name in 1912. That same year, Jim Thorpe, a member of the Sauk and Fox

Nations and a graduate of the Carlisle Indian School (his football coach there was none other than Glenn "Pop" Warner), won two gold medals for pentathlon and decathlon at the 1912 Olympics.[18] In 1915, the Cleveland Indians adopted their nickname. The following decades saw high schools and colleges across the country field teams such as "Braves," "Indians," "Chiefs," even "Redmen."

In 1932, the Boston Braves professional football team was formed. A year later, supposedly in honor of their coach, William Henry "Lone Star" Dietz, who some claim was Sioux, the team changed its name to the R*dskins, and in 1937 the franchise moved to Washington, DC. Deitz, according to the *Washington Post*, "was born in 1884 in the village of Rice Lake, Wis., to white parents."[19] Nonetheless, Dietz told the people who ran the Carlisle Indian School he was one-fourth Sioux and then, after graduation, started his coaching career there as an assistant for Warner. The Washington NFL team has, for years, defended the nickname in court documents by citing Dietz's alleged Native heritage.[20]

Native people have been protesting these mascots since at least the late 1960s. In 1968, the National Congress of American Indians started a campaign to "address stereotypes of Native people in popular culture and media, as well as in sports."[21]

The Cleveland American Indian Movement (Cleveland AIM) has been fighting the Cleveland Indians baseball franchise and its Chief Wahoo image for decades. "In January 1972, Cleveland A.I.M. sued Cleveland Baseball for libel and slander, in an unsuccessful effort to change the 'Cleveland Indians' team name and abolish its shameful, racist dead-Indian-head logo 'Chief Wahoo,'" its website reads. "Through our Campaign for Dignity, we have demonstrated at Cleveland Home Openers since 1973."[22]

As early as 1970, the University of Oklahoma abandoned its "Little Red" mascot. Plenty of schools—including Marquette, Stanford, and Syracuse—followed suit, either retiring mascots completely or eliminating particularly racist images of Native peoples. By the late 1980s, state efforts in Michigan and Minnesota sought to end the use of Native mascots at all levels of education.

At the same time, Charlene Teters, a member of the Spokane

tribe and a graduate student at the University of Illinois, began her protests against the school's name, the Fightin' Illini, and its mascot, Chief Illiniwek. Her journey was chronicled in the documentary *In Whose Honor?*, which premiered on PBS in 1997. "Along the way," the film's description says, "she is spit upon, threatened, even assaulted, yet she never wavers in her mission to protect and preserve her cultural identity for her children."[23] It took another decade for the school to finally ban Illiniwek, but it wasn't until 2016 that it "formed a committee to explore identifying a new mascot." In August 2017 the school finally "confirmed it's ending the 'war chant' at games."[24]

Illinois removed the Illiniwek mascot only when forced to comply by the National Collegiate Athletic Association. In 2005, the NCAA "banned the use of American Indian mascots by sports teams during its postseason tournaments. Nicknames or mascots deemed 'hostile or abusive' would not be allowed on team uniforms or other clothing."[25] Certain schools appealed and were allowed to keep their names: the Catawba College Indians, Central Michigan University Chippewas, Florida State Seminoles, Mississippi College Choctaws, and University of Utah Utes.[26]

It's important to note, however, that opposition to these team names still exists. Take Florida State University (Jessica's alma mater) as one example.

FSU has worked with the Seminole tribe of Florida since the 1970s and over those years has received the tribe's continued blessing to use the nickname "Seminoles." According to the university, the school interacts with the tribe in several ways. "Tribal members . . . travel to Tallahassee each year to crown the Homecoming chief and princess with authentic Seminole regalia"; it established "a scholarship program that pays the way for students from the reservations to attend Florida State"; and in 2006 it erected a statue on campus that depicts "a Seminole family."[27] The school has also tried to be more accurate when using representations of Seminole people. In 2016, the FSU student government passed a resolution to discourage fans from wearing headdresses to games. According to the school's student paper, "Headdresses usually worn and seen by those at Florida State games are closer to those worn by the Plains region tribes, such as the Sioux, rather than those of the Seminole Tribe."[28]

The school also has an FAQ page that seems to exist, in part, as a response to complaints people have with different aspects of the Seminole "traditions" often seen and heard at football games: the war chant (citing FSU's president in 1993: "Some traditions we cannot control"); the accompanying "tomahawk chop" (same FSU president: "It's a term we did not choose and officially do not use"); the Chief Osceola figure created by a Tallahassee businessman and FSU supporter in the 1970s ("Over the years, the costume of Osceola has been tweaked and tailored, always with the say-so of the Seminole Tribe of Florida. In fact, the costume often has been handmade by tribe members."); the fact that Chief Osceola rides a horse (citing a 1978 article in which the then-chief of the Seminole Tribe of Florida "commented that horses were indeed a part of his tribe's tradition"); and the flaming spear that Osceola, astride his horse, spikes into the field before home games ("minor variances [on historical accuracy] such as the warrior's flaming spear have become a cherished part of the FSU tradition").[29]

The site does not address the school's fight song, which is played after every field goal and touchdown and begins: "You've got to fight, fight, fight, for FSU! You've got to scalp 'em Seminoles!" FSU students and staff have made some efforts to distance themselves from the image of scalping. A spirit group on campus who would do things like paint fans' faces outside home games used to be called the "Scalphunters"; they have since changed their name to "Spirit Hunters."[30]

You must add "of Florida" when talking about the specific group of Seminoles who support FSU's use of the name because the horrific history of forced displacement split the Seminoles into different nations during the nineteenth century. After decades of war with the tribe (the Seminole Wars were a series of three separate conflicts from roughly 1816 to 1858), the US government forced more than 3,000 Seminoles to move west of the Mississippi River, which "left roughly 200 to 300 Seminoles remaining in Florida, hidden in the swamps," according to the Florida Department of State website.[31]

In October 2013, "the more populous Seminole Nation of Oklahoma," the *Washington Post* reported, "officially resolved that it 'condemns the use of all American Indian sports-team mascots in the public school system, by college and university level and by professional sports teams.'" The Seminole Nation of Oklahoma, however, has a much less complicated relationship with the state of Florida. For instance, the tribe does not possess casinos in Florida, it does not have to interact with the Florida state government, and it does not risk angering potential customers by standing directly in the way of FSU using the tribe's name. The leaders of the Seminole Tribe of Florida, for their part, are okay with FSU using the name; they also have a lot to lose by opposing it. That doesn't mean, though, that everything is fine.

Jacqueline Keeler is a Navajo/Yankton Dakota Sioux who cofounded Eradicating Offensive Native Mascotry and the hashtag #NotYourMascot. She says, "I spent days interviewing folks from Florida State and, you know, it's very hard on the native students there. And they said the only place they can go on campus where there is not something of the mascot is in the Native American student lounge."[32]

Even when teams make changes, some fans don't accept them. At Dartmouth in 2015, despite the fact that the school had given up its "Indians" nickname more than four decades earlier, "the Dartmouth Indian resurfaced on an unofficial T-shirt denounced by the provost."[33]

The Dartmouth incident highlights the idea that changing mascots destroys long-standing traditions worthy of preservation simply because of their longevity. Daniel Snyder, the owner of the Washington NFL team, has said as much in at least one 2013 interview: "We will never change the name of the team. As a lifelong R*dskins fan, and I think that the R*dskins fans understand the great tradition and what it's all about and what it means."[34]

What, though, of the great traditions of Native peoples and the horrific history in which "R*dskins" is embedded? "People talk about tradition," Lane says. "This has been around for eighty years and I'm like, 'Get out of here. My ancestors have been here for 13,000.'" Dr. Adrienne Keene, an assistant professor of American Studies and Ethnic Studies at Brown University and a citizen of the Cherokee Nation, has a similar reaction: "We've had this culture for conservative estimates of 15,000 years, so your 80 years is really small compared to that." She notes, though, that eighty years can seem like a lot. "To those people, that's their entire lifetime, that's their parents' lifetime. That's their grandparents' lifetime." Or as Lane puts it: "We're at that point right now where blinders are being ripped off and people are like, 'No, fuck you! I want my blinders on!'"

There's a natural instinct to cling to what we know and, more importantly, to believe we are not participating in a racist or hurtful practice. That may be partly responsible for why teams and fans justify the continued use of these images and mascots by claiming that their own intent is to *honor*, not to offend, Native people. That's misguided at best.

"To think that somehow we're supposed to feel proud of being a mascot of a football team or a baseball team and see that as an honor when we can't even get people to recognize our rights over our homelands or to not put a pipeline through our water sources," Keene says. "An honor, to me, would be listening to us as human beings and listening to us as people. So there's no way that a caricature of a stereotype of Native people is somehow honoring to me."[35]

Jackie Keeler echoes this viewpoint. "The promotion of stereotypes doesn't honor anyone," she says. And it's rooted in something more sinister than most people are willing to reckon with. "The United States has created this white-centered experience for all Americans," Keeler says. "You have this white-centered experience of every aspect of life, and just a sprinkling of people of color in the background. For white people who are used to having a plethora of representation in the media and every level of society and history, they have no clue what it's like." And that lack of representation has a dark underbelly, and Keeler believes that mascotry is an example of it. It's "the continuation of the colonial impulse. And that's, to a large extent, what mascotry is about. It's about trophyism. It's about celebration of victory over conquered foes. It's about having the right to do whatever you want with their image. And it can get pretty ugly."

Keene addressed that ugliness in a 2013 post at her website Native Appropriations. She noted that even if anyone, whether a member of the team or a fan, truly wants to honor Native or Indigenous people by using a racist mascot, one still cannot control how rival fans will use that image. "Part of athletic culture is vilifying the other team, creating cheers, images, and slogans that show your superiority over your rivals," Keene writes. "But what happens when that opponent is a real, living, group of people?" For example, a giant banner directed at an opposing team—the Indians, say—might warn them to prepare to "leave in a trail of tears," referencing the forced removal of Native peoples in the nineteenth century that led to the deaths of thousands. Rival fans manipulate the image of Washington's NFL mascot by putting an arrow through his head or showing him drinking. There's a famous image of a Philadelphia Eagles fan holding a stick that is plunged through a dismembered head wearing paint on the face and a headdress. "When they're yelling 'F*uck the Redsk*ns!' or 'Scalp the Indians!,'" Keene writes, "how do you think it feels to be a Native person hearing that? Or a Native *child* going to a sporting event for the first time?"[36]

But many fans don't want to give up their identity with their team. "I can understand if they themselves feel an intricate part of the fabric of the team," Temryss Lane says. "The team becomes a family, and the family, you do everything for [it]. And your gonna defend, defend, defend, no matter who is on the other side of the ball."

Keene says being able to identify as "Indian," even only as a fan of a team with a Native mascot, became part of white Americans' identity long ago. "It goes back to the foundations of America. From the earliest days, like with the Boston Tea Party, colonists were playing Indian. Because in order to formulate an identity as American, you have to be something different than British."

But that's not an innocuous identification, especially when the people with whom we are identifying are still here living among us. In identifying as American/Not British, Keene says, "it gives you a sense of ownership over the land, et cetera. That's something that's baked into the core of American identity from the beginning." Pushing against these mascots pushes on the underpinnings of this identity and exposes, as Keeler puts it, our colonial impulses.[37] And once we do that, once we "admit that the mascot is wrong, you have to admit that you were hurting this person that you actually claim to care about and that you're a part of that problem," Keene says.

Make no doubt: Native mascotry does have a tangible, negative impact. "The mascot fight is just so representative of the way that we as Native people are seen and positioned in society and then also the lack of respect that we receive when we speak out about issues that affect our communities," Keene says. "We are positioned at the same level as animals and inanimate objects and fantasy creatures like wizards, when we're actually a contemporary living group of people."

According to research conducted by a team of psychologists, including Stephanie Fryberg, a member of the Tulalip Tribes and a leading expert on the psychological effects of Native mascotry, "exposure to American Indian mascot images has a negative impact on American Indian high school and college students' feelings of personal and community worth." The team continues:

> The current American Indian mascot representations func-
> tion as inordinately powerful communicators, to natives and
> non-natives alike, of how American Indians should look and
> behave. American Indian mascots thus remind American
> Indians of the limited ways in which others see them. More-
> over, ... the views of American Indians held by others can also
> limit the ways in which American Indians see themselves.

For groups that are "caricaturized by the mascots," according to the research, "the studies suggest that American Indian mascots have harmful psychological consequences, . . . whether the American Indian mascot was represented by a caricature, a European American dressed as an American Indian, or an American Indian figure, and whether the mascot represented an American Indian university, a mainstream university, or a professional sports team." Beyond that—and this is critically important—"two studies revealed that after exposure to various American Indian representations, European Americans reported higher self-esteem compared to the control condition and to a nonnative mascot, namely, the University of Notre Dame Fighting Irish." White Americans feel better about themselves after looking at Native mascots, whereas Native people feel worse. Keene asks: "Why would you want to get rid of an image that makes you feel good?"[38]

In early January 2017, Jody Tallbear sued her employer, the US Department of Energy (DOE), for discrimination. As part of her lawsuit, Tallbear noted

> the scarcity of Native American employees at DOE and the pervasive stereotypical images and racial slurs related to Native Americans represented and promoted by the Washington R*dskins paraphernalia in her workplace. As part of her DOE mission, she attempted through presentations to DOE and to other federal agencies and in other ways to raise an awareness of the harm caused to Native Americans by the stereotypical images of Native Americans, such as Indian mascot portrayals, and the disparaging slur "r*dskin," which is directly tied to the historical bounty hunting of Native Americans.

She says that in the six years she worked for the DOE, "she has been subject to the persistent use of racially offensive language, portrayals, and representations of Native Americans in her workplace." Despite her drawing attention to this situation, no one at DOE attempted to remedy the problem. She says she was banned from doing sensitivity training for fellow employees regarding the Washington NFL team's name and that her direct supervisor retaliated against her by "isolating and ostracizing her for her actions to raise awareness on this issue."[39]

Native mascotry affects daily, mundane interactions between Native and non-Native people that can leave deep scars on Natives, especially Native women. "Native women are the only group, and this is not true of any other ethnic group or racial group in the country, that the majority of their attackers are not members of their own race," Keeler says. A Department of Justice report in 2016 found that "more than 4 in 5 American Indian and Alaska Native women (84.3 percent) have experienced violence in their lifetime," including

"56.1 percent who have experienced sexual violence" and "55.5 percent who have experienced physical violence by an intimate partner." It also notes that "relative to non-Hispanic White-only women, American Indian and Alaska Native women are also significantly more likely to have experienced violence by an interracial perpetrator and significantly less likely to have experienced violence by an intraracial perpetrator."[40] "What white men think about us really matters because it impacts the level of violence," Keeler says.

"It's no surprise that we have the highest disproportionate rates of teen suicide," Lane observes. "It's no surprise that with imagery like this [that there is a] perpetual invisibility around our women who are going missing and murdered by the thousands. Nobody cares because it's systematically designed that way. And the Washington NFL team is the visual image of the systematic oppression for indigenous people."

The hallowed halls where federal legislators craft policy is just down the road from the stadium where the Washington NFL team plays its home games. Keene drives this point home:

I often use the analogy of a lawmaker in Washington who is supposed to be creating legislation that supports tribal sovereignty and seeing the tribal leaders who come through his or her door as leaders of sovereign nations, [a lawmaker who] is [then] going to walk out the door of that office and see the Washington football team logo plastered all over town. How are they supposed to see those human beings as the tribal leaders and the nations that they are when they're only represented as a mascot?

So, knowing all of this, what is a fan to do? How does anyone cheer for a team with a racist mascot? Maybe you personally don't cheer for such teams, at least not without trying to do something to change it.

It's important to talk with people about the issue of native mascotry. For years, Keene says, she has seen that "person to person, you really can change people's minds if they're willing to listen and if you're willing to teach and be patient." But she's practical about it as well: "Of course [one-on-one dialogue] is not going to create lasting change. That's why the legislation that is in the state of Massachusetts or has been passed in other states [is important]. Or here in Wisconsin, they have a bill that went through against Indian mascots. It has to be at that legislative level."

Targeting pocketbooks is another worthy idea. Keene points to the NCAA's ban on postseason events as a particularly compelling example. Not changing a name or mascot "meant they'd lose out on huge amounts of money for those tournaments." Keeler says that her group Eradicating Offensive Native Mascotry is considering "doing more protests at Nike and really trying to put the pressure on Nike to stop selling racism [via its gear]. Putting the Nike [swoosh] next to Chief Wahoo [on a jersey] legitimizes it. It normalizes it." And Native groups have a powerful precedent: "Adidas made an announcement [in 2015] that they would basically underwrite [high school] teams' uniforms that wanted to get rid of their Indian mascot."[41]

At the time adidas made the announcement, roughly 2,000 high schools were still using Native mascots. President Barack Obama praised the move, calling it a "smart, creative approach. If we can't get states to pass laws to prohibit these mascots, then how can we incentivize schools to think differently?" He then mentioned the problematic team down the road: "I don't know if Adidas made the same offer to a certain NFL team, here in Washington. But they might want to think about that as well."

That very team was unhappy with adidas, releasing a statement in response:

> The hypocrisy of changing names at the high school level of play and continuing to profit off of professional like-named teams is absurd. Adidas makes hundreds of millions of dollars selling uniforms to teams like the Chicago Blackhawks and the Golden State Warriors, while profiting off sales of fan apparel for the Cleveland Indians, Florida State Seminoles, Atlanta Braves and many other like-named teams.[42]

Despite the backlash, adidas got something out of this deal. "I do know it made them look like they were a benevolent, socially minded company," Keene says. "But it also meant that all of these schools would then have adidas-branded things." That's called a win-win.

One other idea is to put pressure on media to change how they discuss these mascots, in particular what it means when media prints the word "R*dskins" without any context for its derogatory meaning and terrible history. In October 2017, a Black player on the Washington NFL team, Terrelle Pryor, flipped the bird at fans in Kansas City after they called him a racist slur. In the reporting around the incident, the word he was called was censored ("n****r," for example) while the name of the team he played for was printed throughout the article with no acknowledgment of the ironic juxtaposition. In response to the incident, the NFL said it would be investigating because it has "no tolerance for racial comments directed to anyone."[43] It's hard not to roll the eyes at a statement like that, but it's also profoundly sad on a basic level.

Since the early 1990s different outlets have decided to drop the Washington team's name (some officially, some more informally), beginning with the *Oregonian* in Portland in 1992.[44] As of 2013, according to the Pew Research Center, "at least 76 news outlets and journalists have publicly stated their opposition to the Washington R*dskins name or moved to restrict or ban its use."[45] In 2014, the editorial board of the *Washington Post*, the team's hometown daily newspaper, announced that it would no longer use the team's name in the op-ed section of the paper.[46] But flip over to the *Washington Post* sports page (or follow any of their sports reporters on social media), and readers will be inundated by the word.

There is a long road ahead.

———

"Turn it inside out!," the protesters yelled in Los Angeles, as Washington NFL team fans walked past them. Temryss Lane says that they were asking people to turn the Washington gear they were wearing inside out. "We would say, 'Support the team, not the name.'" There's at least one video on AIMSoCal's Facebook event page showing someone turning a team jacket inside out. "There were some victories," Lane says, "I'd say 5 to 10 people. Which is a statement, you know?"

The fight to end Native mascotry is a struggle for Native people to reclaim their humanity from those who have spent centuries stripping it away. Turning a jersey inside out is a small gesture that is simultaneously a huge one.

"Who knows what they did inside, once they got past us," Lane says. "The point is that they acknowledged us. They recognized us."

CHAPTER 4

EMBRACING TENNIS
DESPITE ITS INEQUITIES

There is nothing in tennis quite like Serena Williams's serve. The lift of her toes closest to the baseline before she tilts that foot down. The toss of the ball high into the air from her fully extended arm, hand, and every single finger. The bend in her legs as she brings them together and lowers her racquet behind her. Her italicized body, leaning into the court before her arm comes across, her body turns forward, and she strikes the falling ball. Where she is going to hit the ball is almost impossible for opponents to guess based on her body position and form. Serena's serve is both sport and art. It is a masterpiece of speed and accuracy, a blistering weapon that has buttressed her game. It is physical skill and psychological battle. It is the glory and brilliance of tennis in a single, fluid move.

Throughout her long professional career, which today spans nearly a quarter-century and a record twenty-three Grand Slam championship titles in the Open Era, Williams has stood across the net from her opponents and served her way to success (though we should be careful never to discount all the other elements of her game, including her forehand, backhand, shot placement, and mental toughness—all of it, really).[1] There are endless articles about Serena's victories that reference the star serving her way through a match or that make puns about her "acing" the competition. In 2016, during the Wimbledon final, she won 88 percent of her first serves, scored thirteen aces, and clocked a 124 mph serve.[2] That was her twenty-second Grand Slam championship. During that tournament, TV analyst and former Grand Slam champion John McEnroe observed that her serve "is the biggest weapon in the history of the sport."[3] A year earlier, women's tennis legend Billie Jean King said the same thing.[4]

Williams is arguably the greatest tennis player ever. Those of us who have been alive to see her play are lucky to be her contemporaries.

And yet, despite Serena's unprecedented success and her crafting of one of the greatest serves in the sport, Williams, a Black woman in a historically white sport, always faced an uphill battle in her career. She's not the first to do so. She often mentions Arthur Ashe, Althea Gibson, Zina Garrison, and her sister, Venus, as being part of the struggle for racial equality in the sport of professional tennis. In 2016, she told Elena Bergeron at The Fader that Ashe, Gibson, and Garrison "had to deal with different things on a different level that I didn't have to deal with, especially in terms of race and racism."[5] That might well be true, but Williams has had to deal with a lot throughout her career. And no Black tennis player, male or female, has been as dominant as Serena—she is unmatched in tennis history no matter the opponent—nor has any played that well for so long under the glaring spotlight of 24/7 international media and in the age of unfiltered social media and comment sections.

As Williams wrote in a 2019 essay for *Harper's Bazaar*, tennis is "a sport that I love—one that I had dedicated my life to and that my family truly changed, not because we were welcomed, but because we wouldn't stop winning."[6] She is a Black woman from Saginaw, Michigan, who learned to play tennis on the concrete courts of Compton, California. Her race, her gender, and her class have all worked against her in a sport that has earned its country club reputation.

———

Wimbledon, the oldest of the four Grand Slams (which include the Australian, French, and US Opens), is famous for many things: its age, its death grip on tradition, and its sheer Britishness (strawberries and cream, anyone?).[7] Visually, it's best known for two colors: white and green.

Green because it is the only major played on grass. Maintaining the grass is a meticulous process that happens year-round and involves careful snipping of the length of the blades to ensure the proper, even height. White because of the strict dress code. For decades, the All-England Club, which owns and runs Wimbledon, has required competitors to wear white while on the court. But in 2014, it got more even strict.[8] The rules apply to all clothing, front and back, including sweaters, tracksuits, caps, bandanas, any undergarments visible during play, and shoes (which they state "must be almost entirely white, including the soles"). Players can have trim on most gear, but the All-England specifies its width ("no wider than one centimetre"). Off-white and cream are banned, as is any "solid mass or panel of colouring."[9]

Snapshots of the winners show them wearing white head-to-toe against the green court. You know you are looking at Wimbledon.

The green and white of Wimbledon is also reflective of the sport more generally. Put bluntly, we're referring to dollars and race: the cost to participate (not to mention the pay inequality between male and female players), and the whiteness of the sport throughout its history.

Serena Williams won her first of seven Wimbledon titles in 2002 and her latest in 2016 (Martina Navratilova has nine Wimbledon singles championships). She is one shy of Roger Federer and tied with Pete Sampras. When Serena and Federer both won the title in 2003, Federer was awarded £575,000, Serena £535,000. By 2009, when they also won the singles championships, they earned equal money: £850,000 each.[10] The change occurred in 2007, when Wimbledon became the last of the four Grand Slams to offer equal prize money, thirty-four years after the US Open became the first.

In 1973, Billie Jean King threatened to boycott the US Open unless it awarded the same amount of money to male and female participants. The tournament relented. The Australian Open had a few years in the 1980s and 1990s when it offered equal prize money, and in 1987 and 1988 women even made slightly more than men.[11] In the midst of these fluctuations, there was renewed effort in the early 1990s by female tennis players to gain equal pay. Monica Seles, then seventeen years old and ranked No. 1, said in a statement: "If you ask tennis fans, the media or the players, they'll tell you that women's tennis has never been better, and I think that if this is the case then we definitely should have equal prize money." Martina Navratilova, who was a board member of the Women's Tennis Association and the reigning Wimbledon champion at the time, added: "It would be ludicrous for anyone to expect us to accept less than equal prize money or draw size at the Grand Slam Cup, and we're certainly not backing off on our long-standing efforts to secure equal prize money at the French and Wimbledon."[12] The Australian Open made equal pay an official rule in 2001. The French Open followed suit in 2006.

It was finally a Venus Williams–led effort that got the All-England Club to join the other three Grand Slams. In 2005, the day before she played in the singles final at Wimbledon, she went to a meeting that included the heads of all the Grand Slams and made her pitch for equal prize money for women. She went out the next day and won Wimbledon in an epic match against Lindsay Davenport. She earned £30,000 less than Federer, the men's champion that year.[13]

After learning in early 2006 that Wimbledon would not be awarding equal prize money that year, Venus published an opinion piece in the *London Times* in June titled "Wimbledon Has Sent Me a Message: I'm Only a Second Class Champion." In it, she wrote:

I'm disappointed not for myself but for all of my fellow women players who have struggled so hard to get here and who, just like the men, give their all on the courts of SW19. I'm disappointed for the great legends of the game, such as Billie Jean King, Martina Navratilova and Chris Evert, who have never stopped fighting for equality. And disappointed that the home of tennis is sending a message to women across the world that we are inferior.

Venus listed several arguments for equal pay, noting that female players are willing and able to play five-set matches (rather than the standard three for ladies' matches), that the tournament treats men and women the same in all other aspects (including the stage and setting of the final match), and that her 2005 singles final victory was forty-five minutes longer than the men's that year—"no extra charge," thank you very much.[14]

That piece was a catalyst that pushed lawmakers in England to take up Venus's cause. Finally, the All-England Club conceded. In 2007, when Venus Williams was once again Wimbledon champion, she became the first woman to be awarded equal prize money for her efforts.

Despite more than a decade of women receiving equal prize money in Grand Glam tournaments, the debate continues. In 2016, Raymond Moore was the tournament director and CEO of the BNP Paribas Open in Indian Wells, California, an event that bills itself as "the largest professional two-week combined ATP [Association of Tennis Professionals, which oversees men's international tennis] and WTA [Women's Tennis Association] Tour tennis tournament in the world."[15] In a news conference during the tournament, Moore was asked about the WTA, to which he responded:

> In my next life when I come back I want to be someone in the WTA, (laughter) because they ride on the coattails of the men. They don't make any decisions and they are lucky. They are very, very lucky. If I was a lady player, I'd go down every night on my knees and thank God that Roger Federer and Rafa Nadal were born, because they have carried this sport. They really have.
>
> And now the mantle is being handed over to Djokovic and Murray and some others. You know, that's good. We have

no complaints. You know, we pay equal prize money. Do all those things. We don't have any complaints.

He went on to say that there were six top players in tennis: four men, Serena, and Maria Sharapova (who at the time was suspended for a doping violation). When asked why women's tennis does not have enough competition overall, Moore happily continued to dig himself a hole: "I think the WTA have a handful—not just one or two—but they have a handful of very attractive prospects that can assume the mantle. You know, [Garbiñe] Muguruza, Genie Bouchard. They have a lot of very attractive players. And the standard in ladies tennis has improved unbelievably." And when asked to clarify what he meant by "attractive," he kept digging: "They are physically attractive and competitively attractive. They can assume the mantle of leadership once Serena decides to stop. I think they've got—they really have quite a few very, very attractive players."[16] Welcome to The Hole of Your Own Making, Raymond Moore.

After Serena lost the final at Indian Wells that year to Victoria Azarenka and had to stand on the court with Moore as he presented the trophies to the two women, she was asked about his comments. "Obviously I don't think any woman should be down on their knees thanking anybody like that," Williams said. "If I could tell you every day how many people say they don't watch tennis unless they're watching myself or my sister, I couldn't even bring up that number. So I don't think that is a very accurate statement." Williams then pointed out that saying any woman should get on her knees for a man is "offensive" and that the US Open women's final the year before sold out before the men's. "I'm sorry," Williams said, "did Roger play in that final or Rafa or any man play in that final that was sold out before the men's final? I think not."

Moore apologized and then resigned. But not before the No. 1-ranked men's player in the world, Novak Djokovic, chimed in to say that the ATP "should fight for more because the stats are showing that we have much more spectators on the men's tennis matches. I think that's one of the, you know, reasons why maybe we should get awarded more."[17]

At the time he said this, Djokovic was on his way to earning

$55.8 million in a calendar year. He also had just earned more than $20 million in the 2015 season, the first player to ever do so, and he was months away from becoming the first tennis player ever to earn more than $100 million in career prize money. As of March 2020, his total lifetime prize money was up to $143 million.[18]

Compare that to Serena, who went professional in 1995, eight years before Djokovic. During her career (as of March 2020), she had earned $92 million in prize money, which was more than double the next closest woman. In 2016, she earned a total of $28.9 million including earnings and endorsements. (Both Williams and Djokovic paled in comparison to Federer's $67.8 million that year.) For Djokovic to whine publicly about how much men were earning, and to suggest that men should make more, is ridiculous on its face. Men already earn more in almost every key category.[19]

Djokovic pressed his argument anyway. And he made the same tiresome arguments for why women tennis players should be paid less: men play more tennis and draw more fans and should get more money as a result. First, equal prize money exists mainly in top-level tournaments, but players participate at all tournament levels throughout the year. Also, only in majors do men play best-of-five sets while women play best-of-three. Most of the time, men play three sets just like the women—and yet they still make more money than women. And anyway, as Venus wrote, women have long said they would play five sets if Grand Slams set up their tournaments that way. It is the tournaments that demure.[20]

Beyond all this, Grand Slams make money on TV rights and ticket sales, and men's and women's tennis is sold as a package deal. Lindsay Gibbs, author of the *Power Plays* newsletter on sports and gender and cofounder of the tennis website The Changeover, says: "You're selling Wimbledon as Wimbledon, not as men's Wimbledon and women's Wimbledon." And as Serena herself countered in response to Moore's comments, people buy tickets to watch her play. In fact, the year before it was Serena's participation at Indian Wells that drew a surge in ticket sales.[21]

Djokovic and others who argue that women deserve less than men miss the point. The BBC's Tom Fordyce put it this way: "People watch women's tennis for the contests and the characters, for the skill and the strategies, for the fact we are witnessing the best in their chosen field. To claim that men should take an even larger proportion of a revenue pool they already dominate would be to denigrate so much of that."[22] More succinctly, Billie Jean King told the *New York Times* that "we have a chance to continue to lead. To have equal prize money in the majors sends a message. It's not about the money, it's about the message."[23]

That is all well and good—but Serena is not just a woman. She is a Black woman in a world that values whiteness. In 2011, Brittney C. Cooper of the Crunk Feminist Collective wrote that "Serena continues to disrupt tennis spaces with her dark-skinned, powerful body, her flamboyant sartorial choices, her refusal to conform to the professional tennis obstacle course, and her willingness to get angry and show it."[24] And she literally pays a price for it.

———

For most of Serena's career, she made less than a white woman—Maria Sharapova—whom Williams has bested time and again on the tennis court. Williams and Sharapova have played twenty-two times in their careers, Serena winning nineteen of those, including their last eighteen meetings. Still, through 2015, Sharapova earned more total money than Serena, most of it derived from endorsements.[25]

This changed in 2016 while Sharapova was suspended for doping. For the first time, Serena was the world's richest female athlete. In 2015, in a profile of Williams and her place in American culture, the author Claudia Rankine asked Chris Evert, herself a tennis legend who won eighteen Grand Slams during her career in the 1970s and 1980s, about Sharapova's marketability versus Serena's. "I think the corporate world still loves the good-looking blond girls," Evert told her. When Rankine pushed Evert, saying that this goes beyond the color of Sharapova's hair and more to the color of Serena's skin, Evert, Rankine writes, "suggested that any demonstration of corporate preference is about a certain 'type' of look or image, not whiteness in general."[26] It's no stretch to say that marketers believe their consumers are more interested in worshipping the beauty of tall, skinny white women over and above well-built, muscled Black ones. Beyond all this, it's a fool's errand to argue that Serena and Venus have not faced a consistent stream of racism throughout their careers.

Columnists and commentators have spent decades critiquing and judging Serena's body, her work ethic, and her overall fitness. The public has taken to social media repeatedly and engaged in sexist and transphobic language to describe the Williams sisters. Jenée Desmond-Harris described one instance of this at Vox: "In the moments surrounding her win at the French Open in June 2015, Williams was compared to an animal, likened to a man, and deemed frightening and horrifyingly unattractive." In 2007, at the Miami Open during one of Serena's matches, a spectator yelled out: "Hit the ball into the net like any negro would!" Serena's good friend Caroline Wozniacki once impersonated Serena's body by stuffing towels in front of her breasts and butt to increase their size. (Serena, for her part, was unbothered by the display.) In 2014, the Russian Tennis Federation's president referred to Serena and Venus as "the Williams brothers." In 2017, after Serena announced she and her fiancé, who is white, were expecting their first child together, Ilie Nastase, the Romanian Fed Cup captain, said, "Let's see what color it has. Chocolate with milk?"[27]

Perhaps most famously, though, is the treatment Serena and Venus endured early in their careers at Indian Wells. In 2001, Venus, twenty years old at the time, was supposed to play her sister, who was nineteen, in a semifinal match, but she pulled out just before, citing knee tendinitis. When Serena took the court for the final two days later and Venus and her father appeared in the stands to watch, the crowd booed. Their father, Richard Williams, who was their coach at the time, said one person shouted, "N——, stay away from here, we don't want you here." Richard Williams also reported: "One guy said, 'I wish it was '75; we'd skin you alive.'" Serena won the title that day, but neither sister returned to the event for fourteen years.[28]

In 2015, Serena entered the tournament draw at Indian Wells. Explaining her return, she wrote in *Time* magazine:

> It has been difficult for me to forget spending hours crying in the Indian Wells locker room after winning in 2001, driving back to Los Angeles feeling as if I had lost the biggest game ever—not a mere tennis game but a bigger fight for equality. Emotionally it seemed easier to stay away. There are some who say I should never go back. There are others who say I should've returned years ago. I understand both perspectives very well and wrestled with them for a long time. I'm just following my heart on this one.

She believed tennis had changed and she was ready to forgive those who had harmed her in the past. But she did it on her terms: at the same time she announced her return, she also revealed she would be doing a raffle (the winner getting to stand with her at Indian Wells) and that all the proceeds would go toward the Equal Justice Initiative, an organization that describes itself as "committed to ending mass incarceration and excessive punishment in the United States, to challenging racial and economic injustice, and to protecting basic human rights for the most vulnerable people in American society."[29]

The choice not to play at Indian Wells in protest of racist treatment was a financial and professional hit for the Williamses. As Paul Oberjuerge explained in the *New York Times* in 2009 (eight years into their boycott of the tournament and under new rules instituted by the WTA that year), skipping Indian Wells meant "the Williams sisters are sustaining injury to their world rankings, losing money from the bonus pool and must perform a day of tennis-related activity within 125 miles of Indian Wells—or face a two-week suspension and a $75,000 fine." Year after year, they defied the rule to attend this now-mandatory tour event and paid the fine. Year after year, they refused to let the tennis world forget.[30]

Then, in her second year back at the tournament, Serena found herself having to respond to the tournament director's comments about women players getting on their knees in thanks to the men's tour.

———

In the end, despite the racism and sexism she encounters on the tour, and even though she has often made less than a white woman she routinely beat throughout their careers, and made less than men who perform at the same level as she, Serena has no financial worries. This is not to argue at all that her financial status among professional tennis players is fair. Rather it's to point out how large the discrepancy is between those in the lower rankings of the sport and those sitting at the top.

We can argue all day about what the top players are making—but it's clear they are making good money. Many on the pro circuit do not.

Tennis players compete as individuals and do not receive the benefit of salaries paid by franchise organizations as in major team sports. The financial burden rests solely on their shoulders. Lindsay Gibbs says that in order for a player to be a part of the professional tour, which is year-round and international, one has to, you know, get there: "You have to get yourself to and from tournaments. And then when you get to tournaments, you don't know how long you're going to stay. It's a lot of buying flights the night before you need them, which is not the most economical way. The player has to pay for the travel for the coach and for the [support] team and for anyone that comes with them."[31]

The consequences of this are stark. Carl Bialik noted in 2014 for FiveThirtyEight that "only 336 men and 253 women made more than they spent playing tennis last year." That sounds like a lot unless we consider other sports. "If you're the 350th best man in the world at baseball, basketball, American football, ice hockey or soccer, you're earning more than $500,000 each year, expenses paid," Bialik wrote. "If you're the 350th best man in tennis, you're probably either falling into debt or getting help from a sponsor or parent."[32]

Gibbs notes that some players' costs are supported by a federation or their home country, and some receive sponsorships. But the difference between the top and the bottom is stark. The worst way this plays out is seen in the sacrifices that those on the lower rungs will make in terms of their bodies and health. In tennis, "there is no salary," Gibbs points out. "You are literally playing for your prize money every week. There's nothing guaranteed, there's nobody paying for you while you are rehabbing [an injury]." A player might be injured and should be resting, but financially that may be a harmful decision. Gibbs suggests this scenario: "There's a Grand Slam the following week where you qualified for the main draw and even just for playing that one match, even if you don't win it, you'll get $40,000, which is a huge chunk of the money you earn every year." In that case, you probably play the game no matter the physical costs. "The temptation to get out there on court even if you're not completely healthy is massive and understandable," she says.

In many ways, it's no wonder that tennis has problems with match-fixing and doping. And while the Grand Slam tournaments increased prize money to participants, payouts at smaller tournaments remain stagnant. Darren Cahill, a professional tennis coach and ESPN commentator, said a few years ago that "there are Futures and Challengers tournaments—$25,000 and $15,000 Challenger tournaments that haven't offered more prize money for the last 30 years." Gibbs noted that "between 2000 and 2014, for instance, the prize money at the Grand Slams nearly doubled. It stayed exactly the same at the lower levels." If a player ranks at the bottom, it's easy to get stuck there with no financial mobilization to help prepare him or her to battle consistently in a physically wearing sport.[33]

For Gibbs, the answer is (at least in part) to trickle money from the top down to provide lower-ranked players a better shot at moving up. She also wants to see more money go into developing the game—especially in areas, say, without country clubs.

What happens, though, when all of this comes together—the racism, the sexism, and the inequity in tennis? Taylor Townsend might know. Townsend, a young Black female tennis player from Chicago, made headlines in 2012 when she was only sixteen. The United States Tennis Association (USTA), then under the direction of Patrick McEnroe (a TV analyst, John's youngest brother, and a former tennis star in his own right), withdrew financial support for Townsend before the US Open and asked her not to attend. This shocking development came despite the fact that Townsend was the No. 1–ranked junior player in the world. Tom Perrotta reported the decision this way: "Her coaches declined to pay her travel expenses to attend the Open and told her this summer that they wouldn't finance any tournament appearances until she makes sufficient progress in one area: slimming down and getting into better shape." McEnroe justified the decision this way: "Our concern is her long-term health, number one, and her long-term development as a player." Few people bought that. McEnroe would eventually admit they were concerned about Townsend's weight.[34]

Townsend—if we were to compare her to anyone else on the tennis tour—looks most like Serena Williams. Her body is black and female; it thus was scrutinized and found wanting in the same ways that Serena's had often been despite their successes on the court. To make matters worse, the USTA's decision affected Townsend financially in a sport that is already economically stratified and hard to succeed in if one doesn't have enough money. Townsend's mother, Sheila, had to pay her daughter's way to the US Open that year. Townsend played in the juniors and lost in the quarterfinals.

Based on what we know about Serena's treatment over two and a half decades because of her skin color and body shape, it's hard not to connect the dots in Townsend's story. Writing for *Sports Illustrated* back in 2012 in the midst of the controversy, Courtney Nguyen characterized the issue in stark terms: "Instead of helping a promising young talent gain that confidence and experience gleaned from competing, the USTA has taken a paternalistic tack, deeming itself the arbiter and architect behind Townsend's past, present and future success. It's the arrogance of [an] institution built on the belief that there is a tried-and-true formula to build a champion."[35] Even as recently as 2012, that formula didn't include Serena—and so it still could not include Townsend.

———

Sometimes, the green and white hallmarks of tennis become overwhelming. They throw into relief too much about the sport that is hard to justify. But as Serena said in her return to Indian Wells in 2015, things are getting better. From Sloane Stephens and Madison Keys to Taylor Townsend, Victoria Duval, Coco Gauff, and Jamie Hampton—in US women's tennis alone—the field has diversified. Anyone can see it.

This list doesn't even include Naomi Osaka, the twenty-some-thing, two-time Grand Slam champion whose mother is Japanese and father is Haitian. Osaka grew up in the United States and plays for Japan. She has said that Serena is her idol and that during important moments during matches she thinks to herself: *"What would Serena do?"*[36]

Seeking her first major women's singles title, Osaka faced none other than Serena Williams at the 2018 US Open final. The events that surrounded her victory, however, showed everyone watching how Serena had already carved a path for younger up-and-coming players of color—as well as the burdens they face today and in the future. In the second set, Serena—already down one set to Osaka, who was playing beautiful tennis—was struggling and she responded angrily to the chair umpire, who had penalized her for her coach violating the no-coaching rule. "I have never cheated in my life!" Williams exclaimed to the chair. "You owe me an apology." When the umpire did not reverse the penalty or apologize, Williams called him a thief for stealing a point from her. At that point—in the final of a major tournament—he issued another violation, costing Serena the game and putting Osaka within one game of winning the title. Serena continued to press her point and directly addressed the tournament referee: "To lose a game for saying that is not fair," Williams said. "There's a lot of men out here that have said a lot of things, and because they are men, that doesn't happen."[37]

Osaka won. Only twenty years old and overwhelmed after winning her first major title, she apologized through tears to the crowd during the trophy presentation: "I'm sorry. I know that everyone was cheering for her, and I'm sorry that it had to end like this." Serena has maintained ever since that the calls were sexist in nature and that she was fighting for the women who are coming up behind her. Some fans and the media came to Serena's defense, citing the long history of sexism and racism she has faced in the sport; others commented that she was an entitled bully who ruined Osaka's moment.

In 2019, Serena revealed in a 2019 *Harper's Bazaar* piece that she wrote Osaka an email in the weeks following: "As I said on the court, I am so proud of you and I am truly sorry. I thought I was doing the right thing in sticking up for myself. But I had no idea the media would pit us against each other." Osaka acknowledged this dynamic—the Williams-versus-Osaka divide—in a 2019 piece written by Soraya McDonald. Talking to McDonald about that US Open final, Osaka, through tears, said:

> If I were to put it bluntly, I know that there's a lot of people that don't like Serena, and I feel like they're just looking for someone to sort of jump on to be against her and I feel like they found that in me. Of course, I don't really like that. . . . I want people to go with me for the right reasons. If I'm being blunt, I feel like that's happened a lot, like after the U.S. Open.

She expressed herself this way: "I love Serena."

> Growing up . . . I really loved watching her matches, and honestly, I wouldn't be where I am without her. That's a fact. She opened so many doors for tennis and especially for people of color. When you're little and you're growing up and you're watching people, like the Indian Wells thing that happened. . . . For me, that was "How can a human be so strong?" That's one of the reasons I love her so much.[38]

In that *Harper's Bazaar* piece, Serena revealed how Osaka responded to her apology email: "'People can misunderstand anger for strength because they can't differentiate between the two,' she said graciously. 'No one has stood up for themselves the way you have and you need to continue trailblazing.'"

———

This is all to demonstrate that the sport has come a long way—especially in the wake of the extraordinary talent of the Williams sisters—but it still has a long way to go. This is reflected in Soraya McDonald's recent tennis fandom.

McDonald, the culture critic at ESPN's The Undefeated, a website that explores the intersections of race, sports, and culture, has only lately become a tennis fan. Well, a fan of women's tennis. "I usually tell people I'm a tennis misandrist," she jokes. "Because I just . . . I really don't care what the men are doing. I don't pay attention to them." She first covered tennis during the 2018 Osaka–Williams US Open final. "I was basically sent to be on Serena watch," McDonald says. "But because she doesn't play against herself, you learn about [her opponents], too, and their quirks, you go to their press conferences and you learn about their personalities. You sort of get submerged." And less than a year later, as she watched Serena play a flawless Simona Halep in the Wimbledon singles final—a match and tournament she wasn't assigned to cover for her work—she realized she'd become personally emotionally invested.[39]

McDonald says that it's been a bit weird covering the sport as a Black woman, that she has been the only Black person in the tennis media center at a Grand Slam. But because of The Undefeated's mission, she has been able to focus on "how these Black women were faring in the sport. Aside from just being athletes and competitors, but also the atmosphere around them and how they're being affected by it. And the discussion around them and how they're affected by that, too."

This means that she is often interrogating the more problematic parts of the sport—but it's also why she is a fan. She has embraced the women's tour, learned these women's stories, and found it all incredibly compelling. She also does what she has to do to enjoy the matches and tournaments. Tennis, McDonald says, is "just like anything else. Screwed up things are gonna happen and screwed up things around identity are going to happen. And you find a way to make your fandom work for you. If that means watching these matches on mute, which is what I do, by all means." She acknowledges that this is a Band-Aid on the problems and that it is messed up that fans even have to do this. But the alternative isn't great, either: "Don't let the big giant screwed up issues of the world that we're not going to solve tomorrow keep you away from the sport, and the people who play it, and their really awesome, interesting stories."

———

As this book goes to print, Serena Williams has gone back on tour after a pregnancy and labor that nearly killed her.[40] She struggled with injury in her return but has made multiple Grand Slam finals. She is still chasing that elusive twenty-fourth championship title. Two of those finals have been at Wimbledon. Once again dressed in all-white, right down to her underwear and the soles of her shoes, she has battled on the green courts. She remains at once a symbol of the traditions of tennis—its whiteness and its money—and where it is headed—her Blackness, her equal pay despite her gender, and the continued popularity of the women's game.

It is because of Serena (and her sister, Venus) that we have a different tennis future to anticipate, one that makes it easier to weather the inevitable racist, sexist, and classist remarks that will dribble from the mouths of tennis players, fans, and officials.

As fans and contemporaries of this epic story, we have lived during the best of tennis. We have witnessed the greatest weapon ever in the game—the Serena serve. And yet, there is no reason to believe that more brilliance is not yet to come.

CHAPTER 5

COPING WHEN THE SPORTS
YOU LOVE ARE ANTI-LGBTQ+

"The first game I ever played was called 'Smear the Queer,'" Wade
Davis, a former professional football player, says as he thinks back
on his early days playing the sport. "I started playing football at the
age of seven in my backyard in Louisiana," and this was the game
they'd play. He explains that it's "this pickup game of football where
you just have a group of kids and you have a football and someone
throws it up in the air, and the queer is the one that tries to pick it
up and score and everyone else tries to smear that queer."[1]

Plenty of people will recognize the game but maybe not the
name, as it has a host of aliases: Throw-up Tackle; Crush the Car-
rier; Throw Them Up, Bust Them Up; Muckle; and Rumble Fumble,
among others. But Davis grew up playing Smear the Queer, which
is ironic given where his life has taken him. After reaching the NFL
and then retiring from football, Davis announced publicly in 2012
that he is gay. He has spent the intervening years working with You
Can Play, an organization "dedicated to ensuring equality, respect
and safety for all athletes, without regard to sexual orientation

and/or gender identity," as well as serving as the NFL's first LGBTQ+ inclusion consultant.[2] He gives talks on the subject, does workshops, consults with technology firms, and created the Men's Gender Equality Development leadership program that he launched with the United Nations.

Looking back now on the homophobically named backyard game he played with friends, Davis says: "It was just interesting for me to be a gay man and how all of this came full circle. To think that that was my introduction to the game that I love."

———

It's not surprising that some of Davis's earliest memories of sports overlap with homophobia. It is deeply embedded in sports (as well as in most parts of most cultures throughout the world), as is transphobia and the erasure of all people whose identities challenge the rigid gender binary sports is predicated on (one plays either men's sports or women's sports, after all).

Because sports are coded masculine in our society, it's assumed that to be good at them athletes can't be girly. As the author Eric Anderson wrote in 2005: "Sport remains an area that reproduces a desire for the toughest form of masculinity, an attitude in which 'men are men'; an arena in which homosexuality, femininity, and other assumed 'weaknesses' are not perceived as being conducive to the ultimate quest for victory."[3]

More than that, it's sports that help make you a man. Misogyny, homophobia, and transphobia are not accidental byproducts of sports; rather those are natural outcomes of sports as currently imagined. On this point, in an October 2017 interview on NBC wide receiver Julio Jones told Hall of Fame NFL coach Tony Dungy that he played Smear the Queer as a kid. Dungy asked him if that is where he got his toughness from, and Jones replied, "most definitely."[4]

There is no denying that strides have been made for lesbian, gay, bisexual, transgender, queer, and nonbinary athletes (shortened to the most common acronym LGBTQ+, which itself is not all-encompassing), especially since 2000. When it comes to visibility, inclusivity, and opportunities in sports, it is seemingly better than it's ever been. This matters because as long as there have been sports, there have been gay, lesbian, bisexual, nonbinary, queer, and trans athletes. In the United States alone, an obvious list includes tennis legends Billie Jean King and Martina Navratilova, soccer superstars Megan Rapinoe and Abby Wambach, former NBAer John Amaechi, LPGA star Rosie Jones, WNBA All-Stars Brittney Griner and Seimone Augustus, and Olympian Caitlyn Jenner. There are many, many more LGBTQ+ athletes around the world, and whether or not they have publicly disclosed it, they are there.[5]

There is an ongoing tension between how far we have come with LGBTQ+ inclusivity in society—and sports specifically—and how far we have yet to go. This rigidly gendered, masculine system chafes at any challenge to it. Homophobia and transphobia still very much exist within sports, as they do within our culture at large. The Mexican national soccer team continually gets in trouble for its fans shouting a homophobic slur; a promising US soccer player refused to wear a rainbow jersey and quit the US national team over it; every few years an NBA player is fined for using a slur during a game; and transgender athletes across the globe are constantly fighting simply to compete.[6] Nonbinary and genderqueer people barely have a place in sports.[7]

There is still so much work to be done. And LGBTQ+ athletes, coaches, agents, administrators, referees, and fans deserve that we all continue doing that work.

———

Because major men's professional sports in the United States get the most attention and media coverage, the lack of publicly out gay male athletes participating in them is the most obvious place to start. It's also a quick place to start.

As this book goes to print, there is no out gay man actively playing in the National Football League, the National Basketball League, Major League Baseball, National Hockey League, or Major League Soccer. But there have been a few in recent years. On June 29, 2018, Collin Martin, a midfielder for Major League Soccer's Minnesota United team, publicly disclosed on Twitter that his team's pride night was "an important night for me—I'll be announcing that I am an openly gay player in Major League Soccer." His family had known for years, and he told his teammates and the team's staff more than a year earlier. He felt it was now time to publicly disclose, because he wants to "maybe see if I can just affect more people, because I think I've affected a lot of people in my daily life and around this locker room positively just by being myself," he told the local paper. "It's important for people to just respect themselves and respect their own timeline but to also just be open and honest and understand that locker rooms are changing." In February 2020, Martin left the MLS and signed with the San Diego Loyal SC, a team in the USL Championship, a lower-division league.[8]

Martin is not the first active male player in major men's professional sports to publicly disclose. Robbie Rogers, another MLS player, did so in 2013, announcing both his sexuality and that he was stepping away from soccer. But his break from the sport was short-lived, and he went back a few months later, joining the LA Galaxy. That next year, in 2014, as a starter much of the season, his team won the MLS Cup.[9]

In between the time that Rogers came out and his return to the soccer pitch, Jason Collins appeared on the cover of *Sports Illustrated* with an accompanying article that he wrote himself. It started: "I'm a 34-year-old NBA center. I'm Black. And I'm gay."[10] Collins was a free agent at the time but joined the Brooklyn Nets the next season. He retired in November 2014, writing again in *Sports Illustrated*— this time about his experience as an active, out player in the NBA: "Among the memories I will cherish most are the warm applause I received in Los Angeles when I took the court in my Nets debut, and the standing ovation I got at my first home game in Brooklyn. It shows how far we've come."[11]

And then, in February 2014, after completing his senior season at the University of Missouri and before the NFL draft, Michael Sam, an All-American defensive lineman and Southeastern Conference Defensive Player of the Year, conducted interviews during which he publicly disclosed he was gay. At the time Sam announced this, the *New York Times* reported that scouts thought he could go as high as the third round in the draft.[12] On draft day in May, however, he went 249th overall in the seventh and final round, barely making the cut. A camera in his home beamed an image of Sam crying on the phone when he got the news and then kissing his boyfriend. People speculated that his fall in the draft was because he was gay. Or that teams feared he'd be a distraction (and based on how sports teams talk about distractions, there's nothing worse). Or for those locked in a fantasy world, that Sam was just not as good as everyone had thought—something they all figured out only after he told the world he was gay.[13]

In his 2016 book *Fair Play: How LGBT Athletes Are Claiming Their Rightful Place in Sports*, Cyd Zeigler, founder of the sports news website Outsports, wrote about his reaction to Sam falling in the draft and then being cut by the team who drafted him: "I had spent a lot of time and energy defending the NFL as a meritocracy where Sam's sexual orientation would not play a factor in his ability to make it in the NFL. That was now crashing down as quite the opposite became more and more apparent."[14]

Sam jumped around from team to team but never played in the NFL, and his time playing in the Canadian Football League—as the first openly gay man to do so—was brief. He eventually left the sport altogether in August 2015, saying that "the last 12 months have been very difficult for me, to the point where I became concerned with my mental health."[15] He left the door open for a possible comeback, which seems increasingly unlikely.

Sam's story shows the risks for gay male athletes to publicly disclose and why so few do. This causes a particular challenge for younger athletes. Wade Davis says that college players have to consider their professional futures when deciding whether to come out publicly. "Will this pro sports league accept me if I'm open in college and then I come to the pros? There is still that fear that I can't do that," Davis says.

Ultimately, we have to stop caring so much about these athletes in these particular sports. The focus on major men's professional sports obscures so many other people. A quick perusal of Outsports on any day will show you LGBTQ+ athletes in all kinds of sports, from track and field, to wrestling, to diving. espnW and a host of other sport websites are telling stories of LGBTQ+ athletes across the sporting world. At the 2018 Winter Olympics, a rugged, bearded freestyle skier named Gus Kenworthy kissed his boyfriend during NBC's primetime broadcast before one of his runs. They are very good looking people. Audiences were thrilled.

During that same Olympics, Adam Rippon, an American figure skater, took the world by storm. It's hard to overstate his popularity during and since those Games. Peter Moskovitz wrote at the time that in trying to figure out why Rippon, more than any other gay male athlete, had made him want to talk to everyone about this gay male athlete, he realized Rippon's "gayness is not an afterthought, but a central piece of his personality."[16]

In response to this piece, Rippon told *HuffPost* that he's "discovered what I perceive as masculine and what I perceive as feminine," and he tries to be as true to himself as possible. This is a particular challenge in sports, Rippon said, because "I think a lot of times, when somebody's out and gay—especially in sports—they try to really overcompensate [be very masculine], because I think being gay is associated with being weak, which isn't true."[17]

We have to move beyond men's professional sports when thinking about visibility and acceptance of gay male athletes. And we have to move beyond the "G" in LGBTQ+ because there is a whole spectrum of people playing sports and breaking barriers. By centering male pro athletes, we lose sight of the barrier breakers.

———

On June 29, 2018, Candice Dupree of the WNBA's Indiana Fever and DeWanna Bonner of the Phoenix Mercury played against each other for the first time since Bonner's return from maternity leave. This was significant because Bonner's partner is Dupree herself, and together they are mothers to twin girls.[18]

Earlier that week, Megan Rapinoe, who plays in the National Women's Soccer League for the Seattle Reign, and Sue Bird, point guard for the Seattle Storm, became the first same-sex couple to appear on the cover of *ESPN The Magazine*'s annual *The Body Issue*. Rapinoe, in an interview with ESPN, spoke of the significance of that cover: "It's pretty amazing to think about, especially in the times we're in. Just think of how far we've come, but also the current climate and defiance in the face of that."[19]

These two events, back to back, illustrate a point made by Katie

Barnes, a writer and reporter for espnW whose work often covers LGBTQ+ athletes. When it comes to visibility and acceptance in sport, they say, "we are seeing the most success across the board with queer women." (Barnes is nonbinary and uses "they/them/their" pronouns.) Wade Davis agrees: "Lesbian athletes do not get the credit for doing really transformative, revolutionary work being openly lesbian in their sport." He says this is because "the intersection of homophobia and sexism has really muted us giving credit to women for being out in their given sport."[20]

That same sexism causes a particular kind of homophobia that female athletes face. "Sports is coded as masculine and queerness is coded as masculine if you're assigned female at birth," Barnes says. "If you're a girl and you play sports, especially at a high level," people assume you are queer. "Queer female athletes," then, "in general do not get the attention that gay men do when they come out, largely because the assumption is like, 'oh, well, of course.'" In a 2017 piece, Barnes wrote: "To fight back against this idea, it is not uncommon to see overt displays of femininity on the field at every level of women's sports. One of the reasons more girls play volleyball than basketball is because volleyball is perceived as being more feminine."[21]

One place that this plays out is on the college level, where student athletes are recruited, rather than drafted or offered financial incentives as free agents, as they would be in a professional league.

In 2007, Rene Portland, the head coach of the Pennsylvania State University women's basketball team, resigned after twenty-seven years and more than 600 wins. She had come under intense public scrutiny for what a former player, Jennifer Harris, called Portland's "no-lesbian" policy. Harris filed a lawsuit in 2005 against Portland and Penn State. According to the Associated Press, "Harris accused Portland of 'humiliating, berating and ostracizing' her, and claimed she was told she needed to look 'more feminine.' The suit alleged Portland tried to force Harris, who says she is not gay, to leave the team." A university investigation led to a reprimand of Portland, as well as a fine of $10,000, and she was forced to undertake personal development about diversity and inclusiveness. Harris, though, was the last in a string of people to report

Portland, who had said as early as 1986 that she didn't allow lesbians to play on her team.[22]

Portland was not an isolated case. In 2013, former Baylor standout Brittney Griner said that she had to remain in the closet while in school because her coach specifically told her not to be publicly out. "It was a recruiting thing," Griner told ESPN. "The coaches thought that if it seemed like they condoned it, people wouldn't let their kids come play for Baylor."[23] In late 2014, two female basketball players sued Pepperdine University for discrimination because their head coach believed they were gay and made it clear they were unwelcome on the team.[24]

Barnes points out that there are almost no out queer women playing at the NCAA's highest Division 1 level, at least not with the visibility we see in professional ranks such as the WNBA (they are more likely to keep their relationships confined to personal Instagram accounts rather than the front page).[25]

All of this, in turn, harms lesbian coaches. Wade Davis says: "If you look at the women's side, one of the challenges that openly lesbian coaches have is that other coaches will use that against her in their recruiting process." Coaches worry that parents will not send daughters to programs that are accepting and inclusive; fearing parents' homophobic responses, coaches create homophobic cultures at their schools.

In 2017, the *Chicago Tribune* ran a piece about former Portland State coach Sherri Murrell, who in 2009 was the first openly gay Division I basketball coach. Murrell told the Tribune's Shannon Ryan: "If (coaches) are outspoken or more public about it, it's just one more thing to cause them to not get a job or cause them to get fired possibly. In recruiting, everyone has this fear. The world is changing, but it seems like there's this cloud that continues to hang over sports and coaching, especially for women coaches."[26]

Of course, there are even fewer publicly gay male coaches. As Davis observes, "If you have an openly gay man as a coach, and people are accepting him and embracing him, then that means that your son, your brothers, are actually being educated and taught in this hyper masculine space by someone who we've historically deemed as less than a man."

The one exception is Curt Miller, coach and general manager of the WNBA's Connecticut Sun. In a 2018 *New York Times* profile of Miller, John Altavilla reported that Miller is "believed to be the first openly gay male coach of a professional sports team in the United States."[27] Miller told Altavilla that he was closeted for years because "during recruiting wars, I wondered if my sexuality would scare families." Ultimately, he publicly disclosed and has, clearly, been successful in his career. The Connecticut Sun came within one game of winning the 2019 WNBA championship. It makes sense, based on everything just mentioned, that he coaches women and has found his highest profile on the professional level.

Wade Davis hopes "we get to a space where you have more openly lesbian and gay coaches in sports." Openly gay coaches, especially at the collegiate level (but also at the men's professional level), will indicate a significant shift in acceptance and opportunity.

———

And we can't overlook bisexual athletes (the "B" in LGBTQ+), because the discussion around them is virtually absent. Society tends to boil everything down to one thing or the other, flattening and even erasing any identities that appear complicated. This is generally how bisexual people are treated—and it's the same within sports.

In August 2019, NFL defensive end Ryan Russell publicly disclosed that he is "a talented football player, a damn good writer, a loving son, an overbearing brother, a caring friend, a loyal lover, and a bisexual man." He said that growing up, "I always felt as though my existence slipped between the cracks of two worlds." He expanded: "I wasn't flamboyant, tidy, or any other stereotypes kids are forced to construct their world around. I wasn't straight, hyper-masculine or aggressive; I cried quite a bit, and, as a young Black man, I didn't fit the bill. I played football—so I put that in the straight column. I wrote poetry and romance stories—so I put that in the gay column." Ultimately, Russell said, he wants to bring all his worlds together, but he wonders: "Can I unify my separate professional and personal lives into a single one?" Russell did not play during the 2018 or 2019 NFL seasons.[28]

In response to Russell's disclosure, Britni de la Cretaz wrote this for MTV News: "While [Ryan] Russell's openness is important for athletes on the field and in the locker room, it's also important for fans watching at home, especially given how the sports world is notorious for being unwelcoming to its LGBTQ+ fans, and stadiums are not exactly known as bastions of queer acceptance." For this piece de la Cretaz interviewed Wade Davis about his views on Russell: "Davis, too, underscores the significance of Russell coming out as bisexual—or, as Davis prefers to call it, 'letting the world in.' 'I hope that it creates a more curious conversation' around identity, and the nuances of identity, 'especially among people who identify as male,' he [Davis] says."[29]

While bisexual athletes have a sexuality that doesn't slot neatly into "straight" or "gay," transgender athletes have a gender identity that does not fit squarely into "man" or "woman." Their struggle for equality in sports is substantial.

———

In 2015, Chris Mosier qualified for the US Men's National Sprint Duathlon Team. In 2016, at the age of thirty-five, Mosier became the first known transgender athlete to compete in an International Triathlon Union championship. At the end of 2019, Mosier qualified for the Men's 50K Race Walk Championship in 2020, the top three finishers of which compete for Team USA at the Summer Olympics in Tokyo.[30]

According to GLAAD (formerly the Gay & Lesbian Alliance Against Defamation), "transgender" is "an umbrella term for people whose gender identity and/or gender expression differs from what is typically associated with the sex they were assigned at birth." Importantly, "many transgender people are prescribed hormones by their doctors to bring their bodies into alignment with their gender identity. Some undergo surgery as well. But not all transgender people can or will take those steps, and a transgender identity is not dependent upon physical appearance or medical procedures."[31]

Chris Mosier has continued to qualify for teams time and again. He has been featured in a Nike ad and in *ESPN The Magazine*'s *The Body Issue*. It's been a journey, though. For a long time, Mosier says, he wasn't sure if he could maintain "my identity as a transgender man and continue to compete in sports at a competitive level. Simply put, I just didn't see it. I didn't have an example of a person that I could look to and say, 'Here's a transgender man competing against men after a medical transition and competing at a high level.' And that's really what I wanted."[32]

Trans athletes face a particular kind of scrutiny, which mainly falls on trans women.[33] In a series at Victory Press in 2017, a writer named Andrew took a deep dive into the unfair ways that trans athletes' bodies are policed and why. It's a long, complicated history that has involved invasive sex testing and "a tendency to medicalize gender identity," which can include trans athletes being forced to "undergo both top and bottom surgeries, including reproductive system surgeries (forced castration or sterilization)." As Andrew notes: "Not only do such mandates violate the human rights of trans athletes, they undermine self-identification as a valid method of declaring trans identity."[34]

This is often all predicated on the belief that women's sports must be protected from interlopers (men somehow masquerading as trans women) because women's sports are easy for men to dominate and, therefore, easy to cheat. It's also dependent on this idea that "men" and "women" are rigid, simple categories. Jennifer Doyle, a professor at University of California, Riverside, addressed this idea that men are better all-around athletes than women: "The truth is: the fastest men are faster than the fastest women. Some men are faster than all women and most men, but some women are also faster than most men. . . . Most men reading these sentences are, in fact, quite a bit slower than the slowest women running her event in Rio [Summer Olympics 2016]."[35]

A trans female mixed martial artist like Fallon Fox is always going to be more critically questioned than a trans male duathlete like Chris Mosier. Mosier is seen as doing better than what his biological body would suggest based on our sexist notions about gendered bodies; Fox, by contrast, is seen as exploiting an advantage that her body provides.

In a post titled "Meet some trans athletes who work hard, train like mad and (almost) never win" at Outsports in December

2019, Cyd Zeigler, in order to work against the misguided notion that being trans is a direct line to the medal stand, profiled four trans athletes who don't win. All four athletes in the piece are trans women.[36]

To be sure, transphobia goes beyond individual athletes. All trans athletes are harmed collectively by antitrans policies and laws. When North Carolina passed an antitransgender bill in March 2016 that barred "transgender people from bathrooms and locker rooms that do not match the gender on their birth certificates" and "prohibit[ed] municipalities from creating their own antidiscrimination policies," the bill was denounced by many people. It put trans people in danger, forcing them into spaces where they didn't feel comfortable. The NCAA pulled events out of the state because it couldn't guarantee the safety of all athletes. The law was repealed a year later.[37]

In some states, trans athletes have no choice but to participate in a gender category that does not match their identity. In a 2018 piece for *ESPN The Magazine*, Katie Barnes wrote about Mack Beggs. "Mack, 19, is a transgender boy who wrestles girls because the Texas high school athletic association, the University Interscholastic League (UIL), determines gender strictly by birth certificate, a policy approved in 2016 by 586 of 620 superintendents. Mack's certificate reads 'female.'" Beggs wants very badly to wrestle with boys (and many of the parents of the female wrestlers want this, too), but the policy denies him this chance.[38]

Chris Mosier believes that education is a first step in the long process to gain more acceptance for trans athletes. "While I think most people in the United States have an understanding or an idea or have heard of the word 'transgender' as an identity—and I do attribute that in large part to Caitlyn Jenner coming out, to Laverne Cox being a transgender advocate and public figure—this is not a topic that people have been taught in school," Mosier observes. "You don't know what you don't know." So Mosier started a site to educate people about trans athletes: Transathlete.com, "a resource for students, athletes, coaches, and administrators to find information about trans inclusion in athletics at various levels of play." He wants people to understand "there's not just one way of being transgender." His site offers information on "all of these things of the very basic LGBTQ 101 for people."

———

Gay, lesbian, bisexual, and trans athletes make people question their own ideas about masculinity, femininity, and how we differentiate and define "men" and "women," but nonbinary and genderqueer athletes shake up the entire notion of gender in sport—a space often defined by the gender binary. Where everyone fits into the modern framework of sport is still very much unsettled.

Katie Barnes grew up in Indiana. Basketball was their first memory, and by age eight they were playing on a girl's team. "Most of my time was spent in basketball," they say. "I started traveling when I was in seventh grade and I did AAU. I played at a couple of pretty high-powered gyms." They played varsity level all through high school, a point guard mostly. "My claim to fame," they say, "I totally played against Skylar Diggins [also an Indiana native and current point guard for the WNBA's Phoenix Mercury]. That was a thing that happened in my life." They were recruited to play college ball but declined. Instead, "I coached basketball while I was in college."

It's hard to overstate what basketball meant in Barnes's life, the role that it played. In 2016, reflecting on it, they wrote:

> The basketball court became my refuge. As an athlete, I created a sliver of space for myself to exist as I truly wanted. My masculinity morphed into athletic performance, ghettoizing a portion of my soul to the baggy shorts I gently sagged, cut-off tees, and cocksure court swagger. I was Peter Pan and masculinity my shadow, and the only time I could sew myself together was when my shoes burned over hardwood. Basketball gave me a breath of life when the rest of the world ripped me apart.[39]

As Barnes got older and gained new language to describe their identity, they realized they are nonbinary, which GLAAD describes as "people who experience their gender identity and/or gender expression as falling outside the categories of man and woman.

They may define their gender as falling somewhere in between man and woman, or they may define it as wholly different from these terms."[40]

This made Barnes's relationship with sports "more complicated, as opposed to resolving it," they say. Because sports demands that people pick one or the other, for a nonbinary person that distinction can be alienating. "The person that I was as an athlete many years ago is very different than the person I am today," Barnes says. "Today, I think, 'where would I play?' I don't know."

"We're a long ways off when it comes to trans inclusion," but "we're even further when it comes to non-binary identities, genderqueer identities," Barnes says. Those identities challenge "the very fundamentals of what we believe to be true about sport, about gender, about sex, about science." "For folks who are non-binary," Barnes says, "it becomes so hard for us to see ourselves reflected not just in athletes themselves, but in the very opportunities to participate in sport at large."

Layshia Clarendon, a point guard for the WNBA's Atlanta Dream, identifies as "biracial, gay, and Christian and, most recently, a gender non-conforming queer person." She has written about the experience of being gender nonconforming and moving through a binary world. "There is no space for the in-between. You have to be either male or female, gay or straight. When you don't fit those rigid molds, you are confronted everywhere you go that there is no space for you." Clarendon says that for anyone who wants to make the world (and sport) a more inclusive place, you need to "listen" and "understand ally as a verb, not just a noun. Have the courage to interrupt transphobic language. Advocate for gender-neutral restrooms anywhere you can. Respect people's gender pronouns."[41]

In 2016, Lauren Lubin competed in the New York City Marathon, the first nonbinary athlete to do so. They did it, Vice reported at the time, as "a protest to the larger world of sports, where non-binary athletes are widely denied access to major events and discriminated against in ways both subtle and overt." Lubin told Mashable in 2018 that because so few people even understand there are people who don't fit into the gender binary, "recognition is the most fundamental step—and our first major obstacle. You can't have hopes, dreams, and aspirations if you're not recognized." "And sports, systematically, is the most entrenched [institution] in gender norms."[42]

As we mention in chapter 2 on doping in sports, athletes whose bodies don't fit neatly into entrenched gender norms (trans athletes, nonbinary, intersex, etc.) also face increased suspicion when it comes to so-called performance-enhancing drugs. Critics of these athletes' participation often compare their inclusion to those of doping athletes—the implication being that they are cheating merely by the fact they are competing. In so many ways, these athletes pay high prices simply by not adhering to the binary that sporting institutions demand.[43]

One idea to help combat the overreliance on gender in sports is, at the very least, to delay when kids are divided into girls' and boys' sports. Do nine-year-old girls and boys and gender nonconforming children need to be split into groups before anyone has experienced puberty? "What would our sport and culture look like if we allowed for a more integrated system longer?" Barnes asks.

If nothing else, today we must ask a question posed by Barnes: "What does fairness look like in this day and age when we have so much more language and understanding around gender identity?"

———

LGBTQ+ athletes have created their own spaces to combat exclusion and discrimination throughout sports.

There are leagues like the National Gay Flag Football League, which is open to LGBTQ+ athletes and in which "no individual shall be excluded from participating on the basis of sexual orientation, gender, race, religion, nationality, ethnic origin, political beliefs, athletic ability, physical challenge, HIV status or gender identity." The league held its inaugural Gay Super Bowl in April 2002 and currently has more than 200 teams in twenty-four smaller leagues through the United States and Canada.[44]

The North American Gay Amateur Athletic Alliance, which formed in 1977, exists to provide "opportunity and access for the LGBT community to participate in organized softball competition in safe environments." It has more than "17,000 players from 46 cities across Canada and the United States." It also hosts an annual

Gay Softball World Series, which its says is "the largest annual, LGBT single-sport, week-long athletic competition in the world."[45]

The Gay Rodeo has been around since 1976 when 125 people took part in the event in Nevada. In 1985, the International Gay Rodeo Association was founded and today has "a policy of total non-discrimination." There are regional events throughout the United States and Canada each year. In 2019, there were eleven different rodeos, including the World Gay Rodeo Finals in Scottsdale, Arizona. Decades of its archives can be found at the Autry Museum of the American West in Los Angeles.[46]

Homoclimbtastic is an organization that hosts "the world's largest queer-friendly climbing convention, annually in Fayetteville, West Virginia." It includes under the "queer-friendly" umbrella "bisexuals, lesbians, ambisexuals, gays, trans'es, questioners, not quite straight people, amphibians with crushes on cephalopods, or however you define yourself." It dubbed itself "the goddamn center of the goddamn queer climbing universe" and has unaffiliated local chapters; the national group is operated by volunteers.[47]

And then there's the biggest of them all: the Gay Games. It will host its eleventh iteration in Hong Kong in 2022, with the first dating back to 1982 in San Francisco. According to the Federation of Gay Games, the inaugural event was one week long and included 1,350 athletes from twelve countries participating in seventeen sports. For the 2018 games in Paris, there were more than thirty-six sports, an academic conference, fourteen cultural events (including band, chorus, and visual arts), and ninety-one nations with more than 10,000 participants. The Gay Games in Hong Kong will include a wide range of sports: water polo, trail running, marathon, dodgeball, volleyball, esports, figure skating, table tennis, powerlifting, dragon boat racing, and many more.[48]

On its website, the federation explains why the existence of the Gay Games is still important, even as more and more LGBTQ+ athletes participate in sports around the world and at the highest levels: "But the Olympics, and mainstream sport in general, remain a very difficult place for homosexual athletes to compete, and certainly to compete without hiding their sexual identity. There are countless potential champions who under-perform, or simply don't participate, in mainstream sport because of homophobia."[49] The Games are open to people of all sexual orientations and gender identities and all levels of athletic ability.[50]

The creation and maintenance of these LGBTQ+-inclusive sporting spaces indicate that homophobia, transphobia, and anger at those who force us to question the binary of gender are very much still a part of sports despite the progress that has been made. It doesn't need to be this way, but it will take considerable work to change it. It's necessary that we do.

In the summer of 2018, the Human Rights Campaign released a report called "Play to Win" that looked at the state of LGBTQ+ inclusion in youth sports. The researchers who assembled the report found that "too many LGBTQ+ youth report that they have witnessed or been targets of anti-LGBTQ+ treatment or exclusion. Transgender and gender expansive youth face even greater barriers to sports participation." They found that "only 24 percent of LGBTQ+ youth say they play a school sport, compared to 68 percent of a national sample of all youth."[51] But it is these youth who give hope to those wanting change. "We have college and high school athletes who are out publicly on their teams and they're open about their identities," Chris Mosier says. "Some of those players are going to go to professional sports. So, we are in this really interesting and awesome time where we are on the cusp of having that sort of major visibility."

Wade Davis agrees. He acknowledges that on the high school level, students continue to face "bullying and homophobia, but I think that schools are trying to be much more intentional to educate their kids on these issues at a different level and at a different pace than what it was 10, 20, 30 years ago."

Katie Barnes is most optimistic when looking at LGBTQ+ youth athletes today: "There is such a huge generational shift happening right now, where we're seeing tremendous amounts of queer youths come out younger, and younger, and younger, and they have access to language so much earlier," they observe. "I wouldn't be shocked if 30 years from now we look back on this time period and we're like, 'I can't believe we thought nobody was ever going to be an out NFL player.'"

WATCHING WOMEN'S BASKETBALL WHEN PEOPLE TELL YOU YOU'RE THE ONLY ONE

Some of the most compelling athletes are also some of the most underappreciated. They play a sport in which their contributions are rarely celebrated, in a league that's often denigrated. You might predict these dynamics would deter fans from watching, but in truth the fans of this sport are among the most passionate. They are part of a growing group yearning for more exposure and, frankly, more respect for the league they love. We're talking about the Women's National Basketball Association.

But there are plenty of other women's leagues deserving of attention. The National Women's Soccer League. The National Women's Hockey League. National Pro Fastpitch and the Women's Flat Track Derby Association. Include women's college softball, basketball, volleyball, and hockey as well. And these are just a few examples from the United States. These same dynamics—amazing athletes, underresourced leagues, scant media attention, rabid fans—play out in women's team sports across the globe.

We focus in this chapter on the WNBA because it is one of the longest-standing women's leagues, founded in 1996. It had its first season in the summer of 1997.[1]

Popular opinion tends to explain away the relative unpopularity of the WNBA by relying on accepted assumptions about women's sports in general that are at times tailored to the specifics of basketball. These assumptions are rarely challenged. Take just one example: the notion that women's basketball is simply less competitive and less compelling than the men's game because of the supposed biological inferiority of women's bodies. In most sports, this idea manifests in tests of strength—men serving faster in tennis or driving the ball farther in golf, for example. In women's basketball, it's the old line that women can't dunk.

It's certainly true that women and men, on average, tend to be built differently, and that women's basketball sees far less dunking than the men's game. In 2012, Baylor's Brittney Griner became just the second woman ever to dunk in an NCAA Tournament game, sparking a renewed conversation about why there are fewer slams in the women's game. The obvious answer is that it's a function of height: the average WNBA player is six feet tall, while the average NBA player is six-foot-seven. At six-foot-eight, Griner is an outlier in the women's game.[2]

Then there's the disparity in leaping ability: on average, men's basketball players at the collegiate and professional levels have a vertical leap eight to nine inches higher than their women counterparts.

But like so much in women's sports, dunking (or the lack thereof) is as much a function of what we imagine women are capable of as anything else. As Natalie Weiner wrote for Bleacher Report: "Encouraging girls and women to feel free to work toward dunking, with all the strength training and practice that requires, is a task for both coaches and the media." Michael Messner, a professor of sociology and gender studies at the University of Southern California, told Weiner: "When you see LeBron James dunking on a highlight reel, they don't say, 'It's a man dunking!' As long as we're gender-marking every time a woman dunks a ball, essentially we're diminishing the accomplishment and marking it as abnormal." Moving toward dunking in the women's game is, Griner told her, "the evolution of basketball."[3]

The dearth of dunks in the women's game led to a call for the WNBA to lower the rim in 2016. Currently, the rims in WNBA games are ten feet above the court, same as in the NBA. The push to lower the rim received high-profile support by then–Chicago Sky star Elena Delle Donne, who contended that fans wouldn't notice or care much about the rim height, especially if it led to highlight-worthy dunks throughout the game. She noted that fans don't seem to care about measurable differences in other sports—a lower net in volleyball, a closer tee in golf, fewer sets in tennis, for example.[4]

The problem is that it is exactly those differences that have been used to justify the claim that women's sports are inherently inferior and therefore that women athletes deserve less attention, lower salaries, and fewer endorsement contracts.

In tennis, women playing three sets compared to five for men has long been used to justify arguments by those opposing equal pay who say that fans don't, in fact, receive equal play from women. But the truth is that the Women's Tennis Association has said for years that it would be willing to expand to a best-of-five model; the International Tennis Federation has blocked that change. Meanwhile, some professional men's players have advocated for the men to play three sets, citing injury and recovery concerns.

As we wrote about in chapter 4 about sexism in tennis, the sport does actually have equal pay in Grand Slam tournaments, but it's telling that the differences between men's and women's tennis that speak to women's supposedly lesser physical abilities are still constantly brought up. We see that in women's basketball all the time: the women play with a slightly smaller ball, to accommodate women's on-average smaller hands, and thus the sport itself must be inferior. That's why some players broke from Delle Donne's call to lower the rim. In 2016, Diana Taurasi expressed her opinion that lowering the rim would be a step backward for women athletes: "Might as well put us in skirts and back in the kitchen," she said.[5]

To that end, sportswriter Kate Fagan, herself a former college basketball player, put it best: "If history is any indication, instead of jaws dropping over these slam dunks, jaws will start flapping—about how anyone can dunk on a lowered rim, about how watching women dunk will never be as exciting as watching men dunk, about how men (or women) won't pay to watch someone dunk on a hoop that they themselves can dunk on." When Griner dunked in her first WNBA game, many commenters dismissed her. She wasn't a great athlete completing an exciting play, they claimed—she was just freakishly tall.

All these circular arguments come around to show how no matter what, people can contort themselves into all kinds of intellectual positions to express how women's sports are a lesser product. Some of this becomes, sadly, the accepted perception.

Imani McGee-Stafford began playing basketball in high school, but she has always been surrounded by the sport. Her mother, Pamela McGee, won back-to-back NCAA basketball championships at USC and was the second overall pick in the first WNBA draft. Her dad played in college and overseas. Her brother, JaVale McGee, is a well-known NBA player. McGee-Stafford spent her college years at the University of Texas, was drafted by the Chicago Sky, played for the Atlanta Dream and the Dallas Wings, and has played ball professionally in Australia, Turkey, China, Lebanon, and Israel. She announced in March 2020 that she would be taking a two-year break from the WNBA to pursue a law degree.

McGee-Stafford, on why women's sports don't get the same institutional support as men's sports, poses a question: "How do we feel about women?" She continues: "If we don't respect our women, we don't enjoy having women in powerful roles, we don't enjoy having women in leadership roles, how can we support something so big as women's sport? Because women's sport is literally women doing something powerful, doing something traditionally male-dominated."[6]

As for basketball itself, Howard Megdal, a WNBA reporter, said this (with somewhat of a wink): "There are, I'm sure, potentially some non-zero group of people that would be passionate WNBA fans if not for the size of the ball." (Megdal started the women's basketball website High Post Hoops, part of the Fansided network.) He added: "I guess that's a possible thing. But I don't believe that's a real thing. But why do those arguments resonate? I think because a lot of the decision-makers in media are also often looking for a reason to justify what they do."[7]

Megdal hits at the core of what's actually holding back professional women's basketball: the willingness of marketing and media executives to accept the conventional wisdom that women's basketball—and by extension women's sports—will never be as popular as men's and therefore don't justify a meaningful level of investment. Amid all the conversation of why women dunk less than men, only a few thought to ask a simple yet important question: How much does it really matter?

One such person was then–Indiana Fever guard Layshia Clarendon, who, in a 2016 column for ESPN, noted that "people don't tune in to the NBA for the sole purpose of watching dunks." Instead, she argued, fans watch NBA games "because it's embedded in our culture to do so. Men's sports have such an immense platform for visibility that even the utility guy on the best teams is revered. They watch because it's the cool thing to do. We don't give women's sports the space to be cool."[8]

Rather than the inherent inferiority of women's basketball, Clarendon and Megdal argue that it's the lesser visibility of the WNBA that explains the league's lower popularity. Sports writers don't cover women athletes nearly to the extent that they cover men, with the few exceptions of transcendent figures like Serena Williams. Accordingly, TV executives who make programming decisions have relegated WNBA games to lower-profile channels and time slots. A common complaint of casual WNBA fans is that they simply don't know when and where to watch games. They've aired on ESPN2 instead of ESPN, in the midafternoon instead of in primetime, and thus are far less discoverable than men's games.

"Elevating the women's game looks like this: Advanced statistics, pregame and post-game coverage, telling our stories. Because they are there, but the system that is in place demands women should be satisfied with coverage at all. It says we should be happy to be here," Clarendon wrote. "The argument that people just don't care about women's basketball is never going to be true and will never be legitimate without giving the sport the same coverage."

The coverage challenges start from the top and trickle down. The most glaring disparity is in the number of beat writers that local and national outlets have dedicated to covering women's basketball, something Megdal noticed early in his sports writing career. "I've covered sports, men's and women's, ever since I got out of school. And every time I would do a WNBA story I would notice that there weren't that many other reporters there and we had a real continuing problem with how often and the way the league was covered," he said. "There's this enormous gap that you can't unsee and I determined if I devoted myself to it I could make some hopefully fundamental changes in the way it was covered moving forward." Before starting his own website, Megdal noticed a much higher barrier when trying to convince an editor to approve a WNBA story that would have sailed through had the subject been an NBA player. This is exactly Clarendon's point when she writes that "even the utility guy on the best team is revered."

McGee-Stafford says she wants to see media get better at storytelling when it comes to the WNBA. "We see the same five faces: Candace [Parker], Skylar [Diggins], Elena [Delle-Donne], Diana [Taurasi], Sue [Bird]. And you can't build a league on that." Instead, like Megdal and Clarendon, she looks at the coverage of the NBA. "Everybody doesn't care about basketball. That is a fact," she says. "But everybody doesn't care about men's basketball either. But they do care about the fact that LeBron [James] is from Ohio. That Steph [Curry] has these beautiful daughters and his wife. It's the storytelling that sells ninety games of basketball. There's no way in hell that 500,000 people just really love basketball and want to watch ninety games. They can get the casual fan because they tell the stories."

By the same token, however, she also wants to see the league get better at packaging its players. "I think just the WNBA does a terrible job of pushing unique stories, of covering the sport in a way that makes people care about it." She said that during the 2019 season, the WNBA social media accounts had typos and would tag the wrong people in the pictures. "It was like, do you care? Do you?"

"It is always more challenging," Megdal said of covering the WNBA.

You can measure the lack of parity in thinking about: Why would a particular figure in the NBA be likely to be the center of a successful pitch, as opposed to a comparable person in the WNBA? A profile on the starting guard for the San Antonio Spurs, whoever that might be at the time, is a far easier pitch to make than the equivalent being Kayla McBride, when she was with the San Antonio Stars, despite the fact that Kayla McBride was a legitimate star in the WNBA. There almost always needed to be a hook beyond just excelling on the basketball court, whereas that was usually more than enough for an NBA equivalent.

He added that not having a set commitment to covering women's basketball means that whatever coverage these athletes do get is sporadic and unthematic, which makes it difficult to build interest over time. "There's no rhyme or reason to it and it's whatever strikes a particular editor's fancy, and the net result of that is that there's no consistency," he said.

The past few years have seen an increase in written coverage of the WNBA, with writers like Megdal, SB Nation's Weiner, Bleacher Report's Mirin Fader, and espnW's Mechelle Voepel, who has been a consistent presence in women's basketball coverage since 1984 and has covered the WNBA since its inaugural season in 1997. Local papers, like the *Chicago Sun-Times* and the *Seattle Times*, have assigned their own WNBA beat reporters. In 2019, the *Sun-Times* also secured sponsorship for its Chicago Sky beat from the University of Chicago Medical Center. That same year, The Athletic announced that it had created a WNBA vertical and hired beat reporters for each of the twelve teams, as well as two additional national writers. There was so much more coverage in 2019 that the *Columbia Journalism Review* had a post titled, "How the WNBA Became a Hot Newsroom Beat," and the *Washington Post* ran a feature titled, "The WNBA Has Craved Mainstream Attention. This Season, It Might Be Turning a Corner."[9]

More basketball websites like The Ringer have also made it a point to expand coverage to the women's game. It seems that many NBA and NCAA men's writers are starting to catch up to those who have put in the work for years, seeing a growth opportunity in a space long ignored. Shea Serrano, a beloved voice on social media, former Grantland staffer, current writer for The Ringer, and author of the 2017 book *Basketball (And Other Things)*, has become a vocal and well-known fan of the women's game in the last couple of years. But he didn't become that fan organically. In October 2017, Weiner tweeted images showing that "WNBA," "Lisa Leslie," and "Becky Hammon" did not appear anywhere in the text of Serrano's book and tweeted that "not every book talks about everything, of course . . . but this is the process by which women's achievements get written out of history." According to an interview Serrano gave nine months later, that tweet made him rethink his relationship to the women's game. And so he reached out to Weiner, who guided him into his fandom—one that led to him watching, tweeting, and writing regularly about the sport.[10]

Some long-standing members of sports media have also expressed regret for the part they've played in relegating women's basketball to second-class citizenship. In 2016, days after the death of legendary University of Tennessee Lady Vols coach Pat Summitt, *Los Angeles Times* columnist Bill Plaschke wrote of his role in "marginalizing Pat Summitt's greatness."[11] "Despite holding a prominent sports columnist position for this prominent newspaper for 20 years, I never covered one of Pat Summitt's games," Plaschke wrote. "Excuses for ignoring such an influential sports figure were easy to find. . . . But to marginalize greatness because you don't think many people are watching is embarrassing, even shameful. Summitt's life showed that, when it comes to women's sports, if you follow the ratings, you miss the point."

In the same column, Plaschke wrote about the types of coverage decisions he made to elevate men's basketball over women's, even if those decisions were not based on editorial newsworthiness. Instead of covering a game between the Minnesota Lynx and Los Angeles Sparks—two undefeated teams that would go on to face each other in the next two WNBA Finals—he chose to cover a press conference held on the same afternoon in which the Los Angeles Lakers introduced their newly hired head coach, Luke Walton. "I made this choice even though I needed no introduction to Walton while knowing nothing about the Sparks," he wrote.

I was sucked in by the metrics, the buzz, the reputation, and made a decision to follow everything but the most basic tenet of good and important journalism. I ignored the better story for the more popular story. I missed a chance to inform and enlighten and, instead, chose simply to replay and reflect. The tired bottom line was, I went for the sparks over the Sparks because, with women playing in a league with scant local interest and minuscule TV ratings, I based their importance on their perception.

That perception is thankfully changing, but so too are the numbers that have always been used to formulate it. The big question surrounding women's sports has always boiled down to a chicken-or-the-egg dilemma: whether increased visibility is justified by poor ratings, or whether those ratings would increase with more coverage. If the push toward equal exposure has been slow, the perception has been changing, and this can be seen perhaps most impactfully on the television side.

———

In 2013, WNBA regular season games airing on ESPN2 averaged 231,000 viewers, a 28 percent jump from the previous year. This followed a particularly grim 2012 season in which the league averaged a record low 7,457 attendance per game. Heading into the 2013 season, 24/7 Wall Street predicted that the WNBA would cease to exist after that year.[12]

However, that year saw the beginning of a marketing and programming push that banked on proving wrong such negative outlooks. ESPN renewed its television deal with the WNBA through the 2022 season, committing to airing games nationally on ABC, ESPN, ESPN2, and what's now known as the ESPN+ streaming site. For the first time ever, in 2013, the WNBA draft was broadcast on ESPN in primetime.[13]

The year 2015 saw another low point for WNBA metrics. Attendance fell 3.4 percent, while combined television viewership on ESPN and ESPN2 dropped 14 percent from the previous year. Yet WNBA viewership on NBA TV rose 8 percent, while the league also saw growth in digital media, with page views on WNBA.com up 26 percent.[14]

In 2018, the WNBA's growth was positive but still mixed. Attendance dropped 13 percent, but half of that decline was attributed to the New York Liberty's move out of Madison Square Garden and into Westchester. ESPN's combined viewership increased 35 percent and saw its most-watched season on ESPN2 since 2014.[15]

In addition to ESPN, at least some other television executives see the potential in the WNBA. In 2019, CBS announced a multiyear deal to broadcast forty regular-season games in primetime on CBS Sports Network. (In 2019, ESPN's deal with the WNBA was for sixteen regular-season games, the All-Star Game, and up to nineteen postseason games.)[16]

According to the *Washington Post*, the WNBA hit some milestones in 2019. 2K Sports, publisher of the popular video game NBA2K, announced that for the first time ever it would feature the WNBA in the 2020 edition. In addition, the "All-Star Game in Las Vegas credentialed 41 percent more media members than in 2018 and 81 percent more than in 2017," and "for the handful of games the league streams on Twitter, average viewership is up 244 percent. (The league declined to share total figures.)" Additionally, "on Disney's networks, helped by more games on ESPN and ABC, viewership is up 31 percent from last season. (CBS Sports Network is not Nielsen-rated.)"[17]

Of course, many sports fans are still skeptical of the WNBA's ability to achieve return on investment because of the belief that men, in particular, don't care. You hear both sides of the argument—either that women don't watch the WNBA, so how can we expect men to? Or, even if it's demonstrated that the WNBA does, in fact, have female fans, people remain doubtful that men would have any interest in watching women's basketball in general.

To Megdal, these arguments still come down to exposure and the ease of access of games. "Why don't men watch the WNBA more? If you're in a near media blackout and it's damn near impossible to get the games without seeking them out and because of a media blackout you don't know how to seek them out, then that's going to be tough for men and women," he said. Additionally, the idea that the burden of elevating women's sports should be placed squarely on the shoulders of women fans despite the institutional barriers to simply finding and watching these games "treats women like these magical, fairy-like creatures. Men get their information from mass media. But women, what, via women's intuition, are somehow going to be knowledgeable about when the WNBA games are, that women are going to somehow be able to get information through some women-only cloud that exists?"

"Women get information the same way as men do: via media," he added. "If you have a media blackout it's very hard for women to find this out. And women don't have, therefore, a special responsibility to intuit, to close their eyes and feel the presence of a WNBA game nearby."

"Have you ever bought a pair of scissors that needs to be opened with a pair of scissors?" McGee-Stafford asks. "That's women's sports coverage and not just basketball. That's what it's like. It's like, 'No one wants to watch the WNBA.' No one can find our fucking game!"

———

One undercovered aspect of the WNBA's exposure problem is the struggle the league has faced in building the personal brands of individual players. While endorsement deals are a huge propellant of popularity for NBA stars, this hasn't translated to women athletes. As Kelly Whiteside wrote in the *New York Times* in 2017, WNBA stars during the early days of the league were actually in a much better position. In the mid-1990s, stars like Sheryl Swoopes, Lisa Leslie, Dawn Staley, and Rebecca Lobo all had sneaker deals with companies like Nike, adidas, Reebok, and Fila. But despite the enormous growth of the athlete-branded shoe market in the decades since, WNBA players haven't benefited accordingly. In 2011, Maya Moore became the first WNBA player signed to Nike's Jordan brand, yet she still didn't get her own shoe. In 2017, not a single WNBA player had her own shoe. In 2018, the WNBA announced a league-wide partnership with Puma, though it's unclear if that will lead to player-specific sneakers.[18]

"Those things matter, especially when you're young," Moore

said in 2017, recalling her first pair of Air Swoopes as an eight-year-old. "There's value there. Her work and talent were being rewarded. The investment was worthwhile because it inspired the next generation of women's basketball players."

There are other barriers women playing team sports face in garnering individual endorsement deals. Whiteside notes that many athletic and lifestyle brands tend to sign women in entertainment and the arts instead of sports to their own shoe deals, even if that seems counterintuitive. Rihanna has her own Puma line, for example, and Stella McCartney has her own adidas shoe.

That could be due to the notion that women athletes still need to adhere to traditional ideals of femininity in order to be seen as marketable. That obviously shouldn't be the case, and it isn't the primary standard to which male athletes are held. Sex certainly sells, but nobody will argue that the best player in the NBA doesn't deserve a shoe deal because he doesn't have a fashion model's good looks. It also belies reality, as there are a bevy of WNBA stars whose accomplishments on the court happen to be matched by their beauty.

But it also comes down to yet another way that WNBA players suffer from lower visibility: they simply aren't in the country as much. That's due to the economic realities of the league. The WNBA season is only four months long, and because of the players' notoriously low salaries, most spend off-seasons playing abroad for bigger money. WNBA players earn roughly 20 percent of the NBA's minimum salary; by the 2019 season, the median women's player's salary was $73,000 and capped out at $115,500. More than half the women in the league play overseas in the off-season, including Australia, Belgium, China, the Czech Republic, France, Hungary, Israel, Italy, Korea, Poland, Russia, Spain, and Turkey. Diana Taurasi makes fourteen times her WNBA salary playing in Russia—roughly $1.5 million.[19]

The detriments to playing overseas extend far beyond visibility, however. McGee-Stafford says playing overseas is also emotionally difficult. "I miss so much with my family because I'm on the other side of the world half the year." But it's a choice many make because "it's more lucrative than WNBA." She says: "The WNBA only pays us during season. We're not like the NBA that gets a year-round check whether we're in season or not. So you get your check for the little five months we play. And then what are you doing for the rest of the year? And so you go overseas to get quick money."

But it also carries risk for players. They are world-class athletes who, if they were paid comparably to men, would rightfully have their off-seasons to rest, work out, and recover from injury. Instead, they risk significant injury playing games overseas, making their entire position within the WNBA unstable. In 2019, the Seattle Storm star Breanna Stewart ruptured her Achilles tendon while playing for Russia's Dynamo Kursk team, forcing her to sit out the entire 2019 WNBA season. Stewart was the first overall pick in the 2016 draft, 2016 Rookie of the Year, 2018 league MVP, and 2018 Finals MVP. It was a huge blow for the player and the WNBA as the league struggles to market its best players and it speaks to the need to invest in both.[20]

The salary disparity has been billed as an economic issue, not a gendered one, dictated by the WNBA's fractional revenues as compared to the NBA's, and is used by the league and anti–equal pay advocates to justify the low salaries. But even when calculating the salaries as a function of revenues, NBA players make 50 percent of league revenues, whereas WNBA players, during the 2019 season, made only 23 percent.

While many people are quick to note that the NBA is far more profitable than the WNBA, players aren't looking for the same salary levels—they just want a fairer share, as well as more structural commitment to their futures. As Los Angeles Sparks star and Women's National Basketball Players Association executive committee president Nneka Ogwumike told Fader in 2018: "What we're discussing and fighting for is a lot more intricate than simply pay us more. It's a lot deeper than that. It's infrastructural." She continued: "Why is this so hard for people to understand? It's kind of business 101. You're not going to make money off a product that you don't invest in. We are the product. The W is the product. And the investment is not there."[21]

In a 2018 piece for *The Players' Tribune* explaining the decision of WNBA players to opt out of their collective bargaining agreement with the league, Ogwumike went further on what the players hope to gain out of the negotiations, including full transparency in the league's financials, numbers the players don't actually get to see. "I'm sure there will be people out there who will judge us harshly for opting out—who will say that we should be grateful for what we already have. They'll probably tell us that our league is losing money. They'll say it's just 'economics.' They'll say it's just 'fair.' And they'll definitely, definitely tell me that they can beat me one on one," she wrote.[22] "Does this mean we're all walking up to the league office tomorrow, arm in arm, and demanding some LeBron Money? You have got to stop it with these wild comparisons, I swear. Get your money, LeBron, we appreciate you," she continued. "This is not purely about salaries. This is about small changes the league can make that will impact the players."

Put simply, "This is not just about business. This is deeply personal. This is about the kind of world we want to live in."

After months of negotiations between players and the league, Ogwumike and WNBA commissioner Cathy Engelbert went on *Good Morning America* on January 14, 2020, and announced a new, eight-year collective bargaining agreement. Under the new CBA, players' compensation will double or triple and they will receive maternity leave with full salary, a dedicated space for nursing mothers, a day care stipend, and reimbursement for adoption, surrogacy, or fertility treatment fees. According to Megdal, who wrote about the CBA for the *New York Times*, the players agreed to these benefits in exchange for being at WNBA training camps when they start. "No more reporting late, or even after the season begins, to finish commitments to clubs overseas," Megdal wrote, "with exceptions built in only for national team play and players in their first three seasons." The CBA also includes better housing for families, no more hotel room sharing while on the road, and looser rules around free agency. It does not, however, allow for chartered plane flights; players will still fly commercial in the economy-plus sections. Engelbert said that "a lot of these elements are setting up the future for the next generation of players to be in a great place—for the current stars to leave behind a legacy for the next generation."[23]

Even though this CBA is a major step forward that will most likely have myriad long-term impacts for the league and players, the sustainability of the WNBA is reliant on more than just what the league itself is doing.

Megdal, who is raising two daughters to be proud WNBA fans, sees this as an issue from the media and coverage perspective, one where it's impossible to fully separate the economics from the gender considerations. In his experience covering and attending WNBA games, he sees the future clearly: he sees little boys "jumping out of their seat" just as much as the girls in the stands at every exciting play. "It's on men to solve this. Every time I hear someone making the insidious argument that, 'Well, women have to support women's sports,' it is absurd when it is disproportionately men in the decision-making process on the media side of things, and it is men who have been conditioned from an early age not to treat it as the same, in sports and in other areas," he says. "The fact of the matter is, this is injustice."

McGee-Stafford agrees. "I think allyship plays a huge role" in growing the game, she says. And she points out that some of the biggest fans of the WNBA are NBA players. "As much as I hate the corny, 'Chris Paul came to a WNBA game,' . . . I think it's a needed thing. It makes me angry. . . . But it's also necessary because we have all these stupid men that live in their basement and think that because they're men, they're inherently better than me at what I've spent my entire life perfecting. So, if their favorite superhero comes to a game and it's like, 'Oh, maybe I can shut the fuck up.'"

Correcting injustice takes time and seeing NBA players courtside doesn't do much for fans who want to watch the WNBA now, today. (Or, for that matter, the National Women's Soccer League, National Women's Hockey League, National Pro Fastpitch, Women's Flat Track Derby Association, women's college softball, basketball, volleyball, and hockey—or whatever league is dearest to you.) The truth of the matter is that today, right now, fans have to do a lot of homework just to be fans. "I always say we just have the best fans in the world because they literally go on a scavenger hunt to be our fans," McGee-Stafford jokes. There are things that can make that hunt easier.

When Weiner was guiding Serrano, she suggested he pick a college and WNBA team to follow. Get invested in the players and coaches on a single team, follow their arc. It's not hard to figure out which teams Serrano picked. In March 2018, he wrote a piece for The Ringer titled, "How to Fall in Love with a Team in the NCAA Tournament," and it's all about the Oregon Ducks. Later that summer, the *Las Vegas Review-Journal* ran a piece titled "Best-selling author, Twitter personality Shea Serrano all-in with the Aces."[24]

There's also a lot of community among women's sports fans on social media. Googling something like "WNBA Twitter accounts" can lead you to lists. Look for hashtags that those accounts are using. Follow especially the social media accounts of sites and journalists dedicated to covering the league or the teams you are interested in. Listen to their podcasts and read their stories. For the WNBA, that includes High Post Hoops, Swish Appeal, Her Hoop Stats, WNBA Nation, and The Slam's and The Athletic's WNBA verticals. Certainly, follow the accounts of teams you root for.

Get knowledgeable about the different ways to watch the games. Some WNBA games are on Twitter, many are on TV split among ABC, ESPN, ESPN2, CBS Sports Network, and NBA TV, but you can also watch the vast majority of them on the WNBA's League Pass. Like social media, it helps to Google. In June 2019, Her Hoop Stats ran an article carrying a title suggesting both its utility and also the frustration many fans feel when trying to figure out how to watch a game: "Making Sense of How to Watch the WNBA on Your TV."[25]

And if you ever get a chance to go see a game in person, don't hesitate. You never know when you'll get to see the next WNBA dunk.

CHAPTER 7

CONSUMING SPORTS MEDIA ...

EVEN IF YOU DON'T LOOK LIKE

THE PEOPLE ON TV

One of the main reasons that devoted sports fans may not feel welcome is that so much of the coverage is created by a specific subset of our population: namely white men, most of them straight, the vast majority cisgender.[1] In fact, the homogeneity of sports media cannot be overstated.

And even though all media suffer from a lack of diversity, especially as we move up the chain into more powerful, decision-making positions, sports has a poor record on this—perhaps the worst.

In 2017, the Women's Media Center (WMC) found that 89 percent of sports coverage is written by men. Of the sixteen categories of news topics that WMC counted, sports had the largest concentration of male reporters, followed most closely by weather, which had 72 percent of its coverage by men, a significant difference between the top two spots.[2]

In May 2018, the Institute for Diversity and Ethics in Sport (TIDES) at the University of Central Florida released the Associated Press Sports Editors (APSE) Racial and Gender Report Card, which looked at the staffs of more than seventy-five newspapers and websites. The last report of this kind was from 2014, and this was the sixth time this data had been collected. "For 2018," the executive summary reads, "the grade for racial hiring practices for APSE newspapers and websites was a B, which was the same grade as in the 2014 study. The APSE newspapers and websites received the fifth consecutive F for gender hiring practices. The combined grade for 2018 was a D+, the lowest of all the reports issued by TIDES."[3] Ouch.

And there was one big reason the report was even as good as it was: ESPN. "If we take away the ESPN hires as editors, assistant sports editors and columnists," Richard Lapchick, the director of TIDES and primary author of this report, says, "the percentages of women and people of color in those positions would plummet precipitously." Still, even in the best of circumstances, we end up with pieces like Caleb Hannan's piece for Grantland outing a transgender woman known as Dr. V (which we discuss below). There is always work to be done.

In an accompanying article for ESPN, Lapchick wrote, "sports media leaders remain largely white and male." He notes that it's good that APSE is interested in these numbers and releases them publicly, but "it has been 12 years since the first report and progress has been very slow."[4]

This uniformity in reporting and editing has multiple consequences. First, and most obvious, it affects what is deemed important enough to cover. For example (and not surprising based on those stats), women's sports in general are barely covered in the sports media. As we wrote in chapter 6 about the WNBA, few beat writers cover women's basketball, something that is true for most women's sports. Games aren't covered, or only streamed, or are shown on less prestigious channels. There often isn't a pregame or postgame breakdown—and forget wishing for anything close to equity on par with men's sports.

The problem is bad enough that in 2018 the director-general of UNESCO, Audrey Azoulay, called on media to provide more equal coverage of women athletes. She pointed out that only 4 percent of sports media is women's sports and that women make up a small percentage of the sports industry. "UNESCO also deplores the stereotypical comments that circulate in the media," the press release reads, "often focusing on physical appearance of athletes or their family status, or even crediting their achievements to their male coaches and trainers."[5]

Second, it can have an impact on how stories are covered. This is laid bare when looking at how sports departments cover gendered violence. In 2015, the WMC released a report about who reports on campus sexual violence and how it is covered. "We also extrapolated sports content—stories on sports pages or written by sports journalists—on sexualized violence on campus. The disparities in this arena were startling: Sixty-four percent, or 137 articles, were written by men, while only 7 percent, or 16 articles, were written by women. An additional 29 percent, or 61 articles, had no byline," the report reads. It continued:

> When it came to what kinds of voices made it into stories about sexualized violence on high school and college campuses within sports sections or by sports reporters, the gap was tremendous: Seventy-five percent of quotes in sports content were from male sources, while only 10 percent were from female sources. Another 11 percent were from organizations. The gender of quoted sources could not be determined for an additional 4 percent of the quotes.

It led the WMC to conclude: "Anyone relying on sports coverage to keep up with stories involving athletes and sexualized violence are receiving a seriously skewed kind of coverage, one that clearly prioritizes the voices of men."[6] Which brings us to the third point: white male hegemony among sports staffs can also affect the people who cover sports. Even when people from underrepresented groups get jobs in sports media, they are often subject to discrimination, harassment, or feelings of being an outsider.

Stories of sexism that female sports reporters face on the job are both old and ever-present. In 2003, the NFL legend Joe Namath told ESPN's Suzy Kolber, who was trying to interview him on the sideline during a game, "I want to kiss you." In 2010, a Mexican journalist named Ines Sainz was harassed by players and coaches from the New York Jets during one of their practices. In 2018, the FARE Network, which works to end all forms of discrimination in soccer, reported that at least three female reporters said they were sexually harassed and/or forcibly kissed while on air doing their jobs.[7]

There are many stories, stretching back decades, about female reporters being banned from locker rooms. *Sports Illustrated* reporter Melissa Ludtke sued Major League Baseball commissioner Bowie Kuhn after she was kept out of the New York Yankees locker room during the 1977 World Series. She won. Still, in 2015, three female sports reporters were initially not allowed into the locker room following an Indianapolis Colts game. "I was just blocked from a locker room by an old, out-of-touch geezer who wasn't sure women were allowed because 'you know how guys are,'" Yahoo! Sports's Graham Watson tweeted at the time.[8]

And finally there is the press box.

In 2011, Dexter Rogers wrote about covering his first World Series in St. Petersburg, Florida, in 2008 at Tropicana Field. The Philadelphia Phillies were in town to play the Tampa Bay Rays. "As I walked into the stadium, it was packed with fans and full of energy, and I was reminded of my love for the beat I work," Rogers remembers. "But when I made my way to the press box, I suddenly realized the real story wasn't on the field. As I entered press row, I was first shocked by how many journalists were there—nearly 1,000— and then more stunned by how few of them looked like me, a person of color." In 2016, after Simone Manuel became the first African American woman to win an individual gold medal in swimming at the Olympics, ESPN's Jesse Washington tweeted that he was the only Black reporter among a whole host of international journalists in the press room.

Rhiannon Walker, an NFL reporter for The Athletic, puts it this way: "There's nothing that makes me happier than seeing someone else in a press box that looks like me—black, a woman, LGBTQ and young. But frankly, it's a very rare event when I find any of those categories that overlap with one another." Ben Baby, who spent time at news outlets across north Texas before landing at ESPN as an NFL reporter, joked that in 2016, when he was covering a Texas

A&M football game, "between myself, ESPN.com's Sam Khan Jr. and ESPN play-by-play anchor Anish Shroff, we may have set the record for the most reporters of South Asian descent covering an SEC game. Someone might need to check with the Asian-American Journalist Association for an official count, but we're fairly confident we made history."[9]

In 2018, after the English football star Raheem Sterling called out UK sports media for racism in reporting on Black players, the BBC's own Hugh Woozencroft wrote on BBC.com: "And the fact is, the sports media industry is failing black people and BBC Sport is no different."[10] Woozencroft continued: "I've had discussions with fellow black journalists who feel that a difference in portrayal between black players and white players is clear, and that it wouldn't have happened had there been more of us in newsrooms."[11]

———

All these issues create a problem. And there are worst-case scenarios when the skewed demographics among writers and editors—intentionally or not—lead to horrible consequences.

In 2014, a much-lauded piece by Caleb Hannan at the now-defunct ESPN spinoff site Grantland outed a transgender woman known as Dr. V. In the process of reporting the piece, Hannan told Dr. V that he was going to out her; she died by suicide not long after her final communication with him. Her suicide added another layer to the piece, one that many readers found fascinating. What Hannan didn't know—what no one at Grantland seemed to know because there was no one in the editorial chain who was trans—is that trans people are twenty-six times more likely to commit suicide than nontrans people. (There were other aspects of the piece that were insensitive to trans readers, but much of the criticism focused on Dr. V's death.) Once trans readers began criticizing the piece and others caught on, Grantland's editor-in-chief, Bill Simmons, wrote a piece apologizing for publishing it and offering condolences to Dr. V's family. He tried to outline the process behind the scenes that led it to being published.[12]

On the same day Simmons's piece posted, Christina Kahrl, a transgender baseball reporter for ESPN, penned an essay explaining why Hannan's piece was harmful, the ethical issues at play, and the difficulties many trans people face in a world that is violently transphobic. "If I had known this story was in the pipeline," she wrote, "my first instinct is that I'd want to help Bill Simmons and his team get the job done right. Even if I really would rather be talking about baseball—my day job, my dream job, my job-job as part of ESPN.com's editorial and writing team for MLB—if I can help my colleagues and simultaneously make sure that the trans people who come up in their coverage get a fair shake, I welcome that opportunity."

The kind of generosity Kahrl offers here can become a trap, though. LGBTQ+ members of the sports media worry about being pigeonholed. In a June 2017 roundtable of publicly out writers and reporters, all of them reported generally positive responses from teams, athletes, coaches, fans, and peers. Still, Dave Doyle, who covers mixed martial arts, wrote: "I want to simply be known as an accurate and fair MMA writer, not 'the gay MMA writer.' Christina Kahrl said something similar in 2016, two years after the Dr. V incident: "I didn't want to become known as 'the transsexual sportswriter.' I'm a sportswriter; I just happen to be transsexual. I'm not afraid of that, I'm totally happy to talk about that, but my day job [is to be] a working professional in sports."[13]

Even if reporters, editors, writers, and broadcasters from underrepresented groups don't want to only be known by a certain identity, until the industry fixes its diversity issues they are going to be called on to help their more privileged peers navigate issues of sexism, racism, homophobia, transphobia, and other issues.

This all feels particularly dire in the media landscape at the beginning of the 2020s. The media industry in general is consolidating and contracting in some ways. And this is particularly acute in sports, where an old, marquee publication like *Sports Illustrated*—which for decades put out weekly issues but struggled financially during the 2010s—was bought by a company that had never owned a magazine; the staff was gutted and it was announced in 2020 that *SI* will publish only monthly. Deadspin, which started out as a blog, kept a lot of its original snarky flavor throughout its ten-year run, but it also moved into investigative reporting and incisive sports media and cultural criticism that constantly brought the industry, teams, owners, and fans to task. It was bought up by a hedge fund who was hostile to Deadspin's tone and anti-owner/pro-labor stance. The site abruptly went dark in 2019 after the entire staff quit following sustained disagreements with management over the content and tone on the site (it relaunched under the same name and ownership but an entirely different editorial team in March 2020). This is on top of the loss of Vice Sports, ThinkProgress, Grantland, and the shutdown of *ESPN The Magazine*.[14]

But there are also new outlets popping up, like The Ringer and The Athletic; Bleacher Report and SBNation continue their coverage, and ESPN isn't going anywhere. On top of all of this is social media, which for all of its ills has boosted marginalized voices, brought communities together across great distances, and allowed for more pointed and timely critique of media stories that fail or harm. Still, there are worries over whose voices will be excluded as the landscape continues to contract.[15]

Shireen Ahmed and Shakeia Taylor wrote perhaps the clearest summation of the issues (and solutions) related to the lack of racial and gender diversity in sports media when speaking to diversity issues more generally:

> Hiring women of color not only gives sports media credibility and the opportunity to hire top talent, but also gives readers and viewers a broader range of perspectives on the teams and topics they love. Speaking to a topic with which one has little understanding or knowledge is reckless. Having white people opine on race in a way that lacks nuance is unprofessional at best. There are critical points in conversations, particularly with regards to marginalized folks, where those who are not the subject should make space, listen, and learn.[16]

So let's do that. It's one thing for us to list these statistics and give examples of failures of diversity in sports newsrooms. Again, it's nearly 90 percent cismen who report on sports, the vast majority of whom are white. We hear from and see them all the time.

Therefore, the remainder of this chapter is an oral history of sorts. Based on interviews and statements, we collected the voices, experiences, wishes, and advice from a variety of people in the sports media industry. All of them are from an underrepresented group (many with multiple identities that are underrepresented), and all are people in sports who have managed to carve out a space for themselves. All of their professional titles were accurate when the book went to print. Some statements have been slightly edited for clarity and consistency.

On having to be an advocate:

JEN RAMOS says they "kind of fell into sports media by accident."[17] Blogging about the San Francisco Giants led to a journalism minor in school and a minor league baseball beat. Then they went on to graduate school for sports and data journalism, and on and on. Ramos, who is nonbinary (meaning they don't identify as a man or woman and prefer the third-person plural neutral pronoun), spent some time doing digital media with the NHL's San Jose Sharks and briefly was an assistant general manager for an independent baseball team in California, which most likely meant Ramos was the first genderqueer executive in professional sports.[18]

When Ramos first started blogging as a teenager, they used a "gender neutral pseudonym" ("Mac") because, they say, "I didn't want to be perceived as someone who didn't know anything just because of my gender."

"I wanted to be a part of the baseball community online," they say, and "I was just worried that I would not be accepted."

Eventually, Ramos revealed their name and, later down the line, that they are non-binary.

> For the most part, I have been supported. There is still quite a bit of misgendering that goes on with my pronouns. But I'm also lucky in that I have a good support system within sports media that comes to stand up for me when I'm not expecting it or I don't even know what's going on. I've become more liberal with the block button [on social media].
>
> It's still hard because I feel like a lot of my sports writing has happened after coming out as nonbinary but, because

of the way society thinks gender is a binary, I keep being pigeonholed into Women In Media roles when I keep trying to say there are more perspectives than just the women's perspective. There is the trans perspective, there are trans men who exist. So it's hard for me to keep banging that drum of, "Hey, there is more than just male and female perspectives in sports." There are trans athletes out there who are not open, maybe. There are still LGBTQ+ athletes who don't want to come out as gay, lesbian, bi[sexual], or queer because they don't know what the environment is gonna be like, especially in the big four sports.

And I kind of feel like I've shifted more in that direction of advocating for representation because I didn't want to be the only person in baseball media who looked like me and has a similar gender identity to me. Because it felt so . . . so mono-demographic, and especially seeing in front offices, it's mostly white, cis, het[erosexual], male from a privileged background with an Ivy League degree. And it's still hard to break away from that mold because it goes down from front offices to sports media.

The first generation of gender nonconforming, nonbinary trans writers coming out into sports media, we didn't really have anyone to look up to. And that's always been hard because it's like, "How do I find a mentor this way? How do I find a mentor who will understand where I'm coming from, why I'm feeling a certain way." A mentor that won't just tell me like, "Oh, just toughen up, this is how sports media is." Rather than saying like, "Hey, this needs to change."

On who writes the stories:

SHIREEN AHMED is a freelance writer based in Toronto, Canada. A former collegiate athlete, she is an expert on the intersection of Muslim women and sports, writes extensively on race and gender in sport, and cohosts the feminist sports podcast "Burn It All Down."[19]

She says she started writing about sports because "I was unhappy with the way that stories were being written about women of color, particularly Muslim women." She sees a direct parallel between "the challenges and obstacles of many women in sports" and the media that covers them, namely "the lack of knowledge at the intersections of race, gender, sexuality. Everything from not understanding geopolitical conflicts to misunderstanding and ignorance can emanate from mediocre reporting."

I am blessed to have made some of my closest friends, and incredible colleagues who are excellent people with a similar interest in amplifying issues of social justice and people in the margins. In my opinion, who is telling the stories is as relevant as the stories themselves.

I will always advocate for women and nonbinary folks sharing their own experiences, but I have had women tell me and ask me to write about them. They trust me and that is one of the most incredible gifts I have been given: the trust of the athletes. They are survivors, they are incredible humans with so much to share.

The stories and moments that change sports, elevate the games, or help fight for inclusion are as critical to understand as scores, analytics, and match reports. Those stories are the ones that sucked me in. And the ones that will keep me here.

On diversifying your experiences:
JOEL ANDERSON hosts the "Slow Burn" podcast at *Slate*. But previously he was a senior writer at ESPN, where he covered college sports. He moved to ESPN in 2017 after a four-year stint at BuzzFeed News and an earlier gig at the *Tampa Bay Times*. Anderson played a year of college football at Texas Christian University, or, as he says it, he was a benchwarmer for a year at TCU.[20]

He believes one of the keys to making it in sports media, especially if a person is from an underrepresented group, is to diversify one's experiences in journalism. "Do everything, not just sports," he says. "It helps if you've covered city hall, it helps if you've done a cop beat, just anything that would help give you a broader understanding about all the other dynamics that go on in the world." This matters, he warns: "Don't think that sports is just points, touchdowns, strikes, three-pointers, it's about a lot of other issues that go on with [the] culture" around sports.

> People that have had this broad-based experience . . . can say, "Hey wait a minute, maybe we should take another angle at this story," or "We should look at this."
> I think that smart editors have seen the value in that. At least for me, I've been lucky enough that there have been editors that have come to value that experience that I've had. I definitely think that it can distinguish you from a way that a guy who's been covering high school football or college football or NFL, and that's sort of all they've focused their professional energy on. I think it can kind of help you to maybe cover a beat in a way that they just could never compete with.
> Sports isn't apart from society, it's part of society and . . . you should bring that degree of seriousness when you cover it, too. You should be prepared to go beyond game coverage when you're gonna do it.

On constantly having to prove yourself:

STEFANIE LOH is a former sports editor and reporter, and now the features editor, at the *Seattle Times*, where she has worked since 2015. Her first job in journalism was covering the University of West Virginia football team for a local West Virginia paper. She has since covered college football in four conferences and on both coasts.[21]

> Many incredible female sportswriters who came before me fought for the right I currently have to cover sports, to walk into locker rooms and clubhouses. I'll forever be grateful to these pioneering women: the likes of Mary Garber, Melissa Ludtke, Lesley Visser, Lisa Olson, and Christine Brennan. They all fought for the rest of us.
> The big difference in covering sports as a woman is that while your male counterparts can walk onto a football field with the benefit of doubt, you don't get that. You have to prove you know what you're talking about before you will be

taken seriously. You have to earn the credibility that men in your shoes might get strictly because they are men.

Fair or not, because of your gender, that is your cross to bear—at least until we get to a place where the percentage of women in sports media is proportional to the demographic makeup of the communities we represent and the communities we cover. You cannot fail because that might adversely affect the opportunities open to the women coming up behind you. So comport yourself with honor and follow your moral compass. You're doing this job so future generations of women can do it, too.

On continuing to show up:
MIRIN FADER, a staff writer for Bleacher Report's B/R Mag, has made a name for herself over the last few years writing features on athletes like Notre Dame's championship basketballer Arike Ogunbowale, the NBA's Nate Robinson, and the WNBA's Liz Cambage.[22]

I am usually the only woman sportswriter at a game or a practice or an interview. I've had male players make inappropriate comments to me. I've had male coaches mock my questions or doubt my sports knowledge. I am often underestimated, walking into locker rooms. I've been mistaken for an intern. These things used to really bother me, especially since I've played college basketball (I played my freshman year for Lewis and Clark College).

But as I've moved forward in my career, I realized I didn't need to prove myself to anyone. I know I belong now. I'm confident in myself now. I think that confidence came from continuing to show up, especially during these difficult moments. I would often think, "What if there is another girl in here watching me? How would I want her to see me react?" That always kept me going.

I also think my relationships with other women sportswriters and editors has sustained me, too. Christina Tapper, my managing editor at Bleacher Report [at the time], has been a mentor to me. It is crucial to have a woman to lean on who understands exactly what you are going through. Sometimes you don't even have to explain the situation fully; they just understand it. That is a relief.

On being underestimated:
EMILY KAPLAN, who worked at the *Philadelphia Inquirer*, the *Boston Globe*, and the Associated Press, made a name for herself writing at *Sports Illustrated*, where she contributed regularly to the football spinoff site Monday Morning Quarterback (MMQB). She is now a national hockey reporter for ESPN.[23]

One of the more offensive things an athlete or coach can say during an interview is something they might view as a compliment. "Oh," the subject says, usually fifteen minutes into our conversation. "You actually know what you're talking about." When you don't look like the people you're writing about—I've spent most of my career covering male professional sports— there's often an assumption that you're unknowledgeable.

This has always been an insecurity for me, and when I was younger, I'd overcompensate. Before an interview, I spent hours researching stats and minutia about the subject, and when it was finally time to talk, I would regurgitate that information in my questions; somehow I thought this would prove I belong.

Then a college football coach called me out on it.

We were sitting in his office when he interrupted me mid-sentence: "You know, I can read my own Wikipedia page. I thought you were here to have a conversation." His comment resonated. I wanted to be a sports journalist not because I love X's and O's; I love that sports have the ability to transcend. Through the prism of a sports story, we can tell larger stories about society or human nature.

So for me, the job is more about finding common ground than pointing out differences. I have a new response anytime someone tells me I "actually know what I'm talking about." "So?" I will say. "I thought we were here to have a conversation."

On using your uniqueness to your advantage:
DEVON POUNCEY is a sports broadcaster, journalist, and cohost of the "Wake Up and Win" podcast. He played collegiate basketball at Pacific University just outside Portland, Oregon. He graduated in 2016.[24]

> Upon entering college, never did I imagine becoming a full-time sports radio host, a podcast host, a sportswriter, or a college basketball color analyst.
> The single most important thing that led me to where I am today was an internship. I had the fortune of interning for "The Bald Faced Truth w/ John Canzano," a radio show based out of Portland, Oregon. I noticed there weren't many people in this profession that shared my race, interests, or lifestyle outside of sports. Although that could be discouraging for a young African American male, Canzano encouraged me to build off of who I was in the profession, and that along with other things led to me having some space in the industry.

On the future of women in sports media:
CHRISTINE BRENNAN is an award-winning sports columnist for *USA Today* and was twice named one of the country's top 10 sports columnists by the Associated Press Sports Editors. She is also a commentator for ABC News, PBS NewsHour, and National Public Radio, as well as the best-selling author of seven books, including *Edge of Glory: The Inside Story of the Quest for Figure Skating's Olympic Gold Medals* and *Pressure Is a Privilege* with Billie Jean King. In 1981, Brennan was the first woman sports reporter ever at the *Miami Herald* and, in 1985, the first woman to cover Washington's NFL team for the *Washington Post*. She has fostered women in sports media for decades through the Association for Women in Sports Media, beginning with her service as the first president of the organization in 1988.[25]

She says she is "bullish" when it comes to diversity in sports media, specifically in terms of gender diversity. Brennan believes we are on the cusp of seeing the full impact of Title IX, the federal legislation passed in 1972 that mandates gender equity in schools, including athletics, on sports media. "We have got this wave cresting in our country of millions and millions of girls and women, girls who grow up and obviously become women, who have played sports at some level," she says.

> They are coming out into the workforce and they love sports. And it makes sense that, some of them at least, will want to have careers in sports. And that means, of course, sports law, sports medicine, administrative work, and it certainly could be sports media.
>
> So, my premise is this: that as we begin to figure out how we're going to move forward in the media, with handheld devices, with technology, with the next Twitter, with the next Facebook, with all the things that we're going through here. . . . And if we can figure out a way to monetize those things, so that we can hire more people, I say we as a whole industry, if we can hire more people, then I fully expect that women, these wonderful women, who are the daughters of Title IX, will be leading the way into the next generation of sports media. Because they are not going away. They keep coming out 500,000, a million a year, whatever the number is.
>
> We need the infrastructure of the sports media to be able to catch up. Because I am totally convinced that there is a huge place in sports media for women.

On socioeconomics:

RHIANNON WALKER is a reporter for The Athletic, where she covers the Washington NFL team. Before her current gig, she spent more than two years at ESPN's The Undefeated, where she wrote profiles and historical features covering all major sports.[26]

> Every time someone talks about students or prospective journalists taking on an unpaid internship for the experience, I roll my eyes. It's a privileged statement, and I say this as someone whose first internship was unpaid. My parents lent me a car, paid for my gas and everything else. Because they paid for everything else, I didn't need another job or have any

other conflicts to prevent me from doing the unpaid internship. I loved my experience, but it's simply not a reality for many folks who would make journalism more diverse. And when we talk about how to diversify journalism, a lot of folks forget that socioeconomics is another way the industry could seriously stand to be improved. You've got a lot of media folks covering athletes who were barely making it to get by, and the media can't relate to them in the slightest, and so many stories about that kind of rags-to-riches transition. I promise you if you have more people who come from lower income backgrounds, they'd find an angle more interesting than the rags-to-riches story which has been done to death.

On starting, and pushing, the conversation:
PATRICK CLAYBON is an anchor and reporter for the NFL Network. He started working in broadcast television in 2007 at WTVY News 4 in Dothan, Alabama, and then for CBS42 in Birmingham. He was a two-time Alabama state high school decathlon champion.[27]

Claybon believes change in the industry will happen when "those of us who value it . . . foster a better conversation about what 'diversity' means."

The first question in the conversation, obviously, is: "Should organizations be tasked with learning and disseminating America's history of white supremacy, homophobia, sexism, etc.?" My answer is: "If not, what is the point of these conversations in the first place?"

My second question would be: "If you claim to have a diverse workforce, are you paying them equitably?" With agency representation at the national level, the large firms know exactly what the compensation is for everyone. If a large agency wanted to start a national conversation about any number of pay gaps in journalism, they'd have all the data they need.

So much of getting and keeping these jobs that we have (and love!) means not asking these questions, especially when we're the only one in the room. That's why I feel like it's important to hold companies accountable to having these discussions in order to educate the *entire* workforce on why diversity is more than just a buzzword.

Because if marginalized women and men could have overcome the structure of American society by ourselves, we'd have done it by now.

On turning your challenge into an advantage:
REEM ABULLEIL is an Egyptian freelance sports journalist and the former managing editor of Sport360. She is based in Dubai, was the resident tennis expert at Sport360 for many years, and is now a freelance journalist. She follows both the ATP and WTA tours throughout the season.[28]

Abulleil says that she is surprised that she was able to make a name for herself in sports journalism because "I am Egyptian, writing in English, my second language, carrying a passport that makes it very difficult to obtain visas to travel the world and cover events, and I come from a region that is not necessarily a hotbed for professional athletes."

On this point: "As an Arab Muslim woman . . . I honestly thought I never stood a chance." But, she says, "while there's a long list of barriers that could have discouraged me, some of those perceived barriers helped me find my niche." As for the very thing she thought would hold her back, she now sees an advantage: "I am an Egyptian female sports journalist covering sport at the highest level. Being an anomaly attracted people to my work."

She also worked hard: learning Spanish, utilizing social media to reach people all over the world, and treating all of her assignments with the same level of seriousness.

I started writing about people barely anyone thought, much less cared enough about to tell their stories. The countless Arab athletes, who against all odds, managed to excel in professional sport. I began sharing the point of view of this part of the world. Showcasing the good and the bad, but from our perspective as Arabs.

I am a sportswriter who has made a living writing about

people. Where I'm from should not matter, yet somehow it does. To some, it may be a challenge. I've turned it into my advantage.

On being Black and expected to cover sports:
KEME NZEREM is a journalist and network TV news correspondent for Channel 4 News in the United Kingdom. He has covered a wide range of topics and in 2007 won the Royal Television Society award in foreign news for his narration of a film about the US troop surge in Iraq. Much of his work, though, has focused on sports, something he says happened "by accident."[29]

I think one of the reasons I ended up as a sports correspondent is because I'm Black. Because sport is one of the editorial areas where people of color are allowed to be experts, expected even.

This first manifested when I was newly graduated from journalism school and found myself doing an internship at Channel 4 News, which is one of the most diverse UK news outlets. This was in 1999 and I remember pitching to do the story about Fulham football club at the time, which was the first British football club owned by Mohamed Al-Fayed, who owns Harrods. In a visionary move way back then, he decided to turn Fulham women's club professional.[30] He would pay them.

To me, that wasn't really a sports story: it was a business story, it was a culture story. But because it was football, it instantly made people take interest. If this had been some other industry where women were not paid the same as men, no one would have cared.

So somehow that was interpreted by the editors then at Channel 4 News as, "Oh, this guy knows about sport. Okay." Now I cannot say it was because I was Black, but I suspect I fit quite neatly into this idea that here's a young Black guy that knows about sports. So, I was effectively still a student and I was offered a job as a sports producer. I was never going to turn that job down.

Nzerem has since stopped focusing on sports reporting, which is fine by him. "I was never particularly interested in who wins and who loses." Still, "I think my experience of being a sports reporter led me to want to cover certain stories that other journalists perhaps would ignore or not feel comfortable enough to deal with them."

On being the "lady in the locker room":
JULIET MACUR, who captained the Columbia University rowing team while she was at Barnard College, is a sports reporter at the *New York Times* and author of *Cycle of Lies: The Fall of Lance Armstrong*, published in 2014. She started at the *Orlando Sentinel* in 1997 and spent time reporting for the *Dallas Morning News* before heading to the *Times* in 2004. In 2016, the Associated Press Sports Editors named her one of the top 10 sports columnists in the United States.[31]

The first time I walked into an NFL locker room, in 1997, the PR guy yelled, "Lady in the locker room!" So much for me, a nervous cub reporter, blending in. He shouted that phrase every time I was there. It made me blush.

For the three years I covered the Jacksonville Jaguars, there was no blending in. I was the only female newspaper reporter on the beat. All but one of the male reporters ignored me or poked fun at me for being a newbie. One guy picked on me, asking me loudly in the press room, "Why are you taking so long to finish your story? This isn't Shakespeare." Or, "How can you write about football if you never played it?" That, from a guy who was maybe 5-feet-2 and who never played a Division I college sport, like I did—I was a rower— much less play NFL football. The negativity was unrelenting. But if I wanted to survive in this business, I needed to ignore the noise.

The best thing I've ever done in my career was to stop worrying about fitting in. Because I always believed that I fit in. I grew up playing sports and loving sports, and several years into my career, I finally felt comfortable covering sports. The Good Ol' Boys Club still exists, and our job as women is to chip away at it. One way to do that is to stay focused and do our jobs—and do them well—even when critics try to distract us.

So these days, when a P.R. man yells, "Lady in the locker room!"—and it does happen occasionally—I look around and say, "Really, where?"

On finding stories that need a platform:

ISHMAEL JOHNSON is an editor with *Dave Campbell's Texas Football.* After graduating from Texas State University in San Marcos, Texas, in 2014, he worked for two years at the *San Marcos Daily Record* as a reporter and editor.[32]

Johnson says he has been fortunate so far in his "still-early career in sports media" to "have been surrounded by colleagues and bosses that either understand the modern hurdles that face people of color or are sympathetic enough to want to understand."

When I approached my former boss at the San Marcos *Daily Record* about a feature on a student-activist organization holding a national anthem protest during a Texas State football game in 2016, I was met with zero pushback. But I also know that there's a chance that the same story/pitch is met with rejection elsewhere.

There are countless stories like that, which often get overlooked or whitewashed. Seek out those stories and give them a platform.

But, Johnson says, change has to also come from the inside:

People who have made an impression in the industry have to use their status and capital. It's not entirely fair to put that kind of responsibility on them, but they're the ones with the power to open doors for other people of color. If you happen to work your way into positions of gatekeeping, use it! When I first became an editor and to this day, I've tried to use my platform to give writers/content creators of color a chance. I seek them out.

On owning your space:

MEG LINEHAN is a staff writer for The Athletic who covers women's soccer. She was formerly the social media manager at the National Women's Soccer League. Her career has included a little bit of everything—writing, editing, photography, and video. She has specifically concentrated on women's sports.[33]

I started out in women's sports as an intern for the Boston Breakers post-1999 Women's World Cup—the infrastructure today is much stronger than it was back in 2000, but we're still really far away from consistent, insightful coverage of women's sports on a mainstream level, as any study of sports media will show you. The fun part and the flip side of that means: we get to build it, and we are building it. Our challenge is ensuring that space is diverse and welcoming, to bring people up with us rather than gatekeep.

It's always easier said than done, and women's sports still have plenty of frustrations, especially when it comes to resources. But the thing I am most excited about is that we're finally starting to see pushback against the culture of straight white dudes in sports who like to comment "kitchen" on anything related to a woman athlete. We're owning our space with attitude rather than asking for permission to have a seat at the table. Instead of justifying, we're able to point at the accomplishments of Serena Williams, of Breanna Stewart, of the North Carolina Courage and say, if you're not watching this, it's your loss. I think it's how we win.

We have to put in the work to find the right people to tell stories, even if it means that personally we lose out on a byline. Many don't have formal training, so we have to teach each other skills we have learned along the way. We have to pull others up onto our platforms, instead of being protective of what we have earned so far.

On managing the scrutiny:

MORGAN CAMPBELL is a former sports features writer for the *Toronto Star*. His work has covered the places sports intersects with business, race, and politics. He won the National Newspaper Award for Sports Writing, and his work has been featured in the *Best Canadian Sports Writing* anthology.[34]

Campbell, who readily admits that he has a big ego, says that part of navigating the sports industry as a Black man is getting scrutiny for things that white counterparts do not—such as, say, having an ego. Or people in higher-up positions paying little attention to you even when you've won major awards or been successful in your position for many years.

One time, Campbell came up against an editor who hadn't done his homework on Campbell's career and contributions to the paper. He told Campbell he wasn't sure if he was going to move him back to the sports beat because "maybe you're just not that good" at it.

> He asked me to justify, he asked to list all the stuff; so I list all the stuff. He says to me at the end, "Well, you're quite full of yourself, aren't you?"
>
> You've been around sports, right? They all have big egos. So, for him to put me on the spot and say, "Well, you're full of yourself." Every successful sportswriter's full of him- or herself in one way or the other. You know, and the difference is whether or not it gets in the way of you doing your job well. Listen, there are people who are too egotistical and still make a lot of money, so one has very little to do with the other.
>
> But the fact that he's pointing this out to me, he thinks is a flaw, because he's not telling the white guy that they're full of themselves. I know he isn't. Because when I talk to white colleagues about this, they're like, "I've never had that talk with him, he's never talked to me like that." I even had a white colleague say to me, "Man, that's just white boy shit. That's all it is."

Campbell says diversity in newsrooms is "self-evidently positive."

> If you don't have that diversity on your staff, you're gonna miss a lot of good stories, or misinterpret a lot of stories, or cover a story in a way that doesn't portray the richness of that story.

On being typecast:

ZITO MADU is a writer for SBNation and contributor at *GQ*.[35]

One of the many problems that comes up when you're a Black person or a person of color in sports media, and in journalism overall, is the issue of being typecast. It's absolutely necessary to have inclusion in the workplace, not just to dispel the homogeneity and stale nature of so much of sports media, but also to have a better understanding of the lives of many of the athletes and a better engagement with them as people. But what tends to happen is that because there's a Black person or person of color on staff, they become the go-to person for any issues that involve race. The same goes for women and cases of sexism. This isn't too bad, and it's understandable to a point, even though sometimes it can be a case of laziness to delegate the articles about race and identity to the Black person or person of color, who already knows and deals with these issues daily, rather than having their white counterparts grapple with it. What is truly annoying is when that's all that's asked of the writer. To only be the "Black" writer. The "Asian" writer. The "Latino" writer. That's using the idea of representation as a limitation. It's not really tokenism, but it's [also] not valuing the writer as a creative and capable person, a valuation that their white colleagues usually have. Unless the writer chooses to focus solely on those subjects that relate to their identity, they should have the freedom to express themselves across a wide range of topics like everyone else.

On navigating the negative:

TAMRYN SPRUILL is a features writer at The Athletic. She is also editor-in-chief at Swish Appeal, a website focused on women's basketball. She is the first woman to hold this position at the site. Her basketball-related content has appeared in Bleacher Report, NPR's "All Things Considered," *Teen Vogue*, Golden State of Mind, and High Post Hoops. She is also an adjunct professor of English, literature, and creative writing.[36]

Working in sports media meant learning to expect nicks and cuts and gashes on a regular basis and develop skills to bandage them quickly. In Spring 2018, I accepted an editor-in-chief position that allows me to curate coverage for a women's basketball site in a way that addresses issues of sexism and gender discrimination head-on. During the 2018 WNBA season, I expected to report on the inequitable treatment of WNBA players, but I had no idea I'd silently suffer mistreatment of my own—with neither ally nor advocate supporting me the way the players were being supported by their fans and each other. I was the first woman (and, therefore, the first African American woman) to occupy this position. As the first, I was undermined and sabotaged by staff members I inherited—brazen wrongdoing I'd never witnessed prior male bosses experience at any point in my professional life. Add in unkind treatment from some readers who didn't appreciate my entry into a space they'd hijacked as their own—and, sometimes, belittling treatment from league representatives—the experience has been unpleasant.

On the days I considered walking away, my conviction to work on behalf of justice, equity, and fairness sustained me. A strong motivating force is required fuel for powering through adversity.

On telling your story:

KERI POTTS is a survivor of sexual violence, a victim's advocate, and the president and founder of A Fight Back Woman, Inc. She is also ESPN's director of communications and has worked hard to teach her colleagues at ESPN how to best cover the topic of gendered violence.[37]

After I was sexually assaulted in Rome, Italy, in November 2008, I worked for more than a year to place an article about my experience. I wanted to (a) find others who had prosecuted their attackers overseas, and (b) call attention to the lack of resources and services for Americans assaulted abroad. The inherent volatility of magazine deadlines meant that my story was published nine months after my attacker had pleaded guilty. I was in the midst of changing jobs, transitioning from publicity for ESPN Films to overseeing publicity for ESPN's college sports properties. So, the article was actually the way most sports media came to know my name.

A month later, at the national championship game, I walked into the media room to run a press conference for ESPN, and after my name was announced, I recall hearing intense whispering. I knew why that was. And I remember thinking to myself, "*Yes. I'm that woman. I'm not ashamed and I'm not going anywhere.*"

Over time, I really came to appreciate that I never had to struggle with that decision. I saw then, and still see now, the value for women and men to work with a woman who has made a very personal experience public, unapologetically so.

It's been ten years since my attack and eight years since the article, and I believe it was important for everyone working with me to see me be open about what happened to me and open about my work in victims advocacy, all while continuing to accomplish professional goals and excel at my craft. In a way, I feel that turns the tired narrative of "a shattered woman" on its head. Survivors are everywhere. It can be anyone harmed by this crime. And we are resilient.

On questioning the status quo:

KARIM ZIDAN is an investigative reporter and author who was born and raised in Cairo, Egypt. His work covers the intersection of sports and politics, especially mixed martial arts and the UFC. His bylines have appeared in the *Guardian*, *Foreign Policy*, Deadspin, Bleacher Report, and SBNation.[38]

When it comes to diversity in media, the onus is on newsrooms to ensure that all races, ethnicities, genders, and sexualities are represented fairly within reported stories. However, it is also on journalists who represent minorities to push the boundaries of journalism and challenge archaic industry standards and journalistic conventions. Diversity is not just about the fair representation of minority voices and stories, but also about applying your own experience and cultural identity to better tell these otherwise ignored stories.

In my case, I used my experience as an Egyptian Canadian who grew up under repressive regimes in Egypt, Bahrain, and Saudi Arabia as the foundation for my niche reporting on the intersection of sports and politics. By shedding the notion of what a traditional sports reporter should do, I focused on highlighting the concerning and oftentimes dangerous ways that politicians interact with sports and use them for propaganda and diplomatic gain. In doing so, I am able to use sports as a lens to view the issues facing Arab societies while simultaneously teaching a Western audience about a topic they did not previously know about.

Journalism is not just about opportunities, but also about how you take advantage of those opportunities.

———

Jen Ramos, who kicked off the testimonies in this chapter, says that some of the best and most accurate advice they've ever received was from a white male cis boss who told them, in so many words: "If it's possible, pretend you have that confidence, pretend you're just like them because that's really the only way the system will work, and if you can fake it the way that they fake it, it will start to break barriers down."

However, the burden should not be placed on the underrepresented to change the system, Ramos says. Even so, "we also know and recognize in this system right now, the only way to break the system is to gain it." They've done so by seeking out mentors (many of them professors), asking blatantly for jobs ("I felt like I had nothing to lose at that point"), and creating supportive spaces and networks for non-cis men in the field to gather and promote each other's work.

Or, as Shireen Ahmed puts it: "My best (and only) advice to folks who feel like they don't have a seat at the table: build your own fucking chair."

And if you are not a chair-builder, go search out the people who are. They are out there, changing sports media one story at a time.

CHAPTER 8

ROOTING FOR YOUR TEAM
WHEN THE STAR IS ACCUSED
OF DOMESTIC VIOLENCE

Stephanie Haberman's first love was baseball, her first team the Mets, her first favorite player Jose Reyes. And yet, she found herself walking to Goodwill, Reyes jersey in hand—the first jersey she ever bought—about to donate a piece of her childhood. So much had changed in thirteen years.

"I laid it there and walked away," Haberman said.

In June 2016, the New York Mets brought back Reyes, who spent his first nine years with the team before joining the Colorado Rockies, where he served a 51-game suspension for domestic violence.[1]

In October 2015, Reyes was arrested for abuse of a family or household member at a hotel in Hawaii. According to local reports, including the NBC affiliate KHNL, Reyes grabbed his wife by the throat and shoved her into a glass balcony door. She told police she had injuries to her thigh, neck, and wrist, and she was taken to a hospital.[2]

Reyes was charged in November, but a judge dismissed the case the following April because his wife refused to cooperate. This follows a long-standing pattern in domestic abuse cases generally—and especially those involving famous athletes. An accuser's unwillingness to cooperate in prosecution is often taken as a sign that abuse didn't occur, but victim advocates cite a bevy of reasons why an accuser might choose not to pursue charges—not the least of which is the threat that she and her partner might lose their livelihood and income.

Nevertheless, the absence of criminal prosecution did not deter Major League Baseball's own investigation of the incident, which resulted in what was then the second-longest punishment under the league's new domestic violence policy, which had been enacted in August 2015.[3]

Following the suspension, the Rockies released Reyes, eating nearly $40 million in salary to no longer have him on the roster. Less than two weeks later, the Mets jumped at the chance to sign him. Many Mets fans heartily welcomed back Reyes and the chance to watch a player with whom they'd grown up. Others, like Haberman, couldn't bring themselves to cheer for this once-beloved player.

"Anger and betrayal" is how Haberman describes her reaction to that decision. A die-hard Mets fan dating back to 2000, Haberman—a digital producer at MSNBC who has worked for NBC Sports and *Sports Illustrated*—to this day can't stomach the thought of her once-favorite player rejoining her favorite team. "As a woman and a fan, I felt betrayed by an ownership that viewed winning above all else," she says.

After the Reyes announcement, it took Haberman nearly two months to return to Citi Field to actually watch a game in person, and even then it was because she received free tickets through work. "I wasn't willing to purchase them."

Instead, she used the opportunity to start a personal ritual to show her true feelings about Reyes. One of the most difficult things about sports is that it not only gives fans a chance to cheer for players, coaches, and teams that have done harmful things; it encourages it. It's peer pressure wrapped around the instinctive nature to support your team. But it also offers a potential platform for protest. So, while other fans cheered at the sight of Reyes on the field, Haberman decidedly sat.

"That game started my tradition of whenever the Mets are announced in the beginning of a game, I will stand up and applaud—I am a fan," she recalls. "And then they announce Jose Reyes's name, and I [sit] down. I do not stand up and applaud for him."

The dynamic of standing to cheer for your team while sitting to condemn an individual player speaks to the heart of the conflict many fans feel in such cases. "He was the first athlete I really idolized," Haberman says about Reyes. As she let go of her admiration for Reyes, she still had to come to terms with her disappointment with the Mets organization. Loving the team and loving the people in charge don't always go hand in hand.

"I kind of balance that in my head by rooting for guys like Wilmer Flores," Haberman says, referring to the young utility player who endeared himself to Mets fans in 2015 when he cried on the field after hearing during the game that he was going to be traded. The trade fell through; two days later, he played hero with a walk-off home run in the 12th inning against a division rival; and Flores was forever cemented as one of the "good guys" in baseball—a Met who simply wanted to be a Met.[4]

But as far as the people in charge, Haberman thinks that the decision by the Mets front office to bring back Reyes willfully ignored her and other female fans. "I felt like the team was betraying me, betraying my values and my womanhood for a couple dollars. . . . It's just another way of taking advantage of women," she says. "That's disregarding a large part of your fan base and their feelings about the situation."

———

What made the Reyes situation worse—especially for Haberman—is that until then the Mets (along with the rest of the baseball world) held the moral high ground over their crosstown rival, the New York Yankees. In December 2015, the Yankees completed a blockbuster trade with the Cincinnati Reds, acquiring All-Star closer Aroldis Chapman, famous for throwing 100-plus miles per hour. Chapman had been the subject of trade talks between the Reds and the Dodgers, but Los Angeles pulled out earlier that month after he became the subject of a domestic violence investigation. The Yankees swooped in to grab Chapman, inciting justifiable ire among fans in New York and across the country.

According to a police report obtained by Yahoo! Sports's Jeff Passan and Tim Brown in early December 2015, Chapman's girlfriend told cops the pitcher choked her and threw her against a wall.[5] As she hid in the bushes outside the house and her infant child remained inside, Chapman fired off eight gunshots in his garage. In March, Chapman became the first player disciplined under MLB's new domestic violence policy, receiving a 30-game suspension.[6]

After hearing about this incident the Dodgers suspended trade talks, but the Yankees were champing at the bit. The Yankees would eventually trade Chapman to the Chicago Cubs in July 2016, where he served as the closer in the team's historic World Series run, breaking a 108-year championship drought. The Yankees then turned around in the 2016 offseason and re-signed Chapman to a five-year deal. Conflicted Cubs and Yankees fans alike essentially played Hot Potato with this talented player whom they could not quite wrap their heads around.

News of the initial trade with the Reds excited some Yankees fans still seeking a viable replacement for Mariano Rivera, the legendary closer who retired in 2013. But like Haberman, other fans found it hard to watch a player with a 100-mph arm knowing that arm was used to choke his girlfriend. "There was really no way around it for me to feel slimy about it," Tanya Bondurant, MLB league manager at SB Nation and former managing editor of the site's Yankee blog, "Pinstripe Alley," says.

"At the time I think I was just glad it wasn't my team involved in it," says Julie DiCaro, a Chicago sportswriter, radio host, and lifelong Cubs fan. But when her team traded for Chapman, "I was very vocally upset about it." Before getting into sportswriting, she previously worked as a lawyer, both as a public defender and with domestic violence victims, making her uniquely qualified to have a well-rounded perspective on this issue.

Like Haberman, Bondurant and DiCaro felt particularly slighted as female fans, and especially as women who cover sports. "Look around the stadium. Look at how many women are at this stadium. Really?" DiCaro asks. But at the same time, they can't just stop rooting for their teams, even when the man on the mound makes them cringe. It gets to a point at which you map out scenarios in which the team can win while the player loses.

"I never felt good. I never cheered for him. I just sort of would zone out and just go to a place where like, whatever happens happens, and then we'll move on. But I really didn't like to think about it," DiCaro says. "I wasn't rooting for him. I wasn't working against my team. I'm sure it's a really dissonant position to take. I'm not cheering for that guy. You can break it down and be like, well how do you cheer for your team when he's on the mound. But I felt icky."

"It does take quite a bit of mental gymnastics," she continues. "I would want him to blow the save and then someone else to come in and the Cubs would rally."

"I don't root for him to do well, but I want the Yankees to win," Bondurant says. "If he blows a save and they win in extras, I kind of chuckle to myself. I can't hope that he would do as badly as I would want him to if he were on a different team. But also, when he does well, it's tough, it's really tough, because you feel like you're rooting for someone that you would never want to associate with."

———

Adding to the internal dilemma of how to think about Chapman is the external challenge of explaining that dilemma to other fans, particularly men. For Bondurant, that challenge is compounded by her being a woman who covers sports, having to deal with readers who don't want to be reminded of Chapman's history of abuse and then use that as yet another reason to question her fandom.

"They see it as, you're not 100 percent for the team if you don't like this person or can't root fully for this person. But at the same time I kind of have to defend my fandom anyway," she says. "I think there are people who say like you are less of a fan because you aren't able to blindly root for a team. But I also feel like . . . there should be a limit to what we're willing to tolerate from the players and the team as a whole."

The "team as a whole" aspect echoes conflicts that Haberman and DiCaro expressed about their front offices. As Bondurant notes, the Chapman trade simply reinforced well-established notions about the Yankees, who have embraced their "Evil Empire" persona while going far beyond the usual characterizations of elitism and disproportionate wealth.

"Can we just stop being a self-parody for like five minutes?" Bondurant asks. "The Yankees have this perception of the bad guys in baseball and it's like, you didn't have to go get this guy who no one else wanted to touch to further cement that reputation. So yeah, you want them to be better, but at the same time they're kind of living up to their billing. And that's also really frustrating."

Set against the Yankees and Chapman, the Mets seemed even more like the good guys in town. The Reyes signing changed all that. "I was proud to be a baseball fan from New York who wasn't a fan of the team who did that," Haberman says. "And then my team went around and stabbed me in the back, too." She notes that the little-brother complex many Mets fans feel was temporarily eased by the outrage over Chapman, but that period was short-lived. "It just added to the sense of, so you gave Mets fans a small sense of pride that you don't normally find against Yankee fans . . . and to have something to hold over Yankees fans (other than the fact that we have better food in our stadium) was really nice for a moment." With the Reyes signing, "they took that away from us."

For DiCaro, the Chapman trade similarly spoke volumes about the character of the front office, but it also sent a message to fans. "I sort of think that whoever comes in to take a team over and to run a team is the steward of that team for the fans," she says. "The goal is for teams to be as educated about this kind of stuff as people who work in the industry, and to know what's right and what's wrong when you're putting women in positions of danger and when you're not." As DiCaro notes, teams that sign and support a player with a track record of violence against women "continue to enable him, and I don't want my team to do that. I want them to be better."

The Dallas Cowboys provide a prime example for enabling a player with a violent past. In March 2015, the Cowboys signed the defensive end Greg Hardy, despite the fact that he had already been convicted of domestic violence more than a year prior. In July 2014, Hardy (on the Carolina Panthers at the time) was found guilty of two counts of misdemeanor charges for assaulting a woman and communicating threats. The charges came from a May 2014 incident in which Hardy beat his then-girlfriend and threw her onto a pile of assault rifles. In February 2015, the charges were dismissed after the woman refused to testify at the appeal and reportedly received a settlement from Hardy.[7]

The Cowboys signed Hardy in March 2015, even as he was still under investigation by the NFL. In an official statement, Cowboys owner Jerry Jones stated that the team took care in "gaining a solid understanding of what he is all about as a person and as a football player."[8]

"It just reaffirmed what I had been believing for a long time. It didn't surprise me," says Dale Hansen, sports anchor at Dallas's ABC affiliate WFAA. "They've crawled into that sewer before so many times that it was just another one. It was just more dirt on the grave as far as I was concerned."[9]

In April, the NFL suspended Hardy for ten games, a penalty that would later be reduced to four games. He made his Cowboys debut in the fifth game of the season on October 11. Then in November, Deadspin published graphic photos and the original police report very clearly showing heavy bruising on the woman.

Hansen says he's long lost his sense of fandom precisely because of teams making moves like the Hardy signing that he's witnessed in his forty-plus-year career. "The more I got to know, the more I got to see, the more the game became a business in part, the more that I will not and never have cheered for bad guys, it just kind of reminded me that I shouldn't be a fan in the first place," he says.

Some Cowboys fans did have a negative reaction to the Hardy signing. According to Hansen, he knows of fans who burned their jerseys and canceled their season tickets. But it still wasn't enough to deter Cowboys ownership—or, for that matter, other fans. "As Jerry Jones has proven time and time again, for every ten people that burn their season tickets, there are fifteen people waiting to buy them," he observes.

As some fans continued to support not just the Cowboys but Hardy himself, others wondered how that could be possible. "Tell me how you explain that to your daughter," Hansen says. "How do you explain it to that little twelve-year-old girl that you are standing and cheering for a man who beat up his girlfriend? I can't begin to understand how you do that."

Like Bondurant, DiCaro, and Haberman, Hansen bemoans the broader message sent when teams condone violent behavior. "There is this attitude that does seep through society that if it's okay for Greg Hardy, if it's okay for Ray Rice, if it's okay for a dozen others, why don't these young men think it's okay?" he asks. "When we continue to excuse it and basically look the other way as long as they can entertain us, we've lost our moral way."

Unlike Bondurant, DiCaro, and Haberman—who, as both fans and journalists, are conflicted in reconciling their rooting interests with their values—Hansen describes many fans as essentially being controlled by their fandom. "For some reason, I think it does define a lot of people who identify as fans that winning and losing is somehow a self-reflection of their own worth," he says. "Fans are willing to sell their soul, sell their integrity, sell their self-respect and dignity, to win a game."

When the winning stops, however, it seems that the moral compass can kick in again. In February 2016, the Cowboys declined to re-sign Hardy after his one-year deal expired. Hardy's lone season in Dallas was embattled both on and off the field. He recorded six sacks in twelve games and failed to reach any of the incentives built in to his contract. He also got into a fight with teammate Dez Bryant and the special teams coach Rich Bisaccia on the sideline during a game. The Cowboys would push the narrative that Hardy was released because he was perpetually late for team meetings, even though the team failed to discipline him for that during the season. All in all, the Cowboys got what they signed up for in taking on a player with a violent past.

"You bring in bad guys and they usually cause bad problems and it doesn't work," Hansen says.

The hope with Hardy—like Chapman, like Reyes, and like with so many before them—is that character can change, and behavior can change. As much as he might be the poster boy for domestic violence in sports, Ray Rice might also be the poster boy for rehabilitation, having come the closest to true contrition that we've seen among accused athletes. But Rice is an outlier: his incident forced leagues to start taking violence against women seriously, but it also involved a player on the tail end of his career who didn't create a win-at-all-costs dilemma for teams and fans looking to sign him.

To that end, second chances are justly afforded in the court of law, but many fans struggle with doling out second chances in the court of public opinion, especially when those second chances only seem to go to players who still exhibit remarkable talent—and primarily when their infraction involves violence against women.

"Why don't murderers get a second chance? Oh, I see, it's only second chances for this," Hansen observes, noting that the notion of second chances brings up the uncomfortable question of where, exactly, the bar should be set. "Why don't the Cowboys sign Osama bin Laden? I mean, he's six-foot-four and obviously no one could catch him."

"I don't think it's unreasonable that, here's our standards, and beating up a woman, you just crossed the red line," he says. Similarly, DiCaro calls out people who tout the "innocent until proven guilty" standard in order to police others' fandom. "That's the standard for a courtroom when we're trying to decide if we're going to take away someone's liberty. That's not the standard for me sitting in my living room watching TV deciding whether or not I want to cheer for a player," she says.

———

At the end of the day, how do fans, women, and sportswriters look past the player to root for the team? For some, continuing to talk about players' violent pasts goes a long way.

"There is, to me, an amorphous Cubs idea that doesn't have anything to do with this team and the people running this team," DiCaro notes. "I was with this team long before Theo Epstein and Jed Hoyer were. Long before the Ricketts family was, long before Aroldis Chapman was. . . . In my head I can always cheer for that team even if I'm not happy about what's happening on my TV at that second."

"The Mets will still be here when Reyes is gone," Haberman

says. "Unfortunately, sports and the world being how it is, Reyes is going to go and someone else is going to come. And I wish that there were something I could do about that, but I don't own a baseball team. All I can do is talk about it and not let the fact that this is happening go undiscussed."

"I was upset with the Chicago sportswriters who wrote pieces about the Cubs trading for Chapman and never once in their story mentioned the fact that he'd been suspended for domestic abuse. A lot of people covering it just wanted to put their heads in the sand and just not talk about it," DiCaro says. She added that every time Chapman took the mound for the Cubs, she would tweet about his domestic abuse or retweet the original report about his incident. "Every time he took the mound . . . I tried to make it as clear as possible that I'm not good with this, I'm not on board with this, and try to sort of keep the Cubs' feet to the fire."

In the end, Chapman made the Cubs World Series run bittersweet for her, though he didn't actually record the final out. Still, it's all the more reason to root for another ring now that he's off the team.

"It's a little bit tainted," DiCaro feels. "Him not being on the mound was the best thing that happened that entire series. I would have been really, really, extremely upset, and I don't think I would feel the same way about it as I do. I have fond memories of it, I get warm fuzzies from it. But whenever I think about him having been a part of it, I still get angry."

Haberman says she'd feel the same way if Reyes were to hit a walk-off home run to lead the Mets to their first World Series win in her lifetime. "It would be bittersweet. I would celebrate as a Mets fan, but the ball would forever have an asterisk on it." (As this book goes to print, Reyes is a free agent and Haberman might not have to worry soon.)

"I'm not really the kind of person that lets it go," Bondurant says. "It shouldn't be a negative thing to bring up that the Yankees are willfully employing someone who did this knowing what he did and still chose to do it twice." She continues: "This issue with domestic violence is one that is so widespread across sports, and I think that if you are a woman, particularly a woman who writes about sports . . . that kind of male energy toward women is something that you become very familiar with." She also adds this:

> And I think it makes it tougher because you see, you get threatened, you have people say just like these horrible, awful things that they would never say to males writing about sports. So I think that it's a definite difference when you're a woman and you see this problem that we have in society with domestic violence and trying to mesh that with, "But I also like sports, and I want to like sports care-free." But we can't do that.

While some fans seem capable of enjoying sports purely as a form of escapism, these women represent a faction for whom that's simply impossible, even among outcries from fellow fans and readers, particularly men, that they basically just get over it. "My brain functions at a level where I can't just think about one thing," Bondurant says. "The 'stick to sports' argument is really lost on me, because we're never only going to be able to say this exists in a bubble, because it doesn't."

Part of the answer is for media organizations and teams to hire more women, especially women of color. It's not that men can't or don't report well on or respond correctly to gendered violence, but as we wrote about in chapter 7, women tend to report differently than men do, in particular by including more female voices. Additionally, race is often an important lens through which to understand who gets punished and who is forgiven, who is making the decisions around that punishment and around how the story gets framed, and how we all collectively talk about the issue of gendered violence. We have to diversify who makes these choices and who tells these stories.

In terms of media specifically, there's the case of former Houston Astros assistant general manager Brandon Taubman. In October 2019, during the locker room celebration after the Astros clinched the pennant and their place in the World Series, Taubman "turned to a group of three female reporters, including one wearing a purple domestic-violence awareness bracelet, and yelled, half a dozen times, "Thank God we got Osuna! I'm so f—— glad we got Osuna!," according to *Sports Illustrated*'s Stephanie Apstein. Taubman's taunt was in reference to the criticism the Astros took for signing Osuna during his 75-game suspension from the MLB for domestic violence. Houston was the only team willing to sign Osuna.[10]

As Dan Solomon wrote at *Texas Monthly*, "Taubman's job, like the job of every coach, manager, athletics director, or executive in sports, is to put a winning product on the field. . . . After the Astros won the pennant, it makes sense that Taubman would have felt a sense of vindication over the decisions the team made in constructing its roster." Solomon notes, however, that "part of the reason this story has caught so much attention is that Taubman's outburst has reminded Astros fans that they've been [celebrating Osuna and feeling complicit in it] for the past year and a half." Taubman shined a bright spotlight on the disconnect between the goals of the team on the field and the reputation of the team off of it.[11]

SI's Apstein was the first to report this incident, and the Astros initially questioned the veracity of it. That led to multiple other reports, many of them by male reporters, corroborating what they had seen and admitting that perhaps they should have considered this worthy of reporting. Taubman eventually lost his job and the Astros apologized for questioning Apstein.

Still, it matters that he directed his emotions at female reporters, one in particular: Taubman had complained about the woman wearing the purple bracelet because, according to NPR, "some of the reporter's informational tweets—promoting domestic violence hotline telephone numbers, for example—appeared moments after Osuna entered several Astros games in relief." It emphasized the continued otherness of women in locker rooms, about the potential cost of speaking out about domestic violence or other gendered violence, and the reality that a lot of this stuff might go and certainly has gone unreported based on who is in the room and sees it as newsworthy.[12]

As for fans, they have come up with ways to continue enjoying sports without being silent. They talk about it with friends, post on social media, and sit when certain players are announced. Some also try to offset at least some of the harm.

For her part, Bondurant started a pledge at "Pinstripe Alley" to donate $1 to the National Coalition Against Domestic Violence for every strikeout Chapman recorded in the 2017 season. "All that I can do right now is put my money where my mouth is," she wrote at the time.[13]

"The least I could do is turn his success into help for [victims] and that would make me feel better in the process," Bondurant says. "I am not so enlightened that I could be like, 'I'm never watching the Yankees again.' But if there was anything that I could do—and it was small," she says, noting that Chapman had sixty-nine strikeouts that season. "But that was something that I felt like I could do that would make me not being willing to just cut the team off entirely a little more manageable, personally."

CHAPTER 9

LOVING YOUR TEAM WHEN
YOU HATE THE OWNER

Most of us became sports fans at an early age, either through family tradition, bonding with classmates and peers, or sheer love for our hometown. Perhaps the team we chose to root for in our formative years had that transcendent star player, that unforgettable play that brought us to our feet, or that glorious celebration when a championship trophy was hoisted at a parade. Most of us, at least at an early age, had little to no conception of the head of the beast: the problematic man (or woman) behind the curtain calling the shots and pocketing the tangible spoils generated by our beloved teams. Beyond the wins and records and history-making highlights there are the owners.

As fans mature, however, it becomes harder to ignore this figure occupying the special suite in the stadium. Still, no matter how much we complain—about that ill-advised contract, that refusal to open the purse strings, that laundry list of cringe-worthy comments, that suspect political affiliation, or even that general feeling that our owners might not actually have our best interests at heart as fans—despite ourselves, fans continue to root for teams with almost religious fervor. Sports and fandom, we tell ourselves, are so much bigger than just one man.

Perhaps no one in the past four decades exemplifies this more than Donald Sterling, former owner of the NBA's Los Angeles Clippers. In 2014, the NBA's newly appointed commissioner, Adam Silver, made Clipper fans' dreams come true when he banned Sterling from the league for life and forced the sale of the team following the release of a recording in which Sterling made overtly racist comments about African Americans that centered on Los Angeles Lakers legend Magic Johnson.[1]

At the time, it felt like a watershed moment for the team and the league, for a city that has been no stranger to racial strife, and for a national landscape—both athletic and political—that had allowed such attitudes to prevail among people in power for far too long. Sterling's indiscretions had been well known for decades, extending far beyond mere words—yet it took a tape published by the celebrity gossip website TMZ to finally topple the man in charge. Slumlord, philanderer, racist, sexist, ageist, penny-pincher—you name it, and Donald Sterling was probably known for it.

None of that was immediately top-of-mind to young basketball fans like Alex Crawford, a native of Newport Beach, California, who first fell in love with the Clippers as a preteen in the mid-2000s, due mostly to his affinity for the underdog in a city ruled by Laker purple and gold. "Growing up it was, and it still is, Lakers everything," he says. "I just remember everything was Lakers and I thought, I'm going to root for this other team." He grew into his fandom rooting for players like Elton Brand, Corey Maggette, Cuttino Mobley, and Vladimir Radmanovic—not exactly names that lit up the back pages alongside Shaq and Kobe. Despite resigning himself to rooting for a team that would forever play second fiddle, Crawford did get a taste of what it was like to align himself with a winning team. In 2005–2006, the Clippers finished above .500 for the first time since the 1991–1992 season, ending the regular season as the sixth seed in the Western Conference and winning a playoff series against the Denver Nuggets, eventually falling to the Phoenix Suns in the conference semifinals.

"That was the first time I experienced rooting for the Clippers when they were actually good," he says, having attended one of the playoff games against the Suns at Staples Center. "I remember that was kind of eye-opening, like this can actually be fun to be a fan of this team."[2]

At that time, Crawford was in high school, still young in his fandom. "I didn't really know that much about Donald Sterling," he says. "Later I was like, oh my god, what have I got myself into." It wasn't until Crawford began reading more and more stories about Sterling's history and business practices that he truly became aware of the man running his team. "This is, you know, a scourge of a human being."

And yet, like so many of us, Crawford couldn't pull himself away from his team of lovable underdogs. "It was like, okay, I'm committed to this," he says. "I guess I kind of asked the question, can you root for a team even if the owner is someone that you strongly disagree with across the board and is someone that negatively contributes to society in my eyes? That was something I grappled with quite a bit."

He sums up his dilemma: "Yeah, I'm still a Clippers fan, but it is weird. Now that I'm older and have more perspective—I'm so thankful that Donald Sterling is not the owner anymore."

———

Donald Sterling bought the Clippers, then based in San Diego, in 1981 for $13.5 million. The next year *Sports Illustrated* was already identifying him the worst owner in the NBA, at a time when the league was mired in financial woes, low viewership, and the threat of a labor strike. Having amassed his nearly $300 million fortune through various real estate holdings, particularly housing complexes in Southern California, Sterling quickly brought new meaning to the word "eccentric," plastering his face across billboards in San Diego, floating the idea of tanking in order to secure the top pick in the draft decades before purposely losing became mainstream NBA thought, and failing to make hundreds of thousands of dollars in payments to former players, team hotels, and employee pension funds.[3]

Within the first sixteen months of owning the team, Sterling developed a reputation for prioritizing his pockets over winning, under the guise of supposedly drafting high in the future. The Clippers finished 17-65 after his first season, which saw the team's roster decimated by injuries to just seven players (one below the league minimum). Sterling made no secret of his desire to move the team to Los Angeles, closer to his Beverly Hills residence. According to *SI*, league officials sent "urgent" telexes (a precursor to faxes) to the team expressing concerns about its business practices. They were largely ignored.[4]

In September 1982, after the NBA Players Association threatened to boycott the All-Star Game due to Sterling's failure to pay players, a committee of six owners voted unanimously to recommend his removal as owner of the team. The proceedings were postponed after Sterling announced he would sell the team, after which he hired attorney Alan Rothenberg as team president to "straighten things up," on the advisement of NBA vice president (and future commissioner) David Stern. Rothenberg then persuaded the NBA not to remove Sterling or force the sale of the team.[5]

The decades that followed saw the team finally move to Los Angeles, but with little progress toward expanding the team's talent or its competitiveness. On a personal level, Sterling continued to engage in sleazy business practices that reflected his prejudices against Black and Latinx people, including players, front-office employees, and tenants in his housing complexes. In February 2009, Elgin Baylor sued Sterling in Los Angeles Superior Court for wrongful termination and discrimination based on age and race. Baylor had been the Clippers' general manager from 1986 to 2008. In the lawsuit, Baylor stated that Sterling had a "vision of a Southern plantation-type structure" for the team, alleging that Sterling had said he wanted the Clippers to be "composed of 'poor Black boys from the South' and a white head coach." Also in the lawsuit, Baylor accused Sterling of racism during contract negotiations with star forward Danny Manning. According to Baylor, Sterling told Manning's agent: "I'm offering you a lot of money for a poor black kid." Baylor also said that three Clipper players—Elton Brand, Sam Cassell, and Corey Maggette—had complained that Sterling brought women into the locker room to gawk at players, saying to one of the women: "Look at those beautiful black bodies."[6]

The laundry list of race-related lawsuits against Sterling is almost too lengthy to cover in full, but it's certainly not limited to basketball. In 2006, Sterling faced a housing discrimination suit brought by the US Department of Justice, accusing him of refusing to rent to Black tenants. According to sworn testimony by one of Sterling's property supervisors, the supervisors routinely harassed Black and Latinx tenants by refusing rent checks before accusing tenants of nonpayment, refusing to perform repairs before threatening to evict, and maintaining all-around unlivable conditions. When Sterling bought a building called the Ardmore, he explained its odor: "That's because of all the blacks in this building, they smell, they're not clean," he said, according to the testimony. "And it's because of all of the Mexicans that just sit around and smoke and drink all day. . . . So we have to get them out of here."[7]

Given this history, the 2014 tape that finally caused Donald Sterling's downfall came as no surprise. In that recording, Sterling can be heard admonishing his girlfriend, V. Stiviano, for posting a photo on her Instagram with Magic Johnson. "It bothers me a lot that you want to broadcast that you're associating with Black people," he said. "Why publicize it on the Instagram and why bring it to my games?" In an extended version of the tape obtained by Deadspin, Stiviano asks Sterling: "Do you know that you have a whole team that's Black, that plays for you?" He responds: "I support them and give them food, and clothes, and cars, and houses."

Amid the fallout from the tape's release and Sterling's subsequent ban, players and former employees came out of the woodwork with tales of the owner's rampant racism. Baron Davis, who played on the team from 2008 to 2011, recalled that Sterling would actually heckle him during games to the point that it affected Davis's on-court performance. "As soon as he walked into the arena, I'd get like the worst anxiety and I never had anxiety playing," he said.[8]

"I remember hearing stories like that, and I'm like, I love Baron Davis," Alex Crawford, the fan we introduced above, says. He added that it was his love for the players that helped him justify continuing to root for the Clippers despite Sterling: "Almost like,

I'm going to support him through this hard time." Even before the tape dropped, "I'd always find myself siding with the players, or understanding why guys didn't want to play in LA [for the Clippers] long-term, until we get rid of Donald Sterling," he says. "I always viewed Donald Sterling as a big detriment to the team's success."

Crawford described a fascinating dilemma he faced as a fan of a historically losing team: wanting to see the team win but understanding the moral and roster limitations of ownership. "It was almost like, masochistic or something being a Clippers fan, almost seeing karma play out in front of you," he says. "Knowing deep down, the basketball gods are not going to let us be successful under him." To that end, when Crawford first heard the tape, it was a blessing in disguise that ultimately exposed the curse under which Clipper fans had lived for years.

The Sterling tape is certainly not the first time a team or league has needed documented proof to take action against an individual. It echoes the way accountability for gendered violence is more likely to be administered if a video (à la Ray Rice) or pictures (à la Greg Hardy) exists. Rice himself said this of the pictures reportedly showing Hardy's abuse: "It really shouldn't take photos, you know, or anything to understand the severity of domestic violence that happens every eight seconds as we speak. It does continue to raise awareness. It's just a tough deal that it takes the visual, the photos, for the severity of it to be known."

In the same vein, all the reports of Sterling's racist actions and choices from Black and Latinx tenants and former employees were never proof enough of the harm he was doing. It took himself—a white man—saying it on a recording before the league finally took action.[9] "I think that's a bigger picture, that this is a societal thing where we don't as a society or as a people really take action on things until we see it on tape or until it's documented right before our eyes," Crawford says. "We can read about war and destruction and this and that but if you see photos or you see video, all of a sudden it brings this reality, I think it's a human issue."

Dr. Susan K. Whitbourne, a developmental psychologist and professor at the University of Massachusetts–Amherst whom we introduced in the introduction, is an expert on the psychology of sports fandom. She agrees with this sentiment. "You've got to overcome the denial factor. And yes, there is something more visceral when you're actually seeing the utterances from the individual than reading about it in the paper," she says. "You've got more sources, more channels of communication. It's hard to deny what somebody is actually saying on tape—though people do it."

In the days after the Sterling tape leaked, as the basketball world awaited commissioner Silver's decision on how to discipline Sterling, many wondered how players would respond. The Clippers were scheduled to play Game 4 of the first round of the playoffs against the Golden State Warriors, and rumors floated of a potential boycott. Instead, the players staged a quiet yet impactful pregame protest, removing their shooting shirts in unison during pregame warmups to reveal them wearing their warmup gear inside out. Maneuvering around the NBA's strict in-game dress code, the Clippers also wore black socks and wristbands. Other teams, including the Portland Trailblazers and Miami Heat, followed with similar demonstrations in solidarity with the Clippers— who went on to win Game 4.

Two days later, Silver banned Sterling.

It wasn't an easy time for Clipper players and fans, having to weigh the importance of a playoff game against the moral imperative at hand. "I remember being really curious as to what the players were going to do. That was a weird time, because I wanted the players to do something," Crawford says. "I remember being torn as a fan. Part of me wanted to see them fully sit out and wanted to see them do something drastic just to really drive home the fact that we're not playing for this dude. And then the other part of me was like, it's the playoffs."

This was one of those rare instances in which the right thing to do would also be the best thing for the fans and team. Sterling's ouster wouldn't just mean a win against racism and bigotry—it would also remove the primary roadblock to the team's on-court success. In that way, the Sterling debacle was ultimately much less of a dilemma compared to other cases. It was addition by subtraction.

Sterling was forced to sell the team to Steve Ballmer for $2 billion—a healthy profit for an owner who was allowed to remain in the league far too long and who was a racist miser who, as Crawford puts it, "would never do what it took to win a title or to be competitive year in and year out." Ballmer has given the team a new energy as an owner who cares about players, and especially fans, holding town halls with season ticket holders and regularly appearing to lose his mind on the Jumbotron at Staples Center. "I love his energy. I love that he seems like he's a fan," Crawford says. "Donald Sterling was just running it like a business where you were trying to scrape by and cut corners, and Ballmer seems so enthusiastic, so committed. It's a total 180 from what it was before, and that's exactly what the franchise needed."

The Clippers still haven't won a title, but ousting Donald Sterling seems like a victory in itself. "I honestly consider that the greatest moment in Clippers history," Crawford says. "We've never won a championship. We've never been to a Western Conference final. We've had a handful of really cool playoff wins. But getting rid of Donald Sterling, to me, it was the greatest moment, because it opened up the door. There's not this guy holding us back anymore."

———

New York Knicks fans could only watch with envy. They know that they will likely never see such a fitting end to their team's tumultuous ownership. Despite all the Yankee glory, one could argue that New York is at its core a basketball town. Street ball is a ubiquitous sight throughout the city's public courts, and the city has historically yielded some of the best talent starting at the youth level. So for Knicks fans, watching their team lose year after year after year strikes at the core of their identity as New Yorkers.

Knicks owner James Dolan essentially inherited the Knicks in 1999 from his father, Charles, when James became chairman of Madison Square Garden and assumed control of Cablevision's sports properties, which also include the NHL's New York Rangers and the WNBA's New York Liberty. The Knicks were coming off a 1998–1999 season in which they reached the NBA Finals for the second time that decade, losing to the San Antonio Spurs in five games. Since James Dolan took over, the Knicks have posted just five winning seasons, making it past the first round of the Eastern Conference playoffs once. As this book goes to print, the Knicks were poised to waste yet another season and miss the playoffs before the NBA season was suspended in March 2020 due to the COVID-19 pandemic.

More than two decades under Dolan have led to countless head-scratching moves, ill-advised player signings, demoralizing trades, and infighting with beloved coaches and front-office personnel—not to mention an inexplicable bromance with former Piston player-turned-executive Isiah Thomas (capped off by a very public and messy sexual harassment suit). In short, it's been a steep decline for Knicks fans who grew up during the 1990s, when the team only had one losing season to start the decade and made a legendary run to the NBA Finals in 1994, falling to the Houston Rockets in seven epic games.

Doug Berns, a New York–based musician and self-described sports fanatic, was six years old when he watched that playoff run, one of his earliest memories of being a Knicks fan. He and his older brother Sam would sneak a Walkman to bed every night to listen to those games, falling in love with a team headlined by players like Patrick Ewing and Charles Oakley, players who embodied the physicality and toughness of basketball, particularly in New York during the 1990s.

"If you grew up in New York, those are iconic teams. What was so great about that team is that they were so tough," Berns says.[10]

New York City at that time was changing from being a very gritty, and tough, and crime-ridden place, to becoming what it is today, which is very ritzy—especially Manhattan. It's very ritzy and gentrified and expensive and it's difficult to live here if you have a lower income. But at that time, those players, they weren't the most skilled—they were just the toughest. And that's what was part of New York identity, and still is. For those of us who've been here for a long time, we identify with that ethos.

During the 1990s in the NBA—dominated by Michael Jordan and the Chicago Bulls—the Knicks fielded Ewing along with Oakley,

John Starks, Anthony Mason—grind-'em-out players who left everything on the court in front of the Garden faithful. "I remember seeing Oak and Mase and Ewing and just that Garden energy. I can't tell you specifically the first game I went to, but I can remember the smell and sound and the colors—the light, sea-foam green-blue of the rails and the sections had those purple numbers," Berns recalled.

> Going in there and that intensity every time Patrick would score, or Starks would hit a three, the whole building would rock. We could only really afford to sit super high up, so you could feel it, like you were about to fall over. Just the environment of it being the most special place in the world, and so many people who loved this team, and identified with it. And when you were all in there together, magic. Just, magic.

The magic has waned since Dolan took over. He shipped off tough players who gelled seamlessly in favor of expensive, washed-up veterans and splashy names that might look good in the bright lights of Broadway but did nothing for clubhouse or on-court chemistry. Berns had never been aware of the ownership during his childhood—there wasn't much of a reason for an adolescent to question the front-office moves of a team that was actually winning. But in 2000, the Knicks traded Patrick Ewing, and the following year beloved coach Jeff Van Gundy resigned just nineteen games into the 2001–2002 season. By the time Berns started high school in 2002, the Knicks no longer resembled the team he fell in love with. Coupled with new interests like music, wrestling, and dating, his interest in basketball started to wane.

The name "James Dolan" didn't really mean very much to Berns until the Isiah Thomas years. A legendary player in his own right, Thomas was hired as head of basketball operations in 2003 despite several red flags on his résumé after his career as a player. In 1994, he became part owner and executive vice president of the expansion Toronto Raptors, only to leave a few years later following public disputes with the head coach and failed attempts to gain greater control of the team. In 1998, he bought the Continental Basketball Association for $10 million, only to run it into the ground. The league declared bankruptcy in 2001 as the NBA established its own developmental league. Immediately before joining the Knicks, Thomas served as head coach of the Indiana Pacers—a disappointing three years that ended with him being replaced by Rick Carlisle. In short, Isiah Thomas had failed at every position he'd occupied since hanging up his kicks, and Dolan still saw fit to hand him the reins to the Knicks.

It's nearly impossible to exaggerate just how bad Thomas's tenure was with the Knicks. He leveraged the future by trading high draft picks—many of whom would eventually become top-level talent, like Gordon Hayward and LaMarcus Aldridge—in disastrous deals including Stephon Marbury, Eddy Curry, Mo Taylor, and Antonio Davis. He threw money at players like Jerome James and Jarred Jeffries. He drafted Renaldo Balkman over Rajon Rondo. The Thomas era created a sense of dread among Knicks fans, who continually saw underperforming players flourish once they left New York—players like Channing Frye and Trevor Ariza.

In addition, the head coaching situation was a persistent disaster. Since Van Gundy's departure, the team has had twelve different head coaches and counting, with the most recent signing and firing of David Fizdale signaling little hope for future success. Still, under Thomas the team went through Don Chaney, Lenny Wilkens, Herb Williams, and Larry Brown—until, that is, Thomas decided to take over coaching duties himself in 2006. Despite failing to see significant improvement from the team, Dolan granted Thomas a multiyear extension. It wasn't until 2008, when Donnie Walsh took over as president of basketball operations, that Thomas finally left the Knicks, being "reassigned" as a consultant to work directly under Walsh.

It was during this time that Berns started watching the Knicks much more closely again. "Then I became astutely aware of who James Dolan was and what he was doing to the culture of the team and how awful it was getting," he says. "The thing that I've always hated about this Dolan franchise is that they act like they're one move away and then they do something really stupid. Every single year. There's no continuity with the coaching. He just does these things that are splashy, and they just leave the franchise with nothing."

To Berns—and countless other Knicks fans—the problem is compounded by one fact: no matter how inept Dolan and the team's front office continue to be, the Knicks franchise lines Dolan's pockets with money. The Knicks perennially place first on *Forbes*'s list of the most valuable NBA franchises, benefiting from the corporate sponsorships and seating opportunities at "The World's Most Famous Arena" in the financial and media capital of the country. "This is really the saddest part about it," Berns says. "When the fans stop coming to the games, Chase Bank is still buying a whole section. Dolan never faces any economic consequences for his actions. And that's really the only way to get a rich man to pay attention to what he's messing up, is if you grab him by the pocket book."

That being said, Knicks fans seem to occupy a special place in masochistic sports fandom by continuing to go and watch their team lose. For whatever reason, Madison Square Garden remains a premier entertainment destination in New York. In 2018, the Knicks had the ninth-highest attendance in the league, averaging 19,331 fans per game. Part of that is due to corporate clients who buy suites and rows of tickets to entertain business associates. Moreover, tickets are so expensive that the average fan—even the diehards—are priced out of attending games on a regular basis. And yet the sea of orange and blue fills the MSG stands, in part because average fans are replaceable by rich fans and corporate clients. And some fans, like Berns, just can't quit this team. "The Garden will sell out regardless because we are crazy people, and we love this team so much."

But every fan has a breaking point. Recent years have seen fan uproar, with protests and calls to boycott the team becoming more frequent and brazen. In February 2014, a group of about forty fans organized a protest outside the Garden in March, a culmination of years of frustration and complaints falling on deaf ears. The "Knicks Fans 4 Life Rally" detailed its discontent on its Facebook page. These included: "Dolan's failure to allow knowledgeable basketball people the autonomy/power to make basketball related decisions"; the lack of transparency and availability of high-ranking executives to speak to fans through the media; and the outsized influence of the Creative Artists Agency in negotiations with players and coaches.[11]

The group concluded: "We understand Dolan will not sell. We understand change may not come of this. We just want our voices heard. We want to remind Dolan and the NBA that our voices matter. We buy the tickets, the jerseys, the NBA League Pass subscriptions. We are frustrated. We are tired. We deserve better."

In the weeks between the announcement of the protest and the demonstration, Knicks fans saw something unfamiliar: the front office maybe, perhaps, actually listening to some of their demands. The day before the protest was scheduled, Dolan held a press conference introducing Phil Jackson as the team's new president of basketball operations. Jackson's tenure with the Knicks would prove ill-fated—Jackson's legendary triangle offense seemed obsolete in today's NBA, among other issues—but the real takeaway was provided by Dolan himself. At the press conference, an uncharacteristically talkative Dolan promised Jackson complete autonomy, stating that he would "willingly and gratefully" relinquish his own authority. Then came the words fans had been waiting more than a decade to hear: "I am by no means an expert in basketball," Dolan said. "I think I'm a little out of my element when it comes to the team."[12]

It was stunning and validating all at once for fans to hear their team's owner finally admit he wasn't the best equipped to build a winning franchise. To fans like Berns, the question was never whether Dolan actually cared about winning—"I think he would be thrilled to lift the Larry O'Brien Trophy," Berns says—but instead whether Dolan could overcome his own ego and hubris to defer to true basketball people to build such a team. There was now reason to be cautiously optimistic that that would be the case.

The day after the Phil Jackson press conference, the rally went on as planned, with the fan group sending an amended message to its owner: "Dolan, we will be hopeful but not blind."

Of course, Jackson didn't prove to be the answer the Garden faithful hoped for, and the Knicks would continue to languish in losing streaks and sub-.500 seasons. In January 2015, with the

Knicks about to fall to a 5-34 record, a group of five fans occupied Dolan's courtside seats at the Garden wearing paper bags over their heads. Fans and media alike continue to call for a boycott of the team until Dolan sells—an unrealistic outcome.[13]

The frustration is understandable even to fans, like Berns, who might not agree with the notion of a protest or boycott. "It's cathartic to do those sorts of demonstrations, but it's also embarrassing to all the fans," he says. "We're fans. We love this team. We love what it represents when it's really working. Don't go to a game if it's going to make you unhappy."

Of course, that's easier said than done. Like most fans, Berns just can't bring himself to quit his team, no matter how much anguish it causes, no matter how terribly the seasons play out. He admits to reaching a breaking point every season, usually around the halfway mark, when he recognizes the campaign is basically over. "There's usually one game every year, when they blow the lead for like the twelfth time in a row," he says, recalling a specific instance during the 2017-2018 season. "I involuntarily threw my remote control and it broke." "That's it. I'm done for the year. I'm packing it in."

And yet, he and countless others keep coming back for more. "To start a fresh season, there's always hope. There's always hope and the expectations within that hope. Every year you just have to take what they present to you and hope it's going to work," Berns says, adding that he's taken a somewhat more realistic (perhaps morbid) viewpoint in order to make sure "that disappointment doesn't crush you."

———

Like most teams, the expectations for the Knicks and Dolan extend beyond the court—as do the disappointments. During Thomas's tenure Dolan faced a significant test of character and failed. In 2006, Anucha Browne Sanders (now Anucha Browne), former senior vice president of marketing and business operations, sued Thomas and Madison Square Garden for sexual harassment just days after her firing. In the suit, Browne, at the time one of the few and most powerful Black female executives in North American sports, accused Thomas of sexually harassing her, creating a hostile work environment based on sex, and calling her a "bitch" and "ho" in private conversations. Browne would eventually expand the suit to include Dolan and said she was fired for complaining about the harassment. In 2007, a jury awarded Browne $11.6 million in punitive damages. Madison Square Garden vowed to appeal but ultimately settled for $11.5 million.

In the years since, neither Thomas nor Dolan has shown much contrition, releasing multiple statements questioning Browne's claims. The most recent episode was in 2015, when Dolan made the shocking decision to hire Thomas as president of the Liberty. The Garden released a statement defending Thomas and attacking Browne's previous claims: "We did not believe the allegations then, and we don't believe them now. We feel strongly that the jury improperly and unfairly held Isiah Thomas responsible for sordid allegations that were completely unrelated to him, and for which MSG bore responsibility." As many commentators noted, the Thomas hiring was especially brazen for two glaring reasons: It seemed ill-advised to appoint a man accused of harassing a Black woman in charge of a team consisting of Black women; and from a pure basketball standpoint Isiah Thomas is simply bad at his job.

If that same immaturity is what prevented Dolan from admitting he wasn't a basketball expert, it also informed some of his interactions with fans—even Knicks legends.

Dolan has a notoriously contentious relationship with Charles Oakley, a beloved former Knick who represents that era of hard-nosed, committed, winning basketball during the 1990s. Over the years, Oakley has been refused opportunities to be a goodwill ambassador for the team and has even been denied entry to the Garden. Oakley told reporters that he buys his own ticket whenever he wants to see a game and that Dolan has to be informed whenever he's in the building.[14]

All of this came to a head in February 2017, when Dolan had MSG security escort Oakley out of the arena in handcuffs, claiming he was intoxicated and belligerent; Dolan banned him from the Garden.

Some fans and players, including Dwyane Wade, immediately jumped to Oakley's defense, circulating the hashtag #FreeOak on social media and implying that racism is fueling Dolan's feud with Oakley. It was also another demonstration of just how petty Dolan can be. "That's embarrassing, childish stuff," Berns says. "'*I don't want to play with him—kick him out of the playground.*' After all that Oakley did for us and for the fans—I mean, he really did it for the fans. Those guys just went as hard as they could, recklessly, because they really believed in the fans of New York."

More broadly, many Knicks fans took this incident as part of a longstanding pattern by Dolan to separate the current Knicks era from the much brighter memories of the 1990s—before Dolan took over. "I just don't understand why he thinks that acknowledging that this team was so great would tarnish his legacy as an owner," Berns says. "It's really sad, because all the fans love that team. I'm going to tell my kids about growing up, 'When I was your age there was this guy Charles Oakley. And I got to watch him play.'"

As much as Dolan might want to distance present failures from past success, it's those very memories of seasons gone by that keep fans like Berns coming back. "For fans like me who've been fans for as long as we have and have seen the team go from what it was to where it is now, what we want is a team that represents what this city means to us. And that starts with guys who can run the ship the right way and organically build something that works," Berns says. "I root for this team because they represent my city and my childhood. I love being from New York. I'm super proud of it. It's a big part of who I am and how I see the world. And you have those formative years where you rooted for the Knicks."

For many fans, childhood memories of greatness are a common theme in their continuing, if tortured, relationship with sports. So are the memories of family bonding rooted in the singular love of a team. "I have all these fond memories of going to games with my brother and my parents and just those moments when we were together around this team. I wish I could describe the feeling in a real way. It's like December 12, 1997, and you're walking out of the Garden, and it's cold out, and you just saw this great game. These moments that define your life are around this team," Berns says. "It's just in your DNA. The Knicks are a part of me."

Fans of other teams often ask Knicks fans why they continue to suffer through their fandom, if there's anything the team could do to make them stop being fans. For Berns, the answer is simple. "Impossible. It's impossible." "My involuntary affinity and love and reaction, there's just nothing I can do about it. It's physical. There's a certain guttural response I have to watching the Knicks. This thing, it starts in your stomach and pulls you up. When the Knicks go up by six, have a little run, my endorphins just go crazy. I can't help it."

"My bond with this team is forged forever, and there's nothing I can do about it," Berns concludes. "If you ask me to not be a fan, it's like asking me to change my name. You just can't fathom that—it's part of who you are. There would have to be some crazy ritual, like [a] brainwashing session, to get me to stop being a fan of the Knicks." Devoted fans like Berns don't need some kind of reverse-brainwashing disinformation program to keep them in the fold. But for fans who find themselves on the fence, perhaps a high-dollar PR campaign will do the trick—or not. In January 2020, the Knicks announced they hired Steve Stoute, a music executive who is the CEO of Translation, an ad agency, to rebrand the entire twenty-year debacle represented by Dolan's ownership tenure.[15] But after Stoute appeared on ESPN's *First Take* morning show on February 11 and offered comments that, as he explained it, "inadvertently insinuated about Knicks personnel," the franchise was forced to immediately release a press statement clarifying that "any decisions regarding the operations of the team will be made by the new President of the New York Knicks."[16] Another illustration of franchise unity, Knicks-style.

———

Fans of both the Knicks and Mets share more than just a city and the blue and orange—they also share a doom-and-gloom mentality, an antagonistic relationship with the owner, and a refusal to let go of their fandom.

Kevin Lauriat grew up in Brooklyn in the 1990s, part of a family with a long history of National League baseball fandom that dates back to his grandfather. Upon arriving in New York from Limerick, Ireland, he promptly adopted the Brooklyn Dodgers as his team. "He wanted to join the culture, and what's more American than baseball?" Lauriat observes.[17]

Like many generations of New York baseball fans, Lauriat's family shifted allegiances after the Dodgers left for Los Angeles in 1957 and the Mets were established in 1962. Lauriat's father and all of his brothers and sisters were Mets fans, setting him up for this life of fandom—for better or worse.

"It was like a bonding thing with my siblings. I wanted to be just like them," Lauriat says.

A self-described "masochistic Mets fan," Lauriat's first live game at a stadium (Shea Stadium) was in 1995. And like many who fell in love with a sport or a team by attending a game, he remembers details about that day. According to Lauriat: "It was Hideo Nomo's first start against the Mets"; going by the schedule, it must have been May 23 when the Mets fell to the Dodgers 6-4. "The big stadium lights, the crowd—that's when I really fell in love with it."

Through the years, Lauriat and his contemporaries among the Flushing faithful have experienced pointed highs overshadowed by ultimate disappointments, most notably the 2000 Subway Series in which the Mets lost to the Yankees and the 2015 World Series when they fell to the Royals. Mets fans born after the team's last championship in 1986 *just gotta believe* in that elusive World Series trophy.

But for all the heartache, for every time the team had to play second fiddle to its crosstown rivals, for every head-scratching personnel move made by the front office, Mets fans remain some of the most devoted and passionate in sports today. Nowhere is the passion more evident than in their attitudes toward ownership.

Brooklyn-born real estate developer Fred Wilpon has owned some part of the Mets since 1980, when he bought a minority stake in the team as it changed hands to the Doubleday publishing company. In 1986, Nelson Doubleday Jr. and Wilpon agreed to purchase the Mets in an equal partnership. In 2002, Wilpon bought out Doubleday's remaining half.[18]

As with the Knicks, the shift in ownership at the turn of the millennium signaled a new direction for the team. After Wilpon took over in 2002, the Mets finished the season atop their division just once over the next fifteen (and counting) seasons. Wilpon's son, Jeff, became more active with the team, assuming the role of chief operating officer and earning a reputation, as sportswriter Joel Sherman put it in the *New York Post*, as "a hot-tempered, know-it-all meddler." For Mets fans, the Wilpon era has meant loss, frustrating roster moves, major financial scandal, and repeated calls for a change in ownership.[19]

Unlike Knicks fans, many Mets fans feel their problems stem largely from the owner's unwillingness to spend money and the general sense that running a successful baseball team at any cost simply isn't a top priority for the Wilpons. "The newspapers say they're cheap, they don't want to pay this and that, and that sort of gets in your head," Lauriat says. "They make all their money on real estate, and it's almost like baseball's a hobby."

Examples of poor baseball decisions under the Wilpons abound. The 2009 free-agent signing of Jason Bay to a four-year, $66 million contract will go down as one of the worst moves in franchise history. Every year, baseball insiders mock the deferred contract deal with Bobby Bonilla, whom the Mets owed $5.9 million in 2000. After releasing him in January 2000, rather than buying out the remainder, the Mets negotiated a deal with Bonilla's agent in which the team would make deferred payments with an 8 percent annual interest rate. The result is that every year on July 1—dubbed "Bobby Bonilla Day"—the Mets are on the hook for more than $1 million. These payments were scheduled to be made to Bonilla from 2011 through 2035. He will be seventy-two years old when he receives his final paycheck from the Mets.

Bonilla's case is an extreme example of the Wilpons putting the cart before the horse, prioritizing the bottom line in the short term at the expense of a long-term strategy to invest in a winning team. The practice of deferring contracts isn't new, but the Wilpons used it more than most, placing those owed dollars with an investment firm so that they could profit off the returns from money that was meant to pay players. That investment firm? Bernard L. Madoff Investment Securities LLC.

When Madoff's Ponzi scheme was exposed in 2008, it didn't

take long for the Wilpon name to surface among his key investors. At the time, Fred Wilpon and Saul Katz (Wilpon's brother-in-law, business partner, and the team president) had more than 500 accounts with Madoff to the tune of $500 million, much of which was money related to team finances in the form of player annuities, sponsorship dollars, premiums from disability insurance, and the aforementioned deferred contracts.[20]

As a result of Madoff's bust, Mets ownership had to initially borrow $430 million against the team and $450 million against its majority ownership stake in the regional sports TV network SNY. Financing those debts alone cost the Mets more than $100 million per year—a full season's payroll for many teams in the league. In addition, reports at the time (vehemently disputed by general manager Sandy Alderson) suggested that one of the team's bridge loans with Bank of America contained a limitation on significantly increasing payroll. In other words, the financial woes stemming from the Mets' involvement with Madoff had a direct impact on the team's ability to field a competitive ballclub for several years. In 2008, when the Madoff scandal came to light, the Mets had the third-highest payroll in the league. In 2014, when the team refinanced the Bank of America loan and supposedly lifted such restrictions, the payroll ranked twenty-second, at about $85 million.[21]

For some fans who didn't need yet another reason to lose confidence in ownership, the Madoff scandal was simply more of the same. "My first reaction was probably #lolMets," Lauriat jokes, invoking the long-standing hashtag that refers to any instance of comical Mets incompetence. "That's when I was really like, 'Just end it already. Just sell the team.'"

Lauriat's not alone in calling for a change in ownership, nor did discontent begin with the Madoff case. Longtime New York Post writer Mike Vaccaro advocated as far back as 2004 to boycott Mets games until the Wilpons agreed to sell. In 2011, after then-commissioner Bud Selig caused the league to assume control of the Dodgers amid a contentious divorce battle between owners Frank and Jamie McCourt, many media and fans wondered if similar action would be taken against the Wilpons and the Mets. That never happened, even if it seemed justified given Selig's reason for seizing the Dodgers. "I have taken this action because of my deep concerns regarding the finances and operations of the Dodgers and to protect the best interests of the club," Selig said in a statement.[22]

Yet despite borrowing against the club, directly involving team finances in a Ponzi scheme, requiring emergency loans from the league, and thus fielding a team that was less than competitive, the Wilpons didn't suffer the same fate as the McCourts.

Many baseball insiders saw this as a sign of Selig's long-standing friendship with Wilpon, dating back to his precommissioner days as owner of the Milwaukee Brewers. "Enough is enough is enough," ESPN's Ian O'Connor wrote in May 2011. "If wresting the Mets from Wilpon isn't in the best interests of baseball, what the hell is?"[23]

When asked if the Wilpons should have been forced to sell the Mets, Lauriat doesn't mince words. "100 percent. If not for the sake of the franchise itself, then for the sake of MLB," he says, reiterating that allowing the Wilpons to continue conducting business as usual sends the wrong message regarding how they value the team. "There needs to be some sort of investment in the team." "I feel like a Major League team should run like a Major League team. And sometimes I feel like I'm watching the movie *Major League*, where the owner wants them to lose just so they don't have to spend the money."

Beyond financial incompetence, Mets ownership rubbed fans the wrong way through several other moves. In 2014, Leigh Castergine, former senior vice president for ticket sales, filed a lawsuit against the team and Jeff Wilpon for "discriminatory and retaliatory treatment," claiming that Wilpon took issue with her being pregnant and unmarried. According to the complaint, the harassment included Wilpon "pretending to see if she had an engagement ring on her finger and openly stating in a meeting of the team's all-male senior executives that he is 'morally opposed' to Castergine 'having this baby without being married.'" The suit was settled out of court in 2015, with the Mets issuing a statement that they would be "more attentive to the important issues raised by women in sports."[24]

"Some of these owners are just horrible owners, but a couple of them seem to actually just be terrible human beings," Lauriat says. "When your owner's being sued because he fired a pregnant woman? Come on, guy. There's no real empathy there."

The Wilpons also have a reputation for using the media to trash their players. In 2011, a widely cited piece in the *New Yorker* by Jeffrey Toobin quoted Fred Wilpon directly criticizing much of his roster, including beloved players like David Wright, Jose Reyes, and Carlos Beltrán. (It should be noted that Beltrán was in the midst of a Hall of Fame–caliber career that would later be marred by his role in the Houston Astros' sign-stealing scandal; Wright, despite his injuries, would retire as the face of the franchise; and the Mets would ultimately bring back Reyes after his domestic violence history for inexplicable reasons.)

When that piece was set to run, Wilpon reportedly called Beltrán and Reyes to apologize. But the precedent of passing blame for the team's woes onto players had already been set.[25] "I feel like Justin Turner is a great example of that," Lauriat says, referring to the Mets' decision to nontender their more-than-competent infielder after the 2013 season. Turner would immediately turn into an absolute stud for the Dodgers, becoming an integral part of two World Series appearances. The Mets would justify letting go of Turner—who was making just $500,000 in 2013—by leaking tidbits to the media about his lack of hustle. To this day, Turner says that rejection by the Mets continues to motivate him.[26]

In Lauriat's mind, the reputation of the Wilpons for being stingy yet meddlesome hampers the team's ability to sign big-name free agents and experienced managers. After all, who would want to deal with such circumstances? "Frankly, it's embarrassing," Lauriat says. "Some things are just a decent thing to do as a human."

Much like Alex Crawford loving Baron Davis and rooting for the players' interests, fans who continue to root for the Mets despite ownership do so because of the players they've grown to love over the years. Alienating a team's players probably isn't the best way to retain fandom, then. "You become attached to these players, like I'm really rooting for this guy. I'm almost not even rooting for the team at this point—I'm just rooting for these players. But if there's no talent to root for, there's not investment in the team," according to Lauriat. "I guess that's what really keeps me invested. That and Keith Hernandez making fun of people."

For his part, Lauriat says he doesn't blame any fan who has supported a boycott of the team, but he also doesn't quite see the point. He might not go to as many games as he used to, but his team is no less a part of him. "I'm not willingly going out and buying a ticket. If someone invites me, I'm not going to say no. It's not really a protest—I just don't enjoy it as much as I used to." And still, Mets fans such as Lauriat keep coming back, year after year, with as much pride as ever coupled with just as much cynicism in ownership. "I can't pull myself away. No matter how disinvolved I get, I can't," adding that he "can't just become a Yankee fan."

At the end of the day, it's beyond the sheer emotional attachment to the team—it's also about the compound effect of fandom, the years that went into building this part of one's identity. "It's almost like when people are in toxic relationships," Lauriat says, careful not to equate a problematic owner with an abusive partner. "I've invested so much time, and I just can't get out of it." After all, Lauriat made the Mets a centerpiece of his life (beyond sports fandom) in September 2014, when he and his wife, Britt, were married at Citi Field.

Lauriat is a particularly interesting fan to speak with. He's completely realistic in how he views ownership; ask him if he thinks whether the Wilpons care about fans, and he's decidedly frank: "On a genuine level, no. They'll pretend to, obviously for press reasons, but at the end of the day it's all about the money."

Mets fans who share Lauriat's sentiment got some stunning and very welcome news in December 2019, when the Wilpons announced they were exploring a sale to hedge fund billionaire Steve Cohen. When he first heard that his team would be sold, Lauriat was "shocked." "I used to joke all the time about them selling the team, but [I] never thought it would ever actually happen," he recalled. Cohen would acquire 80 percent of the team, while Wilpons would retain control until 2025—although Cohen's influence is expected to be felt much sooner. "If Cohen is spending a billion dollars, he's gonna have input in every major decision, I think."[27]

And if Mets fans felt like the current owners don't care enough about the team, that likely wouldn't have been the case with any new owner. Cohen is a self-professed Mets fan with deep pockets. Wall Streeters describe him as a guy who "fucking hates to lose," and he famously bought an Alberto Giacometti sculpture for $141.3 million—more than the team has ever spent on a single player. The hope was that he might infuse new hope and millions of dollars into the team—that he would, essentially, become Mets fans' Steve Ballmer.

Lauriat certainly shared that hope, albeit cautiously (with good reason, as it turned out): "I don't know much about Cohen other than he's super rich and an actual Mets fan," he says. "That second point makes me lean toward optimism, but it is still a business, so who knows what will happen. I'm hoping that we at least go back to being in the hunt for top-tier free agents."

Then again, if the Wilpons' unsavory business practices are under the microscope, then a sale to someone such as Cohen should raise some eyebrows as well. Cohen's now-defunct firm, SAC Capital, saw eight convictions for insider trading, and while Cohen himself was never charged, the US Securities and Exchange Commission fined him $1.8 billion and banned him from managing money for two years.

For Mets fans, it might have come down to which ownership group was the lesser of two evils. "If you're worth billions, I think it's a fair assumption that there's some shady decisions somewhere along the way," Lauriat says. "And I'm just so happy to get rid of the Wilpons that I barely care who it is. Cohen is a hero already." He adds, in true Mets fan form: "But until he's officially the owner, my woes will likely continue."

Alas, on February 6, 2020, the *New York Times* reported that the deal to sell control of the team to Cohen fell apart, reportedly because the Wilpons refused to give up actual control of the team.[28] It seems the younger Jeff Wilpon wanted to retain his role as chief operating officer, which ultimately caused Cohen to pull his offer.

To Lauriat, this was tough to swallow, yet par for the course—part of the "roller coaster" of emotions that comes with being a Mets fan. "It's incredibly disappointing. I'd been operating under the assumption that the Wilpons would own the team forever for my whole life and now the glimmer of hope, the chance of being an actual team, is gone."[29]

For many Mets fans, the prospect of new ownership has been a pipe dream, and the Wilpons' continuing stranglehold on the franchise has done little to deter the devoted Flushing faithful—for better or worse. "If you asked anyone who knows me, they're probably in the top-three things they would say if you asked for my identity. The Mets are already that much in my life," Lauriat says. "It's too late now. I can't get rid of them even if I wanted to."

———

Michael Klopman was born into a family of sports fans. Growing up in Maryland, a half-hour outside Washington, DC, and an hour south of Baltimore, he rooted for the Orioles, the Maryland Terps, and Washington football. "My whole extended family was sports fans, so I remember Sunday, just like everybody coming over. My whole family, everyone watching. . . . It was just so routine, just a part of everyday life."[30]

For Klopman, growing up inside the capital Beltway during the 1990s, nearly everything related to sports fandom centered around Cal Ripken Jr. and the Baltimore Orioles. Klopman was all of four years old when Washington won the Super Bowl in January 1992, but he had little else to celebrate in his formative years when it came to his favorite football team. "We would go to school the next day and everybody would talk about the game and everybody would complain about how bad we were," he recalled. "You just grow into it. And in time, the more you do it, it's like you're brainwashed. Like you're fully invested no matter what."

In 1999, a young marketing executive named Daniel Snyder purchased the Washington football team, with help from family investors and the likes of the former owners of the *New York Daily News* Mort Zuckerman and Fred Drasner, for $800 million—then a record price for an American sports franchise. At the time, the team had missed the playoffs for the sixth straight year, so winning the division that season looked like a leap in the right direction.[31]

Over the years, however, Snyder has cemented a reputation for being fan-unfriendly, for gouging every penny possible, and for doubling down on the team's racist name and logo (which we wrote about in chapter 3 on native mascots)—all, seemingly, out of sheer ego. It's hard to whittle down Snyder's myriad offenses, so let's focus on three lowlights. In 2000, he became the first NFL owner ever to charge admission ($10 a pop) to attend the team's training camp sessions. In 2009, the team sued Pat Hill, a seventy-two-year-old real estate agent, grandmother, and season ticket holder since the 1960s who asked the team to waive her ticket contract for a couple of years in the wake of the housing market crash. And as this book goes to print, Snyder continues to trot out spurious studies of self-identified Native Americans and paid spokespeople in order to maintain his stubborn hold on a name and logo that amount to racial slurs and imagery.[32] On the ticket scandal, Klopman put it succinctly: "It's reprehensible—and that's not even in the top-ten worst things that he's done."

It's true. In addition to the ongoing name and logo debacle, recent years have seen a major scandal involving the cheerleading squad and what can be described only as the unethical and insensitive handling of a front-office hire. In 2018, the *New York Times* reported on a trip to Costa Rica involving the Washington cheerleaders in which the women had their passports confiscated and were required to participate in fourteen-hour photo shoots in front of male spectators and suite holders, after which some women were trotted out as "personal escorts" to nightclubs for the men in attendance.[33]

In 2017, the team fired general manager Scot McCloughan after two seasons, citing his issues with alcohol. Yet these issues were well documented during McCloughan's previous jobs with the Seahawks and 49ers, and he went through rehab before going to Washington. On top of that, various social media posts from his tenure show the open availability of alcohol on team premises, which is in violation of NFL policies and in poor taste given the circumstances.

For Klopman, these latest revelations were the final straw, even after he thought he couldn't suffer more following the team's complete mishandling of quarterback Robert Griffin III, touted as the franchise's savior. "It was just so disgusting," he says. "Before either of those stories came out I had been telling people for two years that I was dead inside. . . . I thought the RGIII era broke me, and then the cheerleading thing came out. It's just so depressing, and yet so not surprising."

Klopman has a unique perspective on his own terrible owner: he worked for years in sports media, first for the *Huffington Post* and then with MLB Advanced Media, before shifting into tech and coding. In addition, the political climate since 2016 gives him a lot to reevaluate when it comes to ownership. He points specifically to the $1 million donation Snyder gave to President Donald Trump's inauguration fund as yet another reason to abandon hope in his team. (Snyder was by no means alone in his largesse; several NFL owners, including the Patriots' Robert Kraft, the Cowboys' Jerry Jones, and the Jets' Woody Johnson, also donated seven-figure sums.)[34]

"This president is supported by white supremacists and the worst bigots." Klopman continues:

> He's not the only one, but he is the owner of the team that I've rooted for since I was born. And after Charlottesville happened [where neo-Nazis clashed with protesters], I just can't justify it, I can't justify rooting for it. If this team wins the Super Bowl, a man who supports the same people will be holding a trophy. They're walking around the streets being emboldened by and empowered by this president and the owner of my football team doesn't give a f*** about anybody, and he doesn't give a f*** about his own team's fans.

Klopman draws a hard line in the sand that some fans often talk about but rarely act on. A combination of identity politics and concerns over players' brain injuries have led him to this point. According to Klopman, the first time he truly felt his enthusiasm draining, giving way to his own sense of morality, occurred while traveling with his future wife.

"I was sad for a little bit, but it's so much easier justifying not being a fan, losing that naiveness. I just got to that breaking point, and I just stopped caring," he says. It was the 2015–2016 season; Washington was playing Philadelphia in the penultimate game of the season to capture the division. Klopman and his girlfriend were returning from visiting her family in Oakland when they had a layover—in enemy territory.

"We got stuck in Dallas, and I had sworn I would never set foot in Dallas because of the Cowboys."

> There was a Dallas Cowboys club in the airport, and I was like, "I can't believe this is happening." And we won the division that night and I was talking with my parents and I was like, "I can't even enjoy this." I really couldn't enjoy it, I was so upset. Because that was the first time that something really good happened with one of my teams, and because of reality, just because of a real-life circumstance, I just couldn't emotionally enjoy it, and I didn't care. And that's when, really, since then, I just don't care.

It's been a difficult adjustment for Klopman, one made slightly easier by his professional transition out of sports media into another line of work, but it still presents challenges of routine and familiarity. "Forever, up until this year, my Sundays revolved around the NFL," he says, "and I'm not sure if I'm prepared for that. I'm not sure how I can enjoy this fall."

It's been a long process—an evolution, even—from the diehard fan who admittedly defended the Washington football team's name, to a fan who will no longer utter it; from the wide-eyed kid from Maryland, to the sports media professional who started to see his team with increased cynicism; and finally to the man whose fandom can no longer be justified by the consequences he sees in the world around him.

And still, he gets it—why others keep coming back even when he can't bring himself to do so. "It's this hope that the same thing you've been doing will somehow turn out right this time. That's kind of sports fandom in general. It's pure joy, and then it goes away so fast," Klopman laments. "Sports just doesn't make sense sometimes."

CHAPTER 10

HOW I LEARNED TO STOP
WORRYING AND LOVE
BASEBALL'S FREE MARKET

The first beauty of baseball is that it's an allegory for life: one's success comes from one's failures. A respectable batting average is .300 or above—failing 70 percent of the time is still considered a great outcome. That's largely because it's about the long haul over a season spanning six months. The best any team can hope for is winning a series, taking two of three games at a time. And if a team (or player) happens to free-fall in May, fans know that there might be a good stretch ahead in September that can make up for it all.

The secondary beauty of baseball is that it might be random: at any time, any given outcome can occur. Within a 162-game season leading up to at least three playoff series, any team in any season might somehow come out on top. If a team gets hot for two weeks in October, it can become the David who defeats Goliath. Despite the sport's reputation for its lack of parity among teams, underdogs have had more of a chance in baseball compared to almost any other major sport, perhaps furthering the somewhat manufactured narrative of America's Pastime. It has long been the sport of the working class, of immigrants, of the marginalized—a diversion that has become a hopeful avenue to Mainstream America. That is baseball in its purest form.

In this country, baseball is among our oldest sports, so steeped in tradition and history that it naturally lends itself to overstated notions of value and virtue. A predecessor to baseball was played as early as the Battle of Valley Forge, in 1777, during the American Revolution. The British precursor of the game (known as "rounders") evolved in different cities with different rules, including "Town Ball" in Massachusetts and "New York Ball," when workers began to acquire leisure time.[1] Union soldiers held in Confederate prison-of-war camps helped proliferate what would eventually become the modern rules of baseball, based largely on the version of the game that was pioneered by the Knickerbocker Base Ball Club of New York.[2]

Outside its development during wartime, the proliferation of baseball in the mid-nineteenth century reflected a growing and changing country and the establishment of a workforce extending from blue to white collar. As historian Steven M. Gelber wrote: "Baseball was a leisure time transition from agrarian to urban life that appealed to the working class not because it compensated for missing elements in the new work environment, but because it was congruent with business life."[3] This is the age during which industrialization coincided with specialization and division of labor on the field. In other words, baseball reflected the trajectory of American capitalism.

It's no surprise, then, that this is also the era during which baseball began its transition from amateur to professional. In 1876, the National League of Professional Baseball Clubs was founded. In 1901, the American League (formerly the Western League, a so-called minor league) established itself as a separate "Major League." In 1903, the National League and the American League agreed to cooperate, culminating their seasons in the World Series.

In the early twentieth century, the idea of baseball-as-life expanded to reflect the nation's cultural and economic values. Sports in general—led, at the time, by baseball, boxing, and horseracing—began to commodify and transform into the big business we see today, with baseball leading the charge. (Of course, as baseball professionalized and became more profitable, women and minorities were increasingly excluded from the sport.)

Attendance and interest soared, and the events that followed were historic and dramatic. In 1922, Major League Baseball received an antitrust exemption under federal law that it still enjoys today—meaning that for nearly a century MLB has enjoyed a loophole that allows the league to engage in certain monopolistic practices. Jackie Robinson broke baseball's color barrier in 1947 by starting for the Brooklyn Dodgers (an important milestone in America's civil rights movement, alongside the integration of the US Army and public schools). And in 1975, MLB's so-called reserve clause (which restricted player movement among teams) was abolished, taking power away from owners and introducing the modern era of free agency and, eventually, setting the table for the massive player contracts we see today.

These advances didn't come without resistance, however. During the 1980s, the players union filed grievances accusing team owners of violating MLB's collective bargaining agreement by circulating a list of impending free agents and agreeing among themselves not to tender competing offers in the name of "fiscal responsibility."[4] As a result of these disputes arbitrators determined that owners had engaged in "collusion" (meaning they had conspired to limit player salaries and movement) and thereby made the free-agent market anything but free. Collusion was a clear violation of the CBA between the players union and the league, and several cases of collusion were alleged and settled in the union's favor during that decade.

After free agency had begun to take hold beginning in 1976, salaries blossomed—as did the parity gap between small-market teams and large-market teams. Competitive disparity within the league came to a head during the 1990s for many owners, who began to push for a revenue-sharing model of some type to address the inability of smaller-market teams to sign high-priced stars. However, most models included a salary cap—that is, a maximum on how much teams would be allowed to spend on total payroll—a condition that the players union viewed as a dealbreaker. Given the owners' long history of trying to limit the ceiling on player contracts, such fears were justified.

In 1994, with MLB's existing collective bargaining agreement set to expire, these conflicting interests came to a head when the players union went on strike, less than two months before the scheduled start of the postseason.[5] In what was then the longest work stoppage in US sports history, more than nine hundred games were canceled, including the playoffs and the World Series. Major League Baseball was on the brink of collapse, with neither side willing to budge. Owners threatened to bring in replacement players, and the union filed a grievance with the National Labor Relations Board (NLRB).

As scabs suited up for spring training, the NLRB issued ruling after ruling in favor of the players, citing unfair labor practices and declaring the illegality of the salary cap the owners had tried to enforce. On March 30, 1995, US district judge Sonia Sotomayor (who today is a justice of the Supreme Court) ordered the owners to adhere to free agency and arbitration as dictated under the previous collective bargaining agreement, effectively ending the strike.[6]

A new CBA was finally ratified in 1997, establishing a revenue-sharing system in which a shared pool would transfer money from richer teams to poorer teams, including a luxury tax on the five highest-payroll teams in the league.[7] Revenue sharing and the luxury tax have evolved under the four CBAs approved since, the most recent taking effect in 2017 and set to expire in 2021. Under this agreement, a luxury tax is levied on payrolls exceeding $195 million in 2017, rising to $210 million in 2021, with the tax rate rising for multiple-year offenders.[8] Teams that can afford to and are willing to spend the money can thus exceed the luxury tax threshold in order to sign the best free agents and stack their rosters in exchange for paying a stiff penalty. Those luxury tax dollars are used to fund player benefits and industry development.

Meanwhile, revenue sharing has even further shifted away from large-market teams. As first established under the 2012 CBA, a formula for a team's "market score" determines whether that team is eligible to receive revenue sharing funds, based on population, income, and cable households. Known as "market rank disqualification," this stipulates under the latest agreement that the top fifteen teams do not receive revenue sharing.

In the years since the 1994 strike, despite fears that efforts toward fiscal competitive balance would hamper player salaries, team payrolls have skyrocketed—as have team revenues. In 1994, the average team payroll was $31,593,617;[9] in 2019, it was $138,436,257.[10] In 1994, the highest-paid player in the league was the New York Mets' Bobby Bonilla, pulling in $6.3 million that season.[11] In 2019, the highest-paid player in the league was the Washington Nationals' Stephen Strasburg, who made more than $39.3 million that season.[12] And it hasn't hurt revenues; the average MLB team is worth $1.78 billion,[13] and the league brought in a record-setting $10.7 billion in revenue in 2019.[14] The business of baseball is clearly booming.

Why, then, are there still complaints on both sides about parity and competitive balance in baseball? One answer has to do with the reputation baseball itself has built over its history. Those so-called storied franchises like the Yankees and St. Louis Cardinals racked up multiple championships in the first half of the century. Before 1975, both teams combined for twenty-eight titles. Gone are the days when dynasties like the Yankees can win six of seven World Series, but those histories have modern-day implications. Regardless of rings, teams such as the Yankees, Cardinals, Dodgers, Giants, Cubs, and Red Sox tend to build incredibly successful traditions into current brands. In addition to benefiting from high market scores, these clubs benefit from their own self-perpetuating legends.

The fear of free agency largely pushed by owners was that the disparity between baseball's haves and have-nots would widen. Yet, as Ronald W. Cox, author of *Free Agency and Competitive Balance in Baseball*, notes, during the first true era of free agency from 1981 to 1993 all twelve National League teams and eleven American League teams finished in first place at least once.[15] But for newer generations of fans, the Yankees' dynasty years in the mid- to late 1990s further solidified the perception of imbalance. A narrative of "buying championships" through free agency emerged—and understandably so. The teams with the highest payrolls always seemed to be the only ones left standing in October.

This view isn't unwarranted; the sheer amount of money pouring into these teams blew up with the advent of local broadcasting rights and team-owned television stations. When the Yankees cried poor in 2006, stating that they spent more on payroll than they brought in in revenue, reports from *Forbes* and the *New York Daily News* estimated these losses at around $50 million due to what the franchise owed in revenue sharing.[16] Reports failed to mention that those numbers didn't include revenue from the YES Network, majority-owned by the Yankees at the time, which the *New York Times* estimated to be around $300 million.[17]

So while teams like the Yankees, Red Sox, and Dodgers perennially sit atop their divisions, and the league's payroll rankings enjoy a level of largesse not afforded to, say, the Tampa Bay Rays, the question remains as to what real effect this wealth gap has on competitive balance. Are calls for a salary cap warranted, and is baseball deserving of its reputation for stifling parity?

The answer lies in the other three major North American sports, each of which imposes some form of a salary cap. Since 2000, the NFL—that bastion of fairness and parity—has seen the New England Patriots appearing in nine Super Bowls, winning six. Since 2000, the NBA has seen the San Antonio Spurs, Los Angeles Lakers, and Golden State Warriors combine for eighteen total appearances in the Finals, winning twelve Larry O'Brien Trophies. Since 2009, the NHL—which is constantly dealing with its own labor issues, highlighted by a season-canceling lockout in 2004–2005—has seen the Pittsburgh Penguins and Chicago Blackhawks each win three Stanley Cups.

Meanwhile, in the years since the Yankee dynasty ended in 2001, MLB has seen thirteen different World Series champions. It shouldn't be too hard, then, for fans to look past the myths of baseball's free market to the realities of the sport's competitive landscape. The proof is seen in the 2001 Arizona Diamondbacks, the 2003 Florida Marlins, and the 2015 Kansas City Royals—small-market teams that often cry poor but have managed to win it all.

In fact, the Royals present an interesting dilemma when discussing free-market economics in baseball. Revenue sharing has absolutely helped small-market teams field better squads—when they choose to actually spend that money on talent. In 2011, the

Royals famously had the lowest payroll in the league at $36 million (in a year in which the average payroll was $93 million). When the Royals won the World Series in 2015, they boasted a payroll of a little more than $112.9 million—still around $13 million less than the league average, but getting closer.[18]

Furthermore, a team like the Oakland A's that has built a reputation as the scrappy underdog, as chronicled in Michael Lewis's *Moneyball*, received $34 million in revenue sharing in 2015 and had a payroll of $84.4 million—the fourth-lowest in baseball.[19] The A's exist in the sixth-largest media market in the country.[20] Given the cognitive dissonance in classifying the A's as a small-market team, the most recent CBA reclassifies Oakland according to its market score and thus disqualifies the team from receiving revenue sharing going forward.

While many teams have legitimate gripes when it comes to their inability to compete with the league's big spenders, the A's are one example of the pitfalls of conflating baseball's free market with a team's futility. A more ridiculous example is the New York Mets. The Mets have always had a little brother complex in having to share the city with the Yankees. Truth be told, the weight of the Mets' brand can't compete with that of their crosstown rivals, even given recent success, including a trip to the World Series in 2015. But the underdog mentality of a team sharing the largest media market in the country serves to justify the small-market practices of its ownership. In 2000, the year the Mets and Yankees met in the Subway Series for the championship, the Yankees had the highest payroll in baseball, at $95.3 million.[21] The Mets had the fourth-highest, at $82.2 million.[22] The Mets' spending rose nearly every year until 2012, when the franchise was forced to slash nearly $40 million in payroll due to the fallout from the owners' investments in Bernie Madoff's Ponzi scheme, as we discussed in chapter 9 on team owners.[23]

Any cries that the Mets are the victim of a have and have-not system in baseball, rather than their own ill-advised management, ring hollow. After the Madoff debacle, the Mets took a loan from Bank of America, the terms of which restricted the amount the team could spend on payroll.[24]

In a sense, then, baseball's free market can be seen as promoting meritocracy. Fiscal progressives can take comfort in the fact that, while the Yankees may have been born on third base, the ne'er-do-well stepbrother Mets haven't been rewarded for bad behavior. Meanwhile, the ever-evolving system of revenue sharing and luxury taxes can help provide opportunities for true underdogs, even if some teams with higher payrolls are now using the luxury tax as an excuse to shed payroll and avoid paying players more. (See the Red Sox trading Mookie Betts to the Dodgers a year before he was set to hit free agency.) It's not capitalism in its purest form, but it is striving for the ideal of capitalism within the American social contract—social safety nets and progressive taxation and all.

Moreover, while the absence of a salary cap in baseball doesn't seem to hinder competitive balance, it does hinder the ability of owners to control players. A free market doesn't just include freedom for management, but labor as well. Until the 1970s, due to the reserve clause, players didn't enjoy any semblance of freedom, and true free agency didn't effectively kick in until after the collusion cases of the 1980s. Equating a salary cap with promoting competitive balance was actually a shrewd narrative strategy by baseball owners seeking to save money and continue exerting control over players. As Rodney Fort and James Quirk wrote in "Cross-Subsidization, Incentives, and Outcomes in Professional Team Sports Leagues":

> Over time, as the reserve clause faced court challenges, owners of sports teams developed the argument that, whatever the consequences of the reserve clause on players' salaries, it was needed to preserve competitive balance. Owners argued that free agency would allow the richest teams to acquire a disproportionate share of the playing talent in the league. Competitive balance would be destroyed, driving weaker franchises out of business.[25]

That was certainly the narrative in 1994, when, days after the players went on strike, MLB's lead counsel trotted out this line: "The question here is a very simple one. The players went out on strike, their average compensation was $1.2 million and all we have been trying to find out is how much more do they want. We never get an answer to that question." *Sports Illustrated*'s Cliff Corcoran wrote this in 2014: "That's an absurd question to ask. The players wanted what every employee wants, which is what the market will bear and not a penny less."[26] Sports owners have done a remarkable job convincing the public that millionaire players are greedy and overpaid without bringing similar scrutiny to the billionaires calling the shots. Baseball players might make exorbitant salaries compared to decades past, when many had to work second and third jobs while owners conspired to control the game's cash flow. But the absolute dollar amount is irrelevant; baseball's "free market" still comes down to the issue of labor versus management.

How did we learn to love baseball's free market? It's been good for meritocracy and good for labor. Baseball—and its fans—are much better for it.

CHAPTER 11

DOUBLING DOWN ON YOUR
MARCH MADNESS BRACKET
EVEN IF THE ATHLETES
DON'T MAKE A DIME

There's something so beautiful about college sports. March Madness—the NCAA basketball tournament—shows us that any team, any athlete, can make a difference at any time. It's the idea (however false it may be) that the "purity" of amateur athleticism might lend itself to righteous upsets and a truly exciting David-versus-Goliath matchup. The ideal of the Cinderella story pervades March Madness. How exciting is it when an 11-seed makes it all the way to the Final Four?

But what happens when you stop to think that these athletes are unpaid? And yet, they are the basis for a billion-dollar business for an association that features huge salaries for coaches, assistant coaches, and athletic directors and spends multimillions on facilities?

That's the question among college athletes, particularly those who play men's basketball and football. And that's the central question among players who often can't afford the partial scholarships offered by other collegiate sports and so choose the revenue-generating sports even though they could very well find immense on-field success in baseball, track, or soccer.

Welcome to the world of big-time college sports, in which the myth of amateurism rules over fans who would otherwise take issue with players being unpaid. And the idea that these athletes also being students should somehow preclude them from making a decent living based on their worth to their employer seems unique to their status within sports. College students who develop a successful social media platform or cookie delivery service or clothing company or one of the most prominent record companies ever aren't denied the fruits of their labor, even though they're clearly both students and workers at the same time.[1]

So why is it different for so-called student-athletes?

That phrase itself is controversial. It implies to many advocates the propagandized notion that a scholarship is compensation enough, or that players themselves serve an equally dual purpose at a school that outweighs their heavy contributions on the field or court.

Consider the NCAA's mission statement:

> Maintaining amateurism is crucial to preserving an academic environment in which acquiring a quality education is the first priority. In the collegiate model of sports, the young men and women competing on the field or court are students first, athletes second.

"They [the NCAA] want you to think that they can't be 'students'" if they're being paid, says Andy Schwarz, a sports economist who has served as an economic expert in congressional hearings involving the NCAA. He points to the fact that not only are a number of nonathlete students on campus employed—many are employed by the schools themselves, through work-study or other programs. Yet the arguments against athletes get made uniquely. "It's like a definitional, axiomatic argument: 'If we pay students to play basketball, they won't be real students anymore,'" yet those same people don't make that argument about students working in, say, the campus library.[2]

"What other Americans are walking around just because of their occupation or their status, at a college even, where they're subject to a national price-fixing scheme?" asks Ramogi Huma, a former football player for UCLA who is now the executive director of the National College Players Association, a nonprofit advocacy group that fights for college athletes' rights.[3]

Another argument that's often made comes down to what Schwarz says people often describe as the corrupting influence of money. "'They wouldn't focus on school if they had a lot of money,'" or so the argument goes. "And, well, everybody in the Ivy League who isn't there on need-based aid?" is Schwarz's answer to that question. "Or the first two hundred years of people going to college when everybody had money."

Still, ask college basketball and football fans about whether players should be compensated, and the idea about the purity of the sport itself comes up. Many fans will say they don't watch professional basketball, for example, because the players are overpaid and the sport seems like a vehicle for individual personalities rather than the game itself. "I just don't think most Americans think that they've been corrupted by money," Schwarz answers. "A lot of people think getting paid for a hard day's work is noble. So then, what is it about these athletes that allows that to resonate with people? Some of it is propaganda, and some of it is just racism, because the majority of the workforce in this case is Black."

And much of it still goes back to this notion of the purity of the game, emphasized by University of South Carolina president Harris Pastides, who testified in 2013 that "fans of college football and men's basketball are loyal to and passionate about their team precisely because they believe they are cheering for students with USC uniforms on their backs that may have the opportunity to live [the] American dream of getting drafted one day in the future, but right now are going to class, getting an education, and are not yet corrupted by money and other financial influences."[4]

The NCAA has been so adept at selling the message that "amateurism" breeds a higher quality in sports that people would apparently otherwise not watch.[5] There's little basis for this line of thinking outside anecdotal remarks from fans that echo NCAA talking points—and it belies what we know from the long-term rise in ratings, merchandise sales, and revenues by the professional leagues, the NBA and the NFL. "The reason the product in the marketplace is successful is because what is being sold is amateurism," Schwarz says. "That's a feature of the product."

There are at least two explanations for this anomalous treatment of sports, one of which comes down to a fairly basic antitrust argument. In 1964, economist Walter Neale published a paper titled "The Peculiar Economics of Professional Sports." In it, Neale essentially described that in order for proper competition to exist, sports teams need other exact sports teams to form, a dynamic he termed the "Louis-Schmeling Paradox." Framing it in terms of two boxers, Neale described a system in which profits are maximized when the product is best, and the product is best when two boxers—or two teams—are directly comparable.

That mentality has since evolved in how we consider modern-day sports, which Schwarz and others describe in terms of a "cartel" whereby leagues and associations determine parameters such as scheduling and, yes, pay.

Extended to college sports, the idea is that schools within the parameters of the NCAA have agreed not to pay its labor force—athletes—on the basis of amateurism. The fact that this is relatively unique to sports isn't difficult to demonstrate. In 2015, Silicon Valley was at the center, and subsequently on the losing end, of a similar debate. Under a deal approved by US district judge Lucy Koh, Apple, Google, Intel, and Adobe agreed to pay $415 million to more than 64,000 workers to settle a wage-fixing scheme in which high-ranking executives from those firms conspired to refrain from competing for talent in order to keep down salaries.[6]

The Silicon Valley case is just one of many that seems to demonstrate that under the law and in our national consciousness, the American economy does not favor suppressing the potential for free-market compensation, and yet we continue to make an exception for college sports. Huma points to a similar scheme that existed within the Ivy League until the early 1990s. In 1991, the eight universities in the Ivy League came under fire for "collaborating" on student financial aid rewards, tuition increases, and faculty salaries. These schools were essentially sharing information in order to keep scholarship amounts down.[7]

"Students and their families are entitled to the full benefits of price competition when they choose a college," then–Attorney General Dick Thornburgh said at the time, according to the *New York Times*. "This collegiate cartel has denied them the right to compare prices and discounts among schools, just as they would in shopping for any other service or commodity."

It's hard to read a statement like that and not apply it to college athletes who seem entitled to the full benefits of salary competition when they commit to a college that will reap the benefits of their labor tenfold—yet are being denied by the college sports cartel the right to compare compensation, just as they would in considering jobs for any other service outside of sports.

———

Two major court cases illuminate this debate in college sports: Ed O'Bannon suing the NCAA for the right to control his own likeness in marketing and merchandise schemes; and Northwestern University's football team filing for unionization with the National Labor Relations Board, led by quarterback Kain Colter and aided by Huma.

The O'Bannon case was filed in 2009 and nearly reached the Supreme Court. O'Bannon, a former UCLA standout, recognized his image being used in a video game from Electronic Arts. It used his exact frame, skin tone, jersey number, and position without compensating him for such use of his image. Certified as a class action, the suit was joined by twenty former college athletes, including basketball legends Bill Russell and Oscar Robertson, as well as sports marketing executive Sonny Vaccaro, known for pioneering sneaker deals (starting with Michael Jordan's).

The initial ruling in 2014 would later be vacated, but it was the most significant acknowledgment that the NCAA violates antitrust rules and that its system based on "amateurism" is tantamount to price-fixing. Federal district court judge Claudia Wilken initially ruled that "the NCAA's compensation rules were an unlawful restraint of trade," proposing that the association allow schools to pay athletes up to $5,000 each in deferred compensation.[8]

Then, in 2015, the US Court of Appeals for the Ninth Circuit limited the scope of that ruling, affirming that the idea of amateurism violates antitrust law but further ruling that schools needed only to compensate athletes with the full cost of attendance—a step up from the previous scholarship model (which failed to take into account the cost of travel, food, and supplies) but a significant step down from the initial ruling. In 2016, the Supreme Court refused to hear the appeal.

The initial ruling by Judge Wilken was especially significant in rejecting the NCAA argument stemming from the 1984 Supreme Court case *NCAA v. Board of Regents*. That case addressed college football television rights and stated that "in order to preserve the character and quality of the 'product,' athletes must not be paid, must be required to attend class and the like."

Five months before the initial ruling in O'Bannon's case, Peter Sung Ohr, a regional director for the NLRB, ruled that Northwestern's football players should be allowed to form a union, answering the central question in their petition: athletes constitute employees, considering they work up to fifty hours per week, receive compensation in the form of a scholarship, and work under a boss whom they call "coach."

A year and a half later in 2015, however, the NLRB declined to assert jurisdiction in the players' push for unionization. It was a unanimous decision that somehow managed to avoid the main issue: whether players are employees. The board played it safe by asserting it did not have jurisdiction over the more than one hundred state-run colleges and universities within the NCAA Division I Football Bowl Subdivision (FBS). Public universities are not governed under the National Labor Relations Act, and thus the board felt any ruling would have created a "patchwork problem" in which football players from private and public institutions would be governed differently.[9] "College athletes deserved an answer, and the NLRB refused to provide an answer," Huma says.

The question of whether athletes are employees was not dead, however. Because the board declined to address this specific issue, Ohr's earlier ruling to grant Northwestern's football players employee status under federal law could be upheld. The university amended its handbook in 2016 to treat them as such, easing restrictions on players' use of social media to communicate with the public and the press after charges were filed claiming that such restrictions constituted unfair labor practices.

In 2017, Richard Griffin, general counsel for the NLRB, sent a memo to the board's regional directors stating unequivocally that "scholarship football players in Division I Football Bowl Subdivision private-sector colleges and universities are employees" under the National Labor Relations Act. Griffin limited the scope of players' rights to one section of the act, but it still allows athletes to form a union, collectively bargain, and request pay without retaliation.[10]

The hope is that every step that continues to chip away at the NCAA's assertion of amateurism will be accompanied by a step toward broader attitudes changing toward these athletes. "I've come to realize that the public follows public policy. A legislature, a city, a judge—someone has to have the courage to say that this is the right thing to do," Huma says. "And then life goes on, and the public follows suit and it becomes a new norm and the world doesn't end."

Perhaps California's state legislature will get credit for demonstrating such courage. In 2019, California passed a law that will allow students, beginning in 2023, to make money off their names, images, and likenesses (collectively known as "NIL"), as well as hire agents. All of that directly challenges NCAA bylaws in fundamental ways, though it does not require any school to pay any athlete—merely that athletes can get paid for sponsorships, appearances, or ads on their social media feeds. The NCAA responded with typical catastrophic language, asserting that this new law is an "existential threat" to the amateurism model.

Soon after California's governor signed the bill into law, legislators in other states (including New York and Florida) announced intentions to follow suit. And within weeks, the NCAA released a confusingly worded statement that its board of governors voted to "permit students participating in athletics the opportunity to benefit from the use of their name, image and likeness in a manner consistent with the collegiate model."

Though several outlets at the time reported that the NCAA's announcement signaled a major shift in its policy toward athlete compensation, that has yet to be determined; it remains unclear how the NCAA plans to interpret its own language. As the NCAA's collegiate model is currently constructed, getting paid for NIL is not, in fact, consistent with it. It will be interesting to see how the NCAA reconciles this inconsistency when its three divisions draft new rules for NIL rights by early 2021. It makes you wonder what other laws will have passed by then and, as Huma predicts, how public sentiment will shift in the meantime.[11]

Huma compares the impending sea change in public opinion on paying college athletes to the uneasiness—yet continued existence—of the country during the civil rights movement. "Some of the same sentiment was there, and that was, 'Hey, you don't deserve the same opportunities that we're giving ourselves,'" he says.

———

The racial dynamics in the college sports debate are impossible to ignore. Many polls conducted over the years have found a significant racial gap among those who favor paying college athletes and those who don't. For example, an HBO Real Sports/Marist poll conducted in 2014 found that 53 percent of African Americans believe college athletes should be paid, while 72 percent of white people and 71 percent of Latinx people think they should not. Also, 61 percent of African Americans believe college athletes are unpaid because they tend to be Black, compared to 25 percent of white respondents.

It's important to look at the undertones that drive this racially based perception gap. In 2017, journalist Patrick Hruby interviewed University of Massachusetts–Amherst professor Tatish M. Nteta, who was inspired to conduct research on the racially coded perceptions of paying college athletes by a radio segment hosted by Colin Cowherd. In the segment, the shock jock said: "I don't think paying all college athletes is great, not every college is loaded and most 19-year-olds [are] gonna spend it—and let's be honest, they're gonna spend it on weed and kicks. And spare me the 'they're being extorted' thing."[12] He continued: "Listen, 90 percent of these college guys are gonna spend it on tats, weed, kicks, Xboxes, beer and swag. They are, get over it!"

To Nteta and others, this was among the more blatant affirmations of what many already suspect to be true: many white Americans opposing paying college athletes believe that basketball and football rosters that consist of majority Black players can't be trusted to handle a sudden influx of income, whether or not they earned it. This paternalistic view of compensation has nothing to do with labor value, market dynamics, or amateurism, but it has everything to do with who we consider to be responsible—or even legitimate—workers. The average Ivy League student is entitled to her rightful scholarship, just as the average app developer on campus is entitled to his rightful profits from a product he created. How might the stereotypical images of those two students differ from those of your average college basketball player?

Nteta and his fellow researchers Kevin Wallsten, Lauren A. McCarthy, and Melinda R. Tarsi took this question literally. In their 2015 study at Amherst, the researchers asked white respondents whether college athletes should be paid, and divided them into two groups, showing one group photos of "young Black men with stereotypical African American first and last names." The percentage of whites who opposed pay increased significantly among those who were shown the photos—both among "all whites" and those who were placed into the category of "racially resentful whites."[13]

"The more negatively a white respondent felt about Blacks, the more they opposed paying college athletes," the Amherst researchers wrote in the *Washington Post* after the study was released in 2015. "In other words, the discussion about paying college athletes is implicitly a discussion about race."

Unfortunately, these notions aren't held only by white people, and they don't reflect simple resentment. Len Elmore, who is Black, was an All-American for the University of Maryland, played for five NBA teams during the 1970s and 1980s, and later received his law degree from Harvard. He holds similar concerns not out of racial resentment but out of concern about the socioeconomic backgrounds of many young Black men. In 2017, he reiterated his stance on paying college athletes to The Shadow League:

> Paying kids obscures the education factor and that hurts kids
> of color more than anybody. Graduation rates are rising and

all these positive things are happening. I'm afraid that if you insert paying these kids all of a sudden their focus goes away from doing the right thing and get seduced by stuff that has nothing to do with education.[14]

Elmore's emphasis on education is not unfounded, and he did affirm his belief, as upheld in the O'Bannon decision, that players should have a right to control their own likeness. But the idea that college players would get "seduced by stuff" by being compensated for their time and labor—when that concern doesn't seem to exist for other students—carries layers we seem to apply only to athletes.

If the worry is that college athletes wouldn't have the financial literacy to handle a substantial income, then we could make the argument that colleges should be teaching its students those life skills anyway—that financial literacy should be part of said promised education. In Schwarz's view, an ideal curriculum for a one-and-done college basketball player would include "a history of labor in sport and financial literacy—things that anybody who's nineteen and in the NBA probably would benefit from. But everyone should get that—even the guys who are going to end up being four [years in college] and graduate and go on and become an entrepreneur. Because financial literacy is good for every eighteen-year-old to learn."

Huma reiterates that the authors of studies on race and paying college athletes "are not saying people are racist who are taking that position. They're saying there is racial resentment. I think everyone has their own biases and prejudices, and that's America." Such notions, as Huma puts it, informs the opposition to paying college athletes, "and it's a force to be reckoned with." He points to those at the top making the important decisions—mostly white athletic directors and college administrators. Yet, it's important to note, as Huma puts it, that "NCAA rules harm white players just as much as they harm Black players. What is clear is that greed has been a primary driver of the status quo—greed from the people who run college sports. I've been saying, the most significant [color] in this mechanism is green, the color of money."

Still, the racial resentment aspect of this debate can't be overlooked and might go a long way toward explaining why many disproven arguments persist. "When I saw those reports, honestly, I was a little shook," Huma says.

> But it made a lot of things clear. You can show as much data as you want, you can point to all the concrete, objective examples as to why reform could take place. No, it's not too difficult to figure out. No, it would not bankrupt college sports, even the small schools. You can dispel each and every myth that has ever been put out there as to why college athletes shouldn't receive more money. But you still have a large number of people who still oppose it and they still just keep talking in circles with the same points that you can disprove handily. And so it kind of makes sense—it's the missing piece of the puzzle.

———

In a video posted on the NCAA's official Twitter account hours before tipoff of the 2018 Final Four, association president Mark Emmert said this:

> This is in the context of higher education. These are educational universities and colleges that are conducting these games, and you have to abide by the educational laws of the United States. You've got to provide women with the same opportunities and support that men receive. If you were going to pay salaries to male athletes you'd have to do the same thing for female athletes and you'd have to come up with some explanation to the federal government as to why you would possibly not do it for one group versus another, and I think that's completely untenable.

The implications under Title IX for paying college athletes are often touted as the trump card against any such argument, without considering the myriad scenarios available. The fact is, however, that without existing case law it's not clear how paying male athletes would affect women's sports or non–revenue-generating male sports. Yet this common refrain is easy to fall back on because of how we undervalue women's sports monetarily and existentially and also because of how we uphold the myth that Title IX has created true equality in higher education.

Yes, the state of the female college athlete is much, much better now than it was before Title IX was enacted in 1972. But according to the National Women's Law Center (NWLC), female athletes at the typical FBS Division I school receive roughly 28 percent of the total money spent on athletics. The NWLC addresses the scapegoating of women's college sports in the name of smaller men's sports by calling for, first and foremost, cost-cutting measures in "bloated" areas of football and basketball.[15] How to cut costs is up for debate, but we could start with coaches' pay and facilities. Of course, many detractors claim that the superstar coach and the aquarium in the locker room are necessary to compete with other schools for top-notch recruits. Yet the same could be said for proper compensation.

Put simply, the idea that paying college athletes would somehow be a blow to women's sports because of Title IX really rests on a question of asset allocation and prioritization. But this entire debate also rests on two of the biggest myths in college sports (other than amateurism): Athletes are receiving the full value of their education; and athletes aren't getting compensated under the table.

In 2014, a report by *Bloomberg Businessweek* exposed what many already knew to be true: many top-tier educational institutions are intentionally failing at educating their athletes. For nearly two decades, the University of North Carolina provided fake "jock classes" to many of its star athletes—even more insultingly, within the African and Afro-American Studies Department—so they could remain eligible to play.[16]

Three years later, the NCAA decided not to take action against the university or its players, essentially giving carte blanche to other big-time sports schools to continue along the status quo. *Bloomberg Opinion*'s Joe Nocera points to the NCAA's aforementioned mission statement, asking with regard to the ruling: "How can anyone possibly take that mission statement seriously anymore?"[17]

Deborah Crowder, the department administrator who set up these courses, claimed in an affidavit that they were meant to correct "problems created by institutional bureaucracy" and didn't solely benefit athletes. But as Nocera wrote, this scheme so egregiously deprived these athletes of the education that is supposed to be their just compensation. "Few scandals in the history of college sports have shined as bright a light on its moral bankruptcy as this one," he wrote.[18]

After letting UNC off the hook, however, the NCAA has bigger problems on its hands. The FBI is currently investigating widespread corruption, kickbacks, and deals among coaches, recruits, agents, and apparel executives. What amounts to an underground recruiting operation involved at least twenty-five players from twenty Division I schools, including some of the biggest names featured every March.

As with the academic scandal, the recruiting scandal is simply more of what everyone knows already goes on. It raises the question, however: What, exactly, would happen should the NCAA finally bring all of that money above the table?[19]

———

If we buy into the notion that college athletes are exploited, then how do we continue to watch basketball every March? How do we continue to huddle around our televisions every December, eating up nearly four dozen bowl games and a national championship in January? The quality of the sports is an easy answer, though hopefully we've established that wouldn't change if athletes were properly compensated.

Cognitive dissonance is another answer. According to Schwarz, the average fan either doesn't know or care about the plight of these young men, most of whom will be left on their own if and when they graduate and fail to make it into the pro leagues. In fact, 52 percent of Division I football players believe they'll make it to the NFL; only 2 percent actually do. And 76 percent of Division I men's basketball players think they'll be drafted by the NBA, but that number is actually 1.2 percent.

Given what they know about these sports, and unwilling to throw in the towel, both Huma and Schwarz seem to be resting on their activism as a way to continue to enjoy these admittedly entertaining showcases. "I feel like the options that fans have are boy-cott or get involved and change it. And I know that's hard—people turn to sports to get away from problems," Schwarz says. "I have to keep working to change public attitudes until they change for real in order to be able to sit down and watch great games of bas-ketball." It's a common refrain heard from those who work within the sports industry, but it bears repeating. It might come across as criticism or cynicism or disillusionment, but in reality it's the love of the game that motivates people to improve it.

"I have had this growing distaste for how the sausage is made—and I still eat the sausage," Schwarz says. "It's why every year I get more active in trying to change the system. Because I'm not ready to boycott—boycott is fine. But I think I can have a bigger impact not boycotting and instead being like, 'I love this sport and want to make it better.'"

CHAPTER 12

LIVING WITH THE NEW STADIUM YOU DIDN'T WANT TO PAY FOR

You walk into the stadium. It's Opening Day, and you've never seen the place look this good. The concourse is peppered with flags and statues of legends past; the concessions now feature gourmet food and craft beer; the bathrooms are actually clean. You find your seat and admire how everything looks brand-new.

And yet, you look around and know that this, somehow, isn't right. It was too soon to say goodbye to your old home—and more importantly, it was too expensive to move into this new one.

Welcome to your shiny new stadium, which may or may not have been necessary to build but almost certainly was built unnecessarily with local tax dollars. This is the world of stadium subsidies, where suckers pay for billionaire owners to construct new dollhouses for their plaything sports teams so that they can pocket revenues from increased ticket prices, more luxury suites, high-end food options, and $15 beers. It's a world where the ever-loyal fan overlooks a grand compromise made in exchange for the local team simply staying put.

One of the greatest American hustles is how a populace taught that we're built on the ideals of freedom, democracy, and capitalism manages to willingly forego those ideals in the name of sports. We can become so enamored with the prospect of a retractable dome, or so frightened by the threat of relocation, that we allow the government to step in where it doesn't necessarily belong and where it's not needed. "We're privatizing the profits and socializing the costs and that's never viable," says Neil deMause, coauthor of the 1998 book *Field of Schemes* and editor of the blog of the same name.[1]

And the thing is, you're paying for *every* new stadium—not just the one in your city. From 2000 to 2014, the federal government lost $3.7 billion in revenue due to subsidies to sports teams building new stadiums, according to the Brookings Institution.[2] These federal subsidies come in the form of tax-exempt municipal bonds. The federal tax exclusion for interest earned on state and local bonds dates back to the first US income tax established in 1913, when it applied to an array of private businesses. Since then, its application has been narrowed and specified several times, yet the financing of sports stadiums remains exempt.

In 1953, Milwaukee County Stadium became a game-changer—it was the first ballpark built entirely with public funding, and it was the first stadium project that actually enticed a team to move to a new city. Milwaukee began construction on the stadium in 1950 without a team to house in it, but the city offered free use of the park to any ballclub that would move there. Three weeks before Opening Day in 1953, the league approved the relocation of the Boston Braves to Milwaukee, beginning the era of teams entering new markets for free stadiums. The Brooklyn Dodgers and New York Giants moving to California in 1958 accelerated this trend—but it wasn't until the 1980s that the prospect of moving to another city with a publicly financed stadium became a viable strategy (some would say threat) used by teams looking for new facilities without paying for them themselves. In 1984, the Baltimore Colts moved to Indianapolis after Baltimore refused to pay for a new stadium, devastating a fan base and creating a prime example for other teams trying to squeeze dollars out of the local government. According to the *Georgia Law Review*: "Before 1948, there were only twenty-eight professional sports stadiums and only four were built with a modest amount of government funds. Over the next half of the twentieth century, American sports teams spent over $20 billion on stadiums for the four major American sports leagues of which, conservatively, taxpayers paid $14.727 billion."[3] By 1992, 77 percent of pro sports stadiums were funded at least in part by taxpayer dollars.[4]

But even as the threat of leaving and the prospect of keeping a team loom large, the actual realized benefit of funding stadiums is questionable at best. A federal exemption highlights the uneven cost and benefit experienced by different parts of the country. In essence, all taxpayers are on the hook for subsidies whether or not they get to enjoy the stadium for which they partially paid. A new stadium in Las Vegas funded with tax-exempt municipal bonds will cost the same number of tax dollars from a resident of Wyoming as a resident of Nevada. "Everybody in the United States is foregoing tax revenues that could have been earned on the taxable bonds that alternatively would have to be used," Brad Humphreys, an economics professor at the University of West Virginia who specializes in stadium financing, says. "Everybody in the United States is providing some sort of subsidy for these private-use sports facilities."[5]

But the federal subsidy represents only a portion of the public cost that goes into new sports facilities. State and local governments must carry most of the burden of financing stadiums. This comes in the form of property tax exemptions to teams or the more direct route: straight out of citizens' pockets in the form of increased general sales taxes, lotteries, and taxes on rental cars, hotels, restaurants, alcohol, and cigarettes. Taxes on hotels and rental cars in particular are sold as a "tourist tax" to reassure locals that outsiders will bear the brunt of the cost. But the underlying unfairness remains: individual citizens are on the hook for a new arena whether or not they personally make use of it.

This dynamic is different from how it works with what might be described as the public good—education, infrastructure, health care—because sports are, essentially, a show. "Why do we subsidize one person's entertainment and not another person's?" Dr. Victor Matheson, a sports economist at College of the Holy Cross, asked, noting that citizens who aren't film buffs don't get tapped to finance new movie theaters. "When I'm sitting in the stands, I can't argue with the fact that I'm having a good time," he says. "As a sports fan, I'm not going to turn down a free ticket—and essentially, what these stadium subsidies are is a free ticket."[6]

That free ticket to local sports fans pales in comparison to the season pass that subsidies represent for owners. As Matheson puts it: "The number one problem with stadium funding is essentially taxpayers and regular middle class taxpayers end up subsidizing salaries for millionaire players and profits for billionaire owners." And therein lies the central dilemma: We tend to scoff at giving handouts to the wealthy, so why do we turn a blind eye when it comes to sports?

"The non-economic reason is this: The fans cannot live without these teams," according to David Berri, an economics professor at Southern Utah University who specializes in sports economics. "I'm not a psychologist, but it seems to me like sports, politics, and religion all activate the same parts of the brain," he surmises. "For a lot of people, this is their whole identity. It's this external thing where I belong to something that's bigger than me and it gives me my identity. And so for a lot of sports fans, their sports team is who they are. So if you take away their sports team, you literally take away their person."[7]

Teams and leagues have perfected the art of exploiting this inherent fervor of sports fandom, transforming fans' loyalty and love for teams into the belief they can't live without them no matter the cost. Teams cry poor, make outsized demands on local governments, pit cities against one another, and make empty threats to pack up and leave. While threats to relocate a team are largely unfounded, the heartbreak when it actually happens resonates for generations. The late New York Yankees owner George Steinbrenner for years lobbied for public assistance for a new stadium, threatening to leave the Bronx for Manhattan[8] or even—gasp!—New Jersey.[9] But as *New York* magazine's Allen Barra wrote in 1998, the owner was bluffing.[10] "Steinbrenner's greatest ally . . . is the ghost of Walter O'Malley, the late owner of the Brooklyn Dodgers, who moved his team to Los Angeles at the end of the 1957 season and who talked New York Giants owner Horace Stoneham into moving to San Francisco," Barra wrote. "By raising the specter of the departed Dodgers and Giants, Steinbrenner is ignoring—or pretending to ignore—one important fact: Failing an earthquake that creates a new coast, there are no major markets left for Steinbrenner to move the Yankees to."

Although a handful of professional teams in the major sports have switched cities in recent years, it's a much more rare occurrence compared to fifty years ago, when many markets in the West were hungry for expansion. "That's the creation myth of franchise relocations," deMause says. "It ignores the fact that nobody's going to invent California again."

And yet, for two decades, the NFL was able to use the city of Los Angeles as the ultimate bargaining chip. After the Rams moved to St. Louis and the Raiders moved back to Oakland, both in 1995, LA was an open market. The Rams would eventually return, the Chargers would leave San Diego to join them (and the Raiders ended up fleeing for Las Vegas), but in the twenty years in between the specter of the country's second-largest media market hung over other NFL cities whose teams only had to cast a gaze west to force the public to meet their demands.

During that span, teams ranging from the Seattle Seahawks[11] to the New Orleans Saints[12] to the Jacksonville Jaguars[13] were said to be considering a move to Los Angeles. But perhaps no team more effectively leveraged that threat than the Minnesota Vikings—a case study in everything wrong with stadium financing.

In 1998, billionaire Red McCombs (a used-car dealer) bought the Vikings for $206 million and immediately began campaigning to replace the Hubert H. Humphrey Metrodome. Opened in 1982, the Metrodome was just sixteen years old and also housed the Minnesota Twins and the University of Minnesota Golden Gophers (as well as the Minnesota Timberwolves for the team's inaugural season in 1989–1990). The stadium was a pioneer of sorts; it was one of only three stadiums at the time to boast an inflatable, air-pressurized, Teflon-coated, fiberglass, fabric roof. But the iconic white roof would prove to be no match for Minnesota's brutal winters, collapsing or deflating under heavy snowfall three times during the 1980s and again in 2010.

When McCombs took over the Vikings, he pushed the idea that the Metrodome was obsolete and that the team would need an entirely new stadium to remain competitive (despite going 15-1 and coming within one missed field goal of a Super Bowl appearance that season).[14] In response to the demand for a new, $500 million stadium, the Metropolitan Sports Facilities Commission (MSFC) put together a proposal for a $200 million renovation of the existing site, which was rejected by the team two weeks later. Over the next six years, the commission and the team would go back and forth trading proposals, with the Vikings seemingly unwilling to budge on the idea of renovation. "We feel that it is our job as agents for the state to put as many options before the Legislature and before the governor as possible," MSFC commissioner Richard Jefferson, a former state legislator, said in 2001. "And to say that we are going to essentially throw away a stadium that was built 20 years ago with no effort to satisfy the needs of our tenants, I think, would be a miscarriage of our charge."[15] McCombs responded by repeatedly insisting that the team could not remain in Minnesota without a brand-new facility.

By 2005—having failed to win legislative support for a new stadium—McCombs cashed in and sold the team for $600 million to a group of investors led by New Jersey real estate developer Zygmund "Zygi" Wilf,[16] who proceeded to pick up where his predecessor left off. By then, the Vikings' proposal had ballooned into a $1.5 billion, 740-acre, mixed-use development in the suburb of Blaine in Anoka County, just north of Minneapolis. The Vikings' lease was set to expire in 2011, after which Wilf planned to move the team to Anoka. After Anoka committed $280 million to the plan, however, it became clear the suburb was being used as leverage, with the team suddenly re-exploring options in downtown Minneapolis; this plan was scrapped.

The public cost of a new Vikings stadium was compounded by the fact that by 2006 both the Twins and the Golden Gophers had each received approval to construct separate, new stadiums, further depleting local coffers. The NFL team's calls for a new facility then slowed in 2007 after a major bridge collapse highlighted the urgent need for public infrastructure improvements—but the pause didn't last long. In November of that year, the MSFC launched an eight-city "Listening Tour" that comprised meetings with local politicians and businesses and town halls for average citizens to sell the idea of a new stadium. The commission's report on the tour offered little hard data on the economics of funding a billion-dollar stadium, but it did highlight survey responses showing that the people of Minnesota wanted the Vikings to stay—a truly remarkable revelation, indeed.

The dramatic images of the roof collapse in 2010, the first in twenty-seven years, and the impending 2011 lease expiration provided some urgency to the debate. Wilf had previously promised to pay for one-third of the new stadium's estimated $700 million cost, but there was little support for public funding of the remaining two-thirds from state legislators dealing with a $6 billion deficit.

In 2011, the Vikings found an ally in newly elected governor Mark Dayton, but the first significant reversal came at the city level, when Minneapolis unveiled a plan that included a new $895 million stadium on the existing site of the Metrodome. The plan put the city on the hook for 22 percent, or $195 million, and the state for 33 percent, or $300 million, bringing the total burden on taxpayers to 55 percent, or $495 million. It was the first time the city proposed extending tax increases to cover the cost, a nonstarter in previous negotiations.[17] The Vikings rejected this plan, scoffing at its requirement that the team cover 45 percent of the cost, or about $400 million. (At the time, *Forbes* valued the Vikings at $796 million, with $227 million in annual revenues.)

The Vikings were meanwhile pursuing a $1.1 billion proposal in Arden Hills, a suburb in nearby Ramsey County, that seemed like little more than a blatant money grab. In September 2011, the team unveiled a map of the proposed site to business leaders in St. Paul that "drew gasps" among attendees, according to a report by the *Star Tribune*.[18] The map featured a red circle around a 120-acre area next to the proposed stadium that was labeled "Potential Convention Center Hotel." In essence, Wilf had included in his proposal land to be used not for stadium facilities but for other real estate developments that would benefit him at taxpayer expense. By providing direct competition to the city's convention center, Wilf's plan "not only would . . . be taking this business from us," Minneapolis City Council president Barbara Johnson said, but "he'd be taking convention business and using state taxes to do it."

In retrospect, it was a brilliant recycling of the strategy employed with the Anoka plan: pitting city against suburb and using the latter as leverage in negotiations with the former.

Sure enough, in January 2012, reports emerged that the Dayton administration was quietly trying to steer the Vikings away from Arden Hills, and the team renewed its interest in downtown Minneapolis.[19] The governor gave Minneapolis and Ramsey County an ultimatum to submit their best offers, giving the city a clear financial advantage (whereas the city promised to fund the proposed project with existing taxes, the county's plan was contingent on raising the food and beverage tax) and using the competition to maximize the public benefit to the Vikings. The strategy, it seems, worked: "Minnesota community leaders are showing fresh zeal for keeping the team and jostling privately to win favor for one of three downtown sites," the *Star Tribune* reported.

In March, the Vikings reached a tentative agreement with Governor Dayton and Minneapolis mayor R. T. Rybak for a new $975 million stadium downtown near the existing Metrodome site. It called for $398 million from the state, $150 million from the city, and $427 million from the team.[20] The plan still had to clear the state legislature, which had been steadfast in its opposition to publicly funding a new stadium. On April 17, the state house decisively rejected the deal, and the plan looked dead in the water.

Having publicly maintained its commitment to staying in Minnesota all along, the team began hinting at relocation. "It's a mistake to think the Vikings and the [NFL] will continue with the status quo," Vikings vice president Lester Bagley told the *Star Tribune*'s Mike Kaszuba, who noted that Bagley "stopped just short of saying that the vote could lead the team to leave Minnesota." With just two weeks remaining in the session, Representative Morrie Lanning, who sponsored the bill, declared that if the bill was going to pass "somebody's going to have to pull a rabbit out of a hat."[21]

While the Vikings tried to dust off the Arden Hills plan, the NFL sent in the big guns. On April 20, 2012, NFL commissioner

Roger Goodell and Pittsburgh Steelers owner Art Rooney II flew to Minnesota for a closed-door meeting with legislators. Goodell maintains that he never threatened that the Vikings would leave for Los Angeles—he simply noted the possibility. "One of us—a legislator—brought the subject up," Governor Dayton told the *Star Tribune*. "[The NFL] said they would like to have a team in Los Angeles [and] they would like to have it not be the Vikings."[22] A report[23] on the league's website reiterated that while the Vikings didn't want to leave the area, the NFL very much did want a team in Los Angeles (wink, wink).

Less than a month later, the Vikings stadium deal in downtown Minneapolis was approved.

Wilf's strategy all along was an ingenious retooling of the usually blunt threat of "if you don't build it, they will leave." And even though Wilf himself never threatened to move the team, reports abounded that he could sell to an ownership group that would. "I don't know that our owners had the stomach to move the team, but I do think there was some question about the state of Minnesota and if we couldn't resolve this issue the team would have gone up for sale," Bagley told the *Los Angeles Daily News* in 2015, adding that the team received interest from potential owners in Los Angeles.[24]

This case highlights how the mere existence of Los Angeles as an open market served as leverage for NFL teams over the years. Wilf never had to directly threaten to move; the media, local officials, and other NFL owners did the work for him. The day before Goodell visited with legislators in the Minnesota state capitol building, Wilf's private plane was spotted on a tarmac in Southern California, setting media speculation ablaze.[25]

Even without the Los Angeles threat, this entire episode demonstrates how teams can pit one local government against another. In lieu of moving to an entirely different region, teams can follow the Yankees' strategy to move from one borough to another, or the Vikings' strategy to move from the city to a suburb, or vice versa.

Strangely, neither politicians nor fans seem to realize that while they may need their teams, their teams need them, too. "There are very few mayors who realize, 'Oh, we as a city actually have some leverage here.' Teams need big markets to play in, and if you run a big market, than you can say, 'Okay, we'd love to have you remain here, but we're of a value to you as you're of a value to us, so let's come together,'" deMause says. "You can't run a sports franchise without selling tickets, and you can't run a sports franchise without selling eyeballs for cable deals, and those things don't just grow on trees."

———

Despite the fact that threats to leave are largely empty, political pressure forces local officials to take them seriously. "Teams don't move nearly as much as they threaten to move," Humphreys says. "But I think local politicians . . . have to take any threat as credible no matter how crazy it sounds on the face of it, because nobody wants to be left holding the bag. You don't want to be the mayor that let the Yankees leave New York."

But don't let this notion fool you into thinking that voters wield significant influence when it comes to stadium financing. While there are a handful of examples of voters approving public money for stadiums, they're lucky if it gets to a vote at all. A poll conducted by KSTP-TV Minneapolis in February 2012 revealed that 68 percent of Minnesotans wanted the new Vikings stadium to be entirely privately funded, with only 22 percent favoring the use of public money.[26] Despite a 1997 amendment to the Minneapolis constitution requiring voter approval for any plan involving at least $10 million of public funding for sports facilities, the new Vikings stadium didn't go to a vote. The city exploited a loophole to bypass the state constitution, promising that its share would come from redirecting existing hospitality taxes already used to pay for the city's convention center. Rybak and others argued that since those dollars are controlled by the state, they don't require a citywide vote for approval.

There's no limit to how creative teams and governments can be in order to circumvent stadium votes. As Matheson notes, Chicago managed to sell its $660 million upgrade of Soldier Field, home of the Chicago Bears, as a "renovation" rather than a rebuild by maintaining the trademark colonnades on the perimeter of the stadium. Because it was a "reno" rather than a "redo," the plan didn't require a vote. Yet the neoclassical columns were so out of place with the "flying saucer" aesthetic of the new stadium that the National Park Service stripped Soldier Field of its landmark status in 2006,[27] stating that "very little of the historic fabric remains."[28]

Then there are those cases where a stadium deal actually manages to get to a vote, the people vote "no," and the deal goes through anyway. The stadiums of the Pittsburgh Steelers and the Pittsburgh Pirates are the quintessential examples of this. Both parks opened in 2001 and were primarily funded by taxpayer dollars. In 1997, voters in the eleven counties surrounding Pittsburgh voted—530,706 to 281,336—against the "Regional Renaissance Initiative," which called for an increase in sales taxes to pay for the two stadiums.[29] Upon its failure, a new plan was developed: the "Regional Destination Development Plan," an $809 million plan to build the two stadiums and expand the city's convention center. Seeing clearly how unpopular stadium financing was with voters, the solution was to bypass a public vote entirely. Instead, the plan required ratification only by the Allegheny Regional Asset District, whose members are appointed, not elected. The board voted 6-1 in favor of the plan, which then passed through the state legislature. Of the $357 million for the Steelers' Heinz Field, taxpayers put up $281 million. Of the $262 million for the Pirates' PNC Park, taxpayers covered $212 million.

At a 2005 conference on mayors and leadership, then–Pittsburgh mayor Thomas J. Murphy told moderator George Stephanopoulos: "You get two messages from the voters: Don't use public money for ball parks to pay for the greedy owners, but don't you dare let these teams leave."[30]

Some fans might vote with their hearts rather than their wallets, but the issue remains: overall, the public isn't well educated on the financial benefit of stadiums or lack thereof.

In the 1990s, a wave of research by economists began to dispel the claims put forth by teams and leagues that new stadiums were huge jobs and revenue creators for their localities. These peer-reviewed studies found, overwhelmingly, no long-term increases in employment or incomes for local citizens.[31] Yet leagues continue to sell the line that new stadiums usher in "neighborhood revitalization," an upbeat euphemism for "gentrification." But that claim is also largely untrue, a fact nearly universally agreed upon by economists not paid to be consultants for teams looking to market a new stadium deal.

———

One of the reasons for this disparity is due to what's known as the "crowding out" effect. Construction jobs are inherently temporary anyway, but as Matheson notes, they're also finite. "Big stadium construction crowds out other sorts of construction projects that could have happened. Your construction workers are working on this project rather than some other project in the area," he said.

In addition, the number of good, sustainable jobs at a stadium is relatively small compared to other businesses that don't receive subsidies. "An NFL team hires about as many full-time, year-round equivalent workers as a regular Macy's department store," Matheson says. "Sure, you have 2,000 workers, but you have 2,000 workers working ten days a year for six hours, and that's just not many full-time equivalent jobs."

The "good jobs" that we always hear about include the players, coaches, trainers, front-office personnel, and some white-collar jobs such as ticket sales and hospitality. But for the most part, stadium employment is seasonal and part-time, such as beer vendors, maintenance personnel, and concession stand workers.

Moreover, the promise of local economic gains from spending and activity in and around the stadium tends to be overstated as well. According to Matheson, there are two reasons for this. The first is what's known as the "substitution effect," whereby people spend money at the ballpark instead of at other local businesses. "This is about what happens in a typical city on Sundays in the months when the NFL isn't playing. It's not like we all sit and hide in our closet and never got out and buy anything or go out to eat," Matheson says. "We just spend our money and our time differently than in the fall when we're watching the NFL."

The second reason is a "crowding out" effect of a different kind: regular tourists. Sports fans—locals as well as out-of-town visitors—descend on the stadium's vicinity and displace other locals and tourists who otherwise would have been there. "Crowding out is outsiders coming in and displacing normal activity; substitution effect is how you shift around your money in the economy," Matheson explains.

All of this comes with a major caveat: it applies mainly to stadiums built in locations where, previously, one did not exist. Any perceived bump in economic activity—whether it's substituting for or crowding out others—is basically rendered moot when a stadium is built in a location that already had one, which is a common occurrence. "You can concentrate economic activity by putting a new arena in a specific neighborhood," Humphreys says. But "how often are they built in the parking lot of the existing stadium? A lot. You can't make that revitalization or that gentrification argument when you're doing that. Although some teams still try."

From the new Yankee Stadium (still in the Bronx) to Fiserv Forum (the home of the Milwaukee Bucks that opened in 2018), no fan should expect a new stadium to perform the revitalization miracle that the old one didn't. "The Yankees have been on the corner of 161st and River for 95 years now," deMause says. "The Yankees moving across the street was never going to make a significant difference on the South Bronx neighborhood."

DeMause contends that the actual presence of a team is "small potatoes." There is an argument to be made, however, that a new stadium can accelerate gentrification if it has already begun. "What teams and city officials are doing is looking for areas that are already ripe for takeoff and relocating there, because it's where everybody wants to be, it's where everybody is already going," deMause explains.

Take, for example, Barclays Center in Brooklyn's Atlantic Yards, home of the Brooklyn Nets. That neighborhood was already a part of the wave of gentrification sweeping through the borough; the new arena simply gave it more buzz. "The actual fans who are going to Nets games and concerts may not have had a huge impact on that neighborhood, but it did help all the commercial real estate developers on Flatbush Avenue say, 'Hey this is a hot neighborhood now, let's open a bunch of boutiques.' I have no doubt that all the housing that went up around the Barclays Center would have been successful with or without the arena," deMause says. "The biggest benefit of Barclays was that it got the name 'Atlantic Yards' in the headlines."

———

This brings us to a dilemma that is central in the stadium debate specifically and the gentrification debate in general: Who, exactly, does it benefit? In recent years, gentrification has come under fire for pricing out longtime locals and further contributing to racial and class inequality in cities, homogenizing the demographics and culture of formerly diverse neighborhoods. "Gentrification, or neighborhood revitalization, has uneven effects on the residents of those areas," Humphreys says. "If you're a renter, revitalization or gentrification is probably not good for you, because it used to be cheap to live in that neighborhood and now it's expensive because of the gentrification and you can't afford to live there anymore."

That's just one of the ways in which stadium development can adversely affect locals who are living in the immediate vicinity. To add insult to injury, because everything in a new stadium costs more—everything from tickets to hot dogs—it means the locals often can't afford to go to games, that is, to actually enjoy the new building their tax dollars helped pay for.

"They're dealing with traffic and they're dealing with the crowds and the trash and the crime that comes with it. And yet they're priced out of going to games," Humphreys says. "There are some equity issues there that are important and largely overlooked. This is not what anybody ever talks about in the debates of whether we should subsidize these facilities." He added that he thinks the leagues are being shortsighted in pricing out local families whose kids could become the future generation of fans. Going to a ballpark is a great introduction to a new sport, a great way to create a new fan.

Pricing out locals who have to bear the brunt of the inconveniences wrought by stadiums not only ignores their potential as fans; it also breeds understandable resentment of a team's very presence in the neighborhood. Ask anyone who lives on Grand Concourse, perhaps returning home from a second job, who has to deal with a packed train full of people who spent $100 a ticket to go watch some baseball in that person's backyard.

Of course, despite what teams say, stadium construction isn't simply about the fans—it's also about making private money on public investment. Some fans (particularly the ever-elusive millennial fan) might view these buildings as entertainment destinations that just so happen to also have baseball. But if you're inclined to agree with deMause, you might think the in-game experience in many new stadiums is actually worse than at the old facility because it's no longer just about the sport—it's about turning the ballpark into a one-stop den for conspicuous consumption.

As deMause notes above, that's exactly what we've seen with places such as the new Yankee Stadium, which aimed to bring spending inside the gates. "That's the main reason that they built the new [Yankee] stadium," he says. "They easily could have renovated [the old venue] and put in snazzier scoreboards. They were just thinking, 'We want more space that isn't devoted to baseball but is devoted to shopping.'" Indeed, while Yankees chief operating officer Lonn Trost contended in 2008 that "the stadium has been built with the fans in mind," he also conceded this nugget: "We tried to reflect a five-star hotel with a ballfield in the middle."[32]

———

For decades, lawmakers have attempted to address public stadium financing to little or no avail. In 2015, President Barack Obama attempted to do away with at least the federal tax exemption on municipal bonds in his budget, but that never made it through Congress.[33] In 2017, a bipartisan bill by Senators Cory Booker and James Lankford eliminating the exemption passed the Senate, but it didn't make it past reconciliation with the House. And neither measure would have addressed the state and local subsidies that are another part of the public giveaway to teams.

Most analysts aren't optimistic that change is imminent. The actual legislation needed is relatively simple to pass, starting with the removal of leagues' monopolistic power to limit the number of teams and where they are located. Unlike, say, MLB's blanket antitrust exemption, which has survived several Supreme Court challenges, this would entail a simple bill by Congress. "When you put a limit on the number of teams, that puts all these cities in competition with one another, and if we were trying to have some sort of grand solution, it would be something that limits this competition between cities, which often ends up in a race to the bottom," Matheson says.

Federal oversight could help, but as Humphreys observes, "I just don't see the appetite for it in DC. Absent the creation of some new bureaucracy that would oversee professional sports, without reducing the monopoly power that leagues have, you're always going to hand the local team owner the trump card in any negotiation over a subsidy."

So what's the solution? Put simply, it comes down to two things: money and political will—and the two aren't separate.

It takes fans and voters and, even more importantly, the politicians who purport to represent us to stop selling short the bargaining power cities may actually have.

It takes us standing tall amid teams' threats to leave so we don't end up in a situation like Wisconsin governor Scott Walker gutting the University of Wisconsin System by $250 million, then turning around and giving that exact sum to the Milwaukee Bucks for their new NBA arena, while being flanked by posters reading "Cheaper to Keep Them."

It takes our representatives standing up not only to all businesses seeking corporate welfare but also—especially—sports teams that claim the inability to afford privately financed stadiums yet refuse to open their books for inspection when demanding hundreds of millions of public dollars. As Paul Beeston, a former Toronto Blue Jays executive and former MLB president, famously said, "I can turn a $4 million profit into a $2 million loss and get every national accounting firm to agree with me."[34]

And it takes calling out rank hypocrisy, such as when Las Vegas throws $750 million at the (former) Oakland Raiders to bring them to town, even as the NHL expansion team, the Vegas Golden Knights, somehow managed to entirely privately finance their own arena. (The fact that two storied franchises—the Raiders and the Warriors—couldn't leave Oakland fast enough is partly a result of the city's unwillingness to cave on public financing, but that's a story for another book.)

Long story short, all of this requires a change in our relationship to money in sports. "Sometimes when people ask me what *Field of Schemes* is about, I say it's actually a book about campaign finance reform," deMause says. "None of this is baked into capitalism. This is all a solvable problem—if not for the fact that it's a completely insolvable problem, because the power of the sports lobby at the federal level and the local level is absolutely tremendous."

The ability of teams to fund PR campaigns for new stadiums parallels the political reality that rich incumbents can easily squash grassroots challengers. In 2004, when owner Jerry Jones was looking to round up support for a referendum on a new stadium for the Dallas Cowboys, the pro-stadium campaign raised about $5.1 million while the anti-stadium group raised $430,000.[35]

Our lobbying system, in addition to the various antitrust and monopolistic powers handed to sports leagues through federal law, reveals another uncomfortable truth: the problem with stadium subsidies is uniquely American. "Sports economists in Europe are somewhat amazed at how socialist the free-market Americans are and how free-market the socialist Europeans are," Matheson says.

Aside from mega events like the Olympic Games and soccer's World Cup, the European Union does not allow public financing for professional stadiums. Furthermore, the European system of promotion and relegation (though creating other issues of competitive balance) means that leagues can't control the movement of teams the way they do in the United States. In 2005, a group of Manchester United fans, angry at the sale of the team to the Glazer family from the United States, started their own club, FC United of Manchester.[36] The team hasn't yet reached the Premier League, but in just fifteen years it's received four promotions and could, during the lifetimes of some of its owners, reach the pros. This would be the equivalent of Marlins fans unhappy with the team's sale to Derek Jeter's investor group starting a new baseball team that could eventually join the Marlins in the National League. As it stands, fans having that much involvement in their sports remains an American pipe dream.

The real takeaway for sports fans, according to deMause, is that teams want to build new stadiums only because they know the public will pay for it. "If subsidies did not exist, they [the owners] would by and large not be building many of these new stadiums. That's the basis of this scam," he says. "You're making money on the stadium because the stadium comes with this enormous pile of cash."

So why do fans pay to sit in these enormously expensive monuments to corporate welfare and enjoy the spectacle? DeMause, a lifelong Yankees fan, had perhaps the most extreme reaction: he couldn't. Tearing down the old stadium was the last straw. He left his future fandom up to his son, and now they root for the Mets.

For Humphreys, it's a matter of accepting reality. "Who doesn't want the government to subsidize your favorite activity? I've got the rest of the country to subsidize my favorite activity, and good for me. Enjoy it," he says. He added that fans could take some solace in the public good that sports teams provide: "a reason to come together." As he puts it: "Team success, you can still take something away from that that it really is part of the fabric of your community."

Finally, Matheson adds that even though the intangible effects of sport might not justify the public cost, the positive benefits are still there. "The one place where economists really are kind of positive is that we do have some evidence that sports make us happy," he says. "For countries that host big events, or places that have teams, especially if they do well, we do see marked increases in self-reported happiness." Matheson notes that while the 2006 World Cup in Germany produced only an incremental economic impact, it did significantly boost happiness in the country, "and we actually have some historical evidence to suggest that a lot of happy Germans is much better for Europe than a lot of angry ones. So I would close with, we do have some evidence that sports make us happy—we just don't have a lot of evidence that it makes us rich."

CHAPTER 13

ENJOYING THE OLYMPICS DESPITE THE HARM TO YOUR COMMUNITY

No one wants to host the Olympics. Literally. The list of cities willing to take on this monstrosity of a mega sporting event is quickly dwindling.

For the 2022 Winter Olympics, Oslo, Stockholm, Krakow, Munich, Quebec City, Davos, and Barcelona all dropped out of the bidding process because they did not have enough public support to justify continuing to compete to be host. That left the International Olympic Committee (IOC) with two choices: Almaty in Kazakhstan (a dictatorship) and Beijing. The latter won, but most events will take place nearly 150 miles away, in Chongli, where there is a winter climate.[1]

For the 2024 Summer Olympics, Boston locals fought hard against the idea and forced the city to remove its bid.[2] Similar action plans for defeating the IOC and local Olympic planning committees spread to other cities around the globe. One organizer told the *Washington Post* that after Bostonians' success, people started calling. "Groups from Hamburg, Rome and Budapest, cities also pursuing the 2024 Games, all had some variation of the same question: How'd you do it?"[3]

Those cities eventually dropped out of the race, leaving only Paris and Los Angeles. In order to save themselves some trouble for a while, the IOC's executive board announced in June 2017 that whichever of the cities they chose to host in 2024, the other would get the honor in 2028. It ended up being Paris in 2024, Los Angeles four years later.[4]

The response in Los Angeles, in particular, has been lukewarm at best. The organization NOlympics LA is attempting to stop the city from hosting despite the winning bid because, as the group's website states: "Regardless of how 'successfully' [the Olympics] are executed, these 'Games' will expose tens of thousands of our fellow Angelenos to incalculable risk and feed the problems which are already devastating and destroying the fabric of our communities today, while depriving us of the resources we need to make the city better."[5]

The IOC, for its part, changed the bidding process in June 2019. Changes include requiring cities vying for the games to hold referendums to gauge local populations' eagerness or lack thereof before bidding; and to use structures that already exist or only to erect temporary ones. As the Associated Press reported, these changes are a direct response to the IOC's trying "to avoid negative headlines and angering local taxpayers following referendum losses and excessive spending on white-elephant venues."[6]

Such changes make sense given that there is one main reason most places are turning away from hosting: cost. In late May 2017, Nancy Armour, a columnist at USA Today, wrote a piece about how the incredibly high price tag for putting on the Olympics may finally be the thing that ends these events. Armour wrote: "Unless the rampant spending is reined in, the IOC will find within a decade that the only cities interested—or able—to host the Games will be a select few that have done it before, like Los Angeles, or are in countries run by despots for whom money is no object."[7]

But the problems with mega events like the Olympics are so much greater than the high costs of putting on the show. In response to Armour's piece, journalist Travis Waldron, who has written often on the myriad costs of hosting mega events, tweeted an emoji of a face in profile screaming followed by these words: "A cost-effective Olympics is still going to take people's homes and lead to security crackdowns on minority groups."[8] Even if we fix the money issue, Waldron is saying, what about displacement of people to make room for venues and Olympic spaces? What about the militarization of local police forces that occurs to protect host cities from possible global terrorist attacks? What about the people who have to live there long after the Olympics are gone but the worst of their legacy remains?

In fact, it's nearly impossible to defend the continued existence of the Olympics as currently staged.

If only it was as simple as getting rid of mega sporting events (not that the IOC would take that lying down or anything, but it is one solution to a corrupt and damaging system). Suggesting such a scenario—even in the face of what we know happens to the cities and countries that host these events—is painful to imagine. The Olympics and their mega-event cousin, the World Cup soccer tournament, serve a purpose and play an important role in the global sports world. They provide a spotlight for sports and athletes that otherwise would never have them. And because of that spotlight, those sports and athletes get resources and support that they otherwise wouldn't receive. They are not just moneymaking engines for the IOC, corporations, and elites in the cities and countries that host them; they are a vehicle for providing legitimacy to sports and athletes that struggle to get it. This is all especially true for women's sports, which has no bigger platform (and often, in many parts of the world, no platform at all) than the Olympics or the World Cup.

If we, as a global sporting community, decide that mega events are not sustainable, what do we do about the lost platform for female athletes? What happens to the sports?

———

It's easiest to start in Brazil. It hosted the Olympics in Rio de Janeiro in 2016, and in 2014 the entire country welcomed the World Cup. The most obvious issues are the costs to put on these events and the abandonment of high-priced venues after they leave town.

The money is egregious. First, the World Cup in 2014 lasted one month. Brazil spent $15 billion to host it, $3 billion of which (roughly equivalent to 13 percent of the country's education budget) went into the renovation of old stadiums and the construction of new ones. The vast majority (90 percent) of that $3 billion was public money despite promises from government officials that private money would fund the World Cup. By March 2015, less than a year after Brazil hosted the World Cup, the BBC reported that "at least six of the 12 stadiums built for the tournament [are] now in financial difficulty," leaving "local governments across Brazil . . . [scrambling] to find productive uses for these costly state-of-the-art venues."[9]

Michael Powell of the New York Times wrote a devastating profile of one venue in Manaus, Brazil, in the heart of the Brazilian rainforest, a piece that published during the Rio Olympics in August 2016. "Years in the making, at a cost of $220 million, it was crafted to resemble a giant white basket of a type common in the region, atop a four-story concrete plaza," Powell writes. The stadium is currently empty, a symbol of sporting decadence, but the construction and maintenance debts continue to harm the city. "The debt for this ziggurat has piled high and requires siphoning off of money intended for schools and hospitals. One-quarter of Manauarans are extremely poor; many lack running water."[10]

The financial problems from the World Cup were not just localized; they affected the entire country, in fact. According to the Associated Press: "Government officials acknowledged that public holidays associated with the World Cup were partly to blame for the country falling into a technical recession late last year."[11]

The Fédération Internationale de Football Association (FIFA), which oversees international soccer, made out well, though. It made $4.8 billion in revenue off the World Cup, $2.6 billion of which was profits. According to the economist Andrew Zimbalist: "FIFA keeps the revenue from TV rights, tickets, corporate sponsorships and marketing. Brazil gets to keep, in my estimate, around $500 million from tourist spending."[12] In 2015, FIFA announced that it was going to return $100 million to Brazil per the World Cup Legacy Fund, which goes toward things like facilities, youth sports, women's sport, and health projects.[13] How kind.

Then, two years later, after paying for and hosting the World Cup, Brazil was hosting another mega event: the Summer Olympics. They occurred over sixteen days in August 2016 and cost $13.1 billion.[14] In February 2017, a mere six months after the games ended, the Associated Press reported a series of terrible outcomes for the host city:

> Four of the new arenas in the main Olympic Park have failed to find private-sector management, and ownership has passed to the federal government. Another new arena will be run by the cash-strapped city with Brazil stuck in its deepest recession in decades. The historic Maracanã stadium, site of the opening and closing ceremony, has been vandalized as stadium operators, Rio state government and Olympic organizers have fought over $1 million in unpaid electricity bills. The electric utility reacted by cutting off all power to the city landmark. There are few players for a new $20 million Olympic golf course and little money for upkeep. Deodoro, the second-largest cluster of Olympic venues, is closed and searching for a management company. The state of Rio de Janeiro is months late paying teachers, hospital workers and pensions. The state also reports record-breaking crime in 2016 in almost all categories, from homicides to robbery.[15]

In April 2017, Bloomberg.com reported that the organizing committee for the Summer Olympics was $32 million in debt and was "trying to pay off suppliers with stuff—air conditioners, portable energy units, electrical cables—in lieu of or in addition to cash."[16]

Then, in June 2017, the former state governor of Rio de Janeiro, Sérgio Cabral, was sentenced to fourteen years in prison after he was found guilty of corruption and money laundering. "Some of the allegations involve construction projects connected with Brazil's hosting of the FIFA World Cup in 2014 and then the Olympic and Paralympic Games two years later," Inside the Games reported. "This includes alleged embezzlement of funds from the renovation work in the Maracanã Stadium used for the FIFA World Cup final and all Rio 2016 ceremonies." Prosecutors think that Cabral's corruption "accelerated and caused the collapse of the State economy to its position of near-bankruptcy today."[17] The former mayor of Rio, Eduardo Paes, who was a great supporter of the IOC and of Rio hosting the Olympics, is under investigation for possibly accepting at least $5 million in payments to facilitate construction projects tied to the games.[18]

In the concluding chapter of *Rio 2016: Olympic Myths, Hard Realities*, an edited collection that looks at the many terrible legacies of these particular Summer Games, Andrew Zimbalist writes: "Perhaps the most prominent and troubling Olympics legacy is the horrific state of Rio's economy." He notes that there were other major issues before the Olympics showed up ("plummeting price of crude oil . . . and reduced demand from China"), but the Olympics, he says, exacerbated all their problems. And so he writes: "The state of Rio owes the federal government over $30 billion. The federal government, in turn, is running an annual budget deficit of 10 percent of the GDP—the equivalent in the United States to a $1.9 trillion budget deficit!" That's one hell of a legacy debt.[19]

Jules Boykoff, professor of politics and government at Pacific University outside Portland, Oregon, is no stranger to the Olympics. He was, in fact, a member of the US Olympic soccer team in the early 1990s. He's now the author of multiple books on the Olympics, including *Activism and the Olympics*, *Celebration Capitalism and the Olympic Games*, and *Power Games: A Political History of the Olympics*. Boykoff says that in his many years of studying the fallout from the Olympics on the communities that host them, there are four main issues: cost, false promises, militarization of public spaces, and displacement of local people.[20]

The cost issue is clear. It is driven, Boykoff says, by "elites who are typically extremely wealthy." They "hoodwink the public, and say it's only going to cost so many billions of dollars, then it costs so many billions more. There is money to be made attaching yourself barnacle-like to the Olympic ship, and these well-connected political elites do it in every city." He offers Sochi, Russia, the 2014 Winter Olympics host, as one example. Sochi, Boykoff says, was "originally slated to cost $12 billion. They cost more than $50 billion, more than all the previous Winter Olympics combined."

Some dissident Russian politicians claimed that up to $30 billion was stolen via padded Olympic construction bills submitted by oligarchs favored by Russian president Vladimir Putin.[21] In thinking about all of these numbers, Boykoff asks, "who bears the cost?" The answer, he says, is "everyday people, the tax-paying public." As this book goes to print, the projected cost of the 2020 Summer Olympics in Tokyo has already hit $25 billion—four times the initial estimate. Originally slated to start in July 2020, the Games were pushed back a year due to the COVID-19 pandemic. Who knows how much that delay will add to the overall cost?[22]

To get tax-paying everymen to go along with plans to host mega events, elites promise a lot of things to the local community that they never deliver. A big part of the problem is the bidding process itself. "Right in the beginning stages," Boykoff says, "when it's a bid and everyone's trying to make it sound as good as possible for the everyday people who are going to be supporting or not supporting it, they say, 'Oh it's only going to cost this amount of money.'" It is never as cheap as they claim—not even close.

Beyond that, promoters promise to do a lot of good for the city, but they rarely come through. For Rio, Boykoff says, one of the biggest promises was that the city said it would clean up the water supply before the Games. Alas, as the *New York Times* reported on the eve of the games: "A major part of Rio's winning Olympic bid was a plan to capture and treat 80 percent of the sewage that flows into Guanabara Bay, something organizers now admit will not happen—certainly not by August, if ever."[23]

Worst of all, as soon as the games are over, those unfulfilled promises are forever lost. "Then, of course, everyone, including myself[,] is guilty of this," Boykoff says. "We go on to the next Games and we talk about the issues and ideals and problems that are going on there. False promises, that one gets me on a level of everyday humans who really suffer the cost after they kick in their taxpayer money."

Another legacy left behind for local communities: a stronger and potentially more lethal police force possessing a new arsenal of fancy military-grade weaponry. "Essentially if you host the Olympics, and you're a local police force, you use the Games like your own private ATM machine," Boykoff laments. "You try to get all the special weaponry and special laws that you'd never be able to get during a normal political time." Police forces use the fact that by hosting the Games, they "become a legit terrorist target," even if it's a place like Rio, which "has zero history of terrorism."

While the Olympics were happening, Boykoff notes, "some of the venues were some of the safest places maybe in all of Latin America." That left other parts of the city more vulnerable. "That left communities on the outskirts of Rio, typically favela and poor communities, open to more violence, and that's exactly what happened, if you look at the human rights report. Militarization of [the] public sphere has all sorts of tentacle problems that spin out of it." As NPR reported at the time: "Police have been conducting more operations inside the favelas to prevent gangs from causing trouble at the Olympics. But the police are also weaker because so many security forces have been redeployed to protect Olympic infrastructure. So the gangs feel emboldened and are pushing back."[24]

When it's all said and done, Boykoff points out, "the police don't box [their new weapons] back up and say, 'All right, return it boys.' They keep that stuff, and they use it for everyday policing afterward, and if there's anything we know about Rio police, they don't need extra difficult and dangerous toys to use against the general population. They're already responsible for killing one in five people who suffer from homicides in the country."[25]

Finally, and perhaps worst of all, Boykoff is troubled with the way that mega events displace people. "Because the Olympics are so big, they require all these specialized venues," Boykoff says. "How many cities and communities have a velodrome? Not too many. You've got to build these things, let alone [something] like one of these zany outdoor alpine canoe racing places. Rio definitely did not have that, so you've got to get rid of people" in order to make room to build such venues. "In Rio, infamously, there were more than 77,000 people who were displaced to make way for venues and transport," Boykoff says. "Those were the city's own numbers. People I talked to from think tanks, they had put the number closer to 100,000 who had been displaced." That is a big number, but it's nothing compared to the estimated 1.5 *million* people that Beijing displaced when it hosted the Summer Olympics in 2008. Beijing will be hosting the Winter Olympics in 2022.[26]

In July 2019, Boykoff, along with sports journalist Dave Zirin, reported for *The Nation* about two women who live in Tokyo, the site of the 2020 Summer Olympics. "They were displaced from their homes 55 years ago to make way for the 1964 Tokyo Olympics, and now, more than five decades later, they have been displaced again." The women said that in 1964, they protested, and after they were forcibly removed the government provided housing with nice amenities. For the 2020 Games, Boykoff and Zirin report, "their community was fractured, as residents were shipped to three different relocation sites, breaking apart a close-knit community." More than three hundred households lost their homes. And even if the Tokyo story is smaller than the numbers from Beijing and Rio, these are real people whose lives have been upended, quite literally, twice over so their city can host a mega event.[27]

Aaron Gordon is a journalist who went to Rio in 2016 and covered the Olympics for Vice Sports. It was his first in-person experience with a mega event. He wrote a piece whose title makes clear his main takeaway: "The Rio Games Were an Unjustifiable Human Disaster, and So Are the Olympics."[28] When asked what made him feel that strongly about his time there, Gordon said: "There was no singular thing, and I think to a large extent I felt that it was the degree to which the International Olympic Committee and its members feel no remorse, no obligation, and no dedication to improving the lives of the people in the city that they profit off."

Gordon was particularly put off by how IOC officials were purposefully separated from everyone else. He had booked an apartment across from the hotel where the IOC officials were staying, which meant he got a good look at the intricate coordination that went into moving them from place to place. In his pointedly titled piece about the disaster that was Rio, he expanded on this idea:

After arriving at the airport, members and assorted apparatchiks were ushered into private cars, ferried along exclusive highway lanes—look out the window, and there were Rio 2016-branded walls to mask the favelas—and dropped off at their exclusive hotels ringed by security, so only those with credentials could enter. They then took the same private cars to all of their events. Some even got motorcades. Once they got to the various sports venues, they went in the Olympic Family entrances, passed through the Olympic Family security lines, mingled in the Olympic Family club lounges, and watched athletes compete from the Olympic Family seats. When they were hungry, they surely put their $900 per diems to use at the city's most exclusive restaurants and bars, never risking having to interact with anyone who wasn't wealthy. Except, perhaps, for the people serving them.

Seeing all of this in practice made Gordon keenly aware of how the IOC has constructed an Olympic experience that centers on IOC officials and walls them off from everything else: "It was the way that nothing else in Rio worked as it was supposed to except the things that touched the IOC, then everything seemed like clockwork." He mentions how athletes were stranded and couldn't make it to venues on time.[29] Or how budget cuts and lack of training caused a slew of problems with doping testing and that 50 percent of the tests didn't happen because athletes couldn't be found.[30] "The only thing that [the IOC] make sure works are the things that are for them and anything else is inconsequential. That was when I realized that's all they care about." It drove home for Gordon the unfairness of the Games and the problem with the group that oversees them. "It really solidified for me that all of the things that I've reported on," Gordon says, "all of the injustices, all the wasted money, all the billion dollars that they [the IOC] make, [that] the whole city spends so that they [the IOC] can profit off of it, all the ways in which they restrict athletes rights to benefit from their own labor, all the ways in which they enable multinational corporations to profit off this as well—all of that is not an accident."

None of this was new to Rio, nor to the World Cup, nor the Olympics. And it did not, of course, end in Rio.

Pyeongchang, South Korea, hosted the Winter Olympics in 2018 and caused environmental damage when constructing the venues. "To make way for a ski run, organizers clear-cut 58,000 trees from an ancient forest on Mount Gariwang," Boykoff wrote in a February 2017 piece. That forest was "a conservation area home to rare species like the yew tree and the wangsasre tree, the latter of which only exists on the Korean peninsula."[31]

That same year, Russia hosted soccer's World Cup. Human Rights Watch has reported that "construction workers building stadiums . . . face exploitation and labor abuses."[32] The report said that "workers on six World Cup stadium construction sites faced unpaid wages either in full or part, several months' delays in payment of wages, work in temperatures as cold as -25 degrees Celsius without sufficient protections, and employers' failure to provide work contracts required for legal employment." Seventeen workers died.

Qatar, which will host the World Cup in 2022, has been under intense criticism since the moment FIFA awarded the event. Amnesty International has a campaign dedicated to shining a light on the horrific labor conditions under which workers are building stadiums in Qatar. It is titled "Qatar World Cup of Shame." "Migrants from Bangladesh, India and Nepal working on the refurbishment of the showcase Khalifa Stadium and landscaping the surrounding gardens and sporting facilities known as the 'Aspire Zone' are being exploited," the site says. "Some are being subjected to forced labour. They can't change jobs, they can't leave the country and they often wait months to get paid. Meanwhile, FIFA (football's global governing body), its sponsors and the construction companies involved are set to make massive financial gains from the tournament."[33]

It is the same old, same old for mega events—just on bigger and more devastating levels each time.

————

It's hard to follow this with a defense of these events, so there's no reason to try. But there is something these events do well that can't be ignored: they showcase sports, teams, and athletes who don't otherwise enjoy the international platform that mega events afford. We could focus on what this means for sports like handball and weightlifting, or what it means for teams from countries that rarely make international news. Instead we'll focus on what the Olympics and the World Cup mean to female athletes and women's teams.

There is no bigger global platform for female athletes than the Olympics and the World Cup. The last Women's World Cup in 2019 was the most watched ever, with an audience of more than 1 billion. And 3.5 billion people watched the Summer Olympics in Rio.[34] If we get rid of or radically scale down these mega events, what do we do with women's sports?

In 2007, the United Nations released a 44-page study (titled "Women, Gender Equality, and Sport") looking at disparities in access to sports for girls and women across the world, as well as the benefits accrued by everybody when girls and women are allowed that access. "In addition to improvements in health, women and girls stand to gain specific social benefits from participation in sport and physical activity," the introduction to the study states. "Sport provides women and girls with an alternative avenue for participation in the social and cultural life of their communities and promotes enjoyment of freedom of expression, interpersonal networks, new opportunities and increased self-esteem. It also expands opportunities for education and for the development of a range of essential life skills, including communication, leadership, teamwork and negotiation." Women and girls (and the communities they live in) all do better when women and girls are allowed a meaningful opportunity to compete in sports.

The United States thinks sports is so important for girls and women that the US State Department partners with the University of Tennessee's Center for Sport, Peace & Society, and espnW runs the Global Sports Mentoring Program. According to the program's website, it draws "on the principles of Title IX—the landmark US law that afforded equality for American women in sports and education"—to create global initiatives that spread gender equality in sports worldwide.[35] And if sports are crucial to girls' and women's lives, then it's important for people to see and support girls and women as athletes. Female athletes need the coverage and exposure they receive by participating in mega events.

Moya Dodd, a former player on Australia's national women's

soccer team, is a longtime executive committee member of the Asian Football Confederation and rose to become one of the most influential women within FIFA. She was a member of the organization's executive committee between 2013 and 2016 and has used her platform to advocate for gender equality in sport.[36]

Dodd says that mega events are crucial to women's sports because they bring awareness to places where women's sports have little visibility. "There are still vast parts of the world in which women and girls have very few sporting options," Dodd says. "And to turn on the television and see the Women's World Cup, that is something that can spur the imaginations of millions of women and girls who are only discovering what their sporting lives could be." These international tournaments, she says, drive "participation and makes sport more accessible." They make these female athletes legitimate in a way that they otherwise would not be. "To see these big brand names around a well organized tournament," Dodd says, "the delivery of it, the coverage. We had twenty-two cameras in each game at the World Cup [in 2015]. You see all of that assembled together and devoted to the women's game, absolutely, that legitimizes it."[37]

But even with the platforms that exist now, there is room for much-needed growth in women's sports throughout the world. "The women's side of the game has been suffocated by neglect for as long as anyone can remember," Dodd says. She's right, of course—no matter the sport.[38] Thus we have far to go in many places. For Dodd, the necessary changes to get more gender equity in sport are twofold. First, place more women in decision-making positions onto sports governance bodies. "The minimum target is 30 percent women in all decision-making forums, which is the tipping point at which the presence of women becomes normalized and at which the benefits of gender diversity in decision making are realized," Dodd says. And second, provide female athletes "access to resources." Without better and more resources, "the women's game just remains as a pale shadow of the men's."

One example of how this works in practice: the Australian women's rugby sevens team got a huge boost in funding from the Australian Sports Commission after winning gold at Rio (the first

Olympics that included rugby sevens), and the "AIS Director Matt Favier said [the] women's gold medal performance at the Rio Olympics played a significant role in securing the extra cash."[39]

Without the legitimacy gained through participation in mega events, achieving Dodd's goals would be even harder. That's not fair to everyone involved: not to the communities who face the long-term financial and physical burdens of hosting these events, and not to female athletes who rely on mega events to prove they deserve to play sports.

It is unfortunate that the biggest international platform for women's sports is married to the oppressive and destructive mega event. It is not worth it. But how do we unwind these two things? Is that even possible? These are hard questions to answer when the only model we currently have is so flawed.

———

To repeat: no one wants to host the Olympics. The fear is real. As the cost to host the Games continues to rise, only the worst governments (namely, dictatorships) will bid for them. And the corrupt, greedy members of the IOC will go along with it, acting as if their hands are tied and they have no other options. Public money and horrific labor practices will continue to be part and parcel of sporting events that are supposed to bring the global sporting community together.

What to do about the Olympics and the World Cup, then? How and can we fix mega events?

Part of the problem is that most people never actually experience mega events except through television and the packaged versions served up by networks. "I think the biggest thing they don't understand," Gordon says about the normal Olympics TV watcher, is "the expansiveness of this bubble that the IOC and its media partners create in the host city, and how the Olympics itself is just a completely different entity from the host city in which it's occurring." Most of us know only the flattened, sanitized, celebratory scenes that divorce mega events from the myriad problems that accompany them.

Boykoff says people need to resist the temptation to flatten everything from the comfort of our living room couches. "We can both cheer on the athletes who I think are amazing myself, and also at the same time really put a spotlight on all these problems that the Olympics bring. We don't have to pick a side in terms of that."

And now, more than ever, there is critical media of these events (leading into and during), even if not part of the TV coverage. If people want to understand the impact of the Olympics and the World Cup or the corruption at the heart of the major bodies putting them on, that information is readily available.

As for how to change the system, Boykoff thinks people should look to corporate sponsors. They should air their grievances with companies who can simply pass the buck to the IOC and FIFA. "They're a very severely untapped resource when it comes to putting pressure on the International Olympic Committee," he says. Sponsor corporations "actually have a seat at the Olympic table in ways that we don't. They don't want to look bad. They've put hundreds of millions of dollars into this, and they want to get the maximum out of it."

More than anything, Boykoff encourages people to get behind athletes who use mega events to speak out against what is happening at them. "When you see an athlete who has the courage to speak out, [people should] boost them, appreciate their courage," he says. "If you have the platform, write about them and get the word out about them, and normalize this kind of behavior, because it is. It's humane and it's normal [to dislike what is happening with mega events]. So the more spaces created for athlete activists who are asking the big questions, the better."

And athletes speaking out is no small thing. As part of the Olympic charter, IOC Rule 50 says that "no kind of demonstration or political, religious or racial propaganda is permitted in any Olympic sites, venues or other areas." In a three-page document released in January 2020 and in anticipation of the 2020 Summer Games in Tokyo, the IOC Athletes' Commission said this is a necessary prohibition because otherwise "the life's work of the athletes around us could be tarnished." Unsurprisingly, the IOC does not admit that its overall goal is to make a hefty profit off of a smooth-running and noncontroversial Olympic Games. It will allow athletes to give opinions during press conferences and interviews and through the media.[40]

Laurence Halsted is one athlete who has spoken up in the press. A fencer for Great Britain at London 2012 and Rio 2016, Halsted says that his personal experiences at the Olympics were "incredibly positive" and that the Olympics were "an amazing thing to be a part of." But he has also been publicly critical of the Olympics. In May 2016, months before heading to Rio, Halsted wrote a piece for the *Guardian* in which he said: "As an athlete proud to represent my country at the Games, I have been forced to grapple with the fact that the Olympics come with negative side effects for the host nation. Silence in the face of such injustice could be wrongly interpreted as implicit approval."[41]

Halsted credits his wife with his shift in thinking surrounding mega events. "I knew that there were some negatives, but I felt they were entirely outweighed by how great it was. She was pretty much the opposite. She kind of thought that it shouldn't be around, it was a travesty. That was eye-opening, those conversations for me, and then I just started looking into [them]." And, he adds, "as with lots of things, once you start looking you can't really ignore the truth."

As to the answer for how athletes should handle the contradictions between how great the Games are for them personally and the cost to the host city and country more generally, Halsted says that "it's not necessarily about whether you choose to boycott or not, it's about whether you choose to make yourself aware and do anything about it or even hold an opinion."

"Athletes have a responsibility to put some pressure on the IOC," Halsted says. "I would like us to be more aware and more conscientious as a group." He recognizes that it's one thing to say such things as one is transitioning out of being an athlete and quite another to do it at the height of one's Olympic or World Cup career. "But I think then it would be nice to start talking, for those mature athletes, to start talking and mentoring the younger ones to come around to this idea quicker." Now that he has retired and is training aspiring Olympians himself, his knowledge of these systems "has affected me a lot," he says, "in terms of how I want to develop the next generation of athletes." Everything is ultimately bigger than any one sport. "Athletes have a responsibility," he believes, "to think about the world that they inhabit. In a micro sense in the team around them, the club around them, but also in a macro sense of where they fit into society and where sport has meaning."

No matter where we are headed with mega events, some things seem clear. For our moral selves, we need to do away with the current rotating bidding/hosting structures that FIFA and the IOC use. They encourage corruption, overspending, abuse, displacement, and militarization—the long-term local legacies of mega events. But if we are to imagine a world without the Olympics or the World Cup as they currently function, then we must figure out how and what to do with all the sports, teams, and athletes that rely on that platform for support and to generate resources.

We—as sports fans and as citizens of this world—need to think beyond the accepted storyline about mega events served up by the IOC and FIFA. This is imperative.

CHAPTER 14

EMBRACING THAT ATHLETES—
AND SPORTS—ARE POLITICAL

It took three games for anyone to notice, and even then only a handful did. On August 26, 2016, during the US national anthem before the start of the San Francisco 49ers' third preseason game, Jennifer Lee Chan, a writer for SBNation's 49ers blog, tweeted a wide shot of the field and the 49ers sideline. And there, toward the bottom of the screen, was Colin Kaepernick, the team's backup quarterback, sitting down.[1]

After the game, reporters had a chance to ask Kaepernick about this during a press conference, but none did. Steve Wyche, who writes for NFL.com (of all places), pulled the quarterback aside afterward and, in an exclusive interview, gave Kaepernick the space to explain why he had sat down on the bench during the anthem.[2]

The following morning, Wyche published his piece and launched one of the biggest stories in the world. In it, Kaepernick explained his decision to sit: "I am not going to stand up to show pride in a flag for a country that oppresses black people and people of color. To me, this is bigger than football and it would be self-ish on my part to look the other way. There are bodies in the street and people getting paid leave and getting away with murder." He was referring, of course, to a spate of high-profile killings of young Black men by white police officers.

In the days following, Kaepernick met with Nate Boyer—a former Green Beret who had a short NFL career as a long snapper—who encouraged him to kneel instead of sit, seeing it as a more respectful gesture. At his next game, Kaepernick kneeled and was joined by his teammate Eric Reid. Other players on other NFL teams began to protest as well, some sitting or kneeling, some linking arms together, others raising their fists. The US women's national team soccer star Megan Rapinoe took a knee before a National Women's Soccer League game. High school players began to kneel, too, then university cheerleaders, members of bands, singers of the national anthem, and WNBA players. A year after Kaepernick's protest began, Lindsay Gibbs wrote at ThinkProgress: "Over the past 13 months, we have found evidence of more than 3,500 people taking steps to join Kaepernick's movement. We tracked more than 200 protests during the national anthem at sporting events in 41 states (including Washington, D.C.) and four countries. Fifty colleges and 68 high schools have seen some type of protest activity on their fields."[3]

The backlash was just as large—led by none other than Donald Trump. Within days of Wyche's story, Trump, then a presidential candidate on the campaign trail and speaking on a conservative radio talk show, said of Kaepernick: "Maybe he should find a country that works better for him. Let him try. It won't happen." A year later, giving a speech as president, Trump said: "Wouldn't you love to see one of these NFL owners, when somebody disrespects our flag, to say, 'Get that son of a bitch off the field right now. Out! He's fired. He's fired!'"[4]

While some people burned their Kaepernick gear, it also became the top-selling jersey in the NFL. Fans on both sides of the issue said they would boycott the league. (*Sports Illustrated*'s Monday Morning Quarterback site published a post that simply reproduced emails from fans who were giving up the NFL because the protests made them so upset.) In September 2018, the Palm Beach County Police Benevolent Association asked its members not to purchase NFL tickets after some Dolphins players continued to kneel at the start of that season.[5]

Kaepernick never played in the NFL again after the end of the 2016–2017 season even though he said repeatedly that he wanted to, and by most measures he was good enough. He instead focused on charity work and created the Know My Rights Camp "to raise awareness on higher education, self empowerment, and instruction to properly interact with law enforcement in various scenarios." Kaepernick, along with his teammate Eric Reid, sued the NFL, claiming the league colluded against them to punish them for their protest. In February 2019, Kaepernick and Reid settled with the league for an undisclosed amount. And in the middle of all of that, Kaepernick became the face of a major new Nike ad campaign, one that did not specifically mention police violence or his protest but featured words over Kaepernick's face: "Believe in something. Even if it means sacrificing everything." Nike made billions from it.[6]

This is all to say that Kaepernick and everything around him was a Big Deal. He serves as an example—the quintessential illustration even—of the tension that erupts whenever an athlete (especially any athlete who is not white, male, cisgender, and/or straight) uses the platform of the traditionally conservative space of sports to push for change. Yet, there is a long, storied history of athletes doing exactly this. Whether or not sports fans want to believe it, the intersection of sports and politics is always there—as it has always been there. But Kaepernick's stand is also contemporaneous, part of a wave of athlete activism and protest during the second decade of the twenty-first century.

When we think about whom sports loves and whom it does not, the athlete who is politically silent falls into the former camp. The outspoken one—especially if espousing culturally progressive ideas—certainly falls into the latter.

Researchers Michael Serazio and Emily Thorson contend that "sports fans tend to harbor more right-leaning attitudes on economic and foreign policy issues, even as Republicans are no more likely than Democrats to follow most sports." Leagues and teams are risk-averse, striving for unruffled feathers, leaning hard on a status quo that works, and fearing anything that could upset that calm. Serazio and Thorson also argue, however, that fundamental ideas behind sports track more closely with conservative political ideas: "First and foremost, sports tell us fairly consistently—if not consistently fairly—that winners work hard and losers are lazy. That's not an irrelevant message in an era of economic inequality; you might even say that it helps determine your views on income taxation and government welfare." They found a correlation between sports fandom and the belief "that personal factors such as ambition and effort were more important than structural advantages such as hailing from a rich family or knowing the right people." Sports fans have more hawkish beliefs than nonfans and also "remain deeply conservative when it comes to gender norms or what scholars like to call hegemonic masculinity."[7]

Sports loves those who don't push against any of these beliefs, and so it is the actions of those who do that most often get told when we tell the story of how sports and politics overlap. But it's more complicated than that, to say the least. Although sports often serve as a space of activism and protest, they are also a site of propaganda. There are athletes—both conservative and progressive—who protest via the platforms afforded them by sports, including the physical space where they play; wealthy team owners who donate to politicians and lobby for tax breaks or subsidies for their teams; fans who use sports as a site for protest; governments who use them as sites for building nationalism; and politicians who use them on the campaign trail.

Watching sports will inevitably expose fans to politics, as sports and politics constantly become intertwined. How we each decide to respond to that reality will vary, but it is a reality we cannot escape—no matter how much we desire to do so.

————

Let's start with the athletes, as we so often do. Their activism tends to fall into two camps: active and passive. Amira Rose Davis, an assistant professor of history and African American studies at Pennsylvania State University, as well as an expert on the history of Black female athletes, differentiates between the two. Passive activism looks something like the first Black and brown athletes to desegregate a sport that was previously open only to white men, whereas active activism is an intentional action over and above participation in the sport that draws attention to social injustices.[8]

For example, Wilma Rudolph, a Black woman, won gold in the 100-meter, 200-meter, and 4x100-meter track relay at the 1960 Olympics. Those gold medals represent passive activism—a participation in sport that pushes on the comfortable and acceptable. Cheering for the US team meant cheering for a Black woman, and her success meant she received accolades and support that she otherwise would be denied in the Jim Crow South. But Rudolph also participated in active activism as well. She refused to participate in the parade that her hometown (Clarksville, Tennessee) wanted to hold in her honor because it was originally to be a segregated event. "Wilma's refusal to participate in this parade and with parade officials deciding to finally integrate the parade— which becomes one of the first integrated events that happened in Clarksville, Tennessee—that's activism," a type that Amira Rose Davis says was "under the radar." "It was a very clear marshaling of her platform."

Athletes who participate in either kind of activism face retaliation, mental and physical violence, and possible damage to their careers. And so, the history of athletes marshaling their platforms— passively as well as actively—is always one of change as much as it is one of backlash.

Athlete activism has a long history and is full of famous names. In 1947, Jackie Robinson broke the color barrier in Major League Baseball and went on to champion civil rights after his sports career ended. Muhammad Ali was the boxer who floated like a butterfly and stung like a bee. He also converted to Islam and was convicted of draft evasion for refusing to serve in the Vietnam War. The Supreme Court later overturned his conviction and he was granted conscientious objector status, but he still lost years from his career. Tommie Smith and John Carlos won the gold and bronze medals, respectively, for the United States in the 200-meter race at the 1968 Olympics and then raised their black-gloved fists while standing on the medal podium. Billie Jean King pushed for gender equality in tennis, and in 1973 she created the Women's Tennis Association, secured women the same paycheck as men at the US Open, and won a nationally televised exhibition match (dubbed "the Battle of the Sexes") against Bobby Riggs. As we discussed in chapter 4 about tennis, Venus Williams, in 2007, after years of work, persuaded Wimbledon—the last holdout for equal pay for women in tennis Grand Slams—to give equal prize money. She won the women's singles championship that year.[9]

But alongside the famous athletes who used their platforms for good are those who are less well known. "Rose Robinson was a high jumper out of Chicago who refused to go on a State Department-sponsored tour of West Africa at a time when the State Department was using black athletes, in particular, to be soft propaganda during the Cold War," Davis says. Robinson "refused to go and, coincidentally or not, about six months after her refusal to go on this trip that was sponsored by the [Amateur Athletic Union] and the State Department, she was jailed for tax evasion over $386."[10]

You may have heard (though most likely haven't) of Craig Hodges, an NBA player in the late 1980s and early 1990s who never played in the league again after attending the White House celebration of the 1992 champion Chicago Bulls. Hodges wore a dashiki ("the loose-fitting pullover which originated in West Africa as a functional work tunic for men") to the event and handed president George H. W. Bush a letter in which he urged the politician to take more seriously the issues facing Black Americans. After Hodges filed a lawsuit in 1996 against the NBA because he believed it blackballed him from the league for his political beliefs, he told the *New York Times*: "After the 1992 season, I or my agent had called every team in the N.B.A. and not one would even give me a tryout, let alone sign me." The lawsuit was dismissed because the judge believed Hodges hadn't filed it within the statute of limitations for racial discrimination cases.[11]

———

Toni Smith-Thompson is another of those lesser-known athletes, and her story shows that activism by athletes happens at all levels of sports, and for different reasons, but with similar intense pushback.

Smith-Thompson grew up in New York City and began playing basketball when she was nine or ten. She attended Manhattanville College, a small liberal arts college just outside the city. The school was predominantly white. Smith-Thompson is the daughter of a Black man and a white woman. She identifies as Black. Halfway through her time at Manhattanville, 9/11 happened. There were, she says, "significant changes on the court after the attacks." The American flag was added to the team jersey, and ceremonies were dedicated to alums who had died that day.[12]

These changes paralleled her studies, which included courses on "the prison-industrial complex, military-industrial complex, [and] gender studies," and furthered her development as an activist. "Senior year, I became the co-captain of the team and at the same time was . . . knee-deep in research on the impact that media has on our society and our consumerism."

Then she had a conversation with her boyfriend, who, like Toni, had a white mom and Black dad. "We shared those experiences of living in a country, being born in a country that does not want you and has targeted you, but knowing no other home," she says. "I really got clear that the way the flag and patriotism are used is not really representative of my life experience or my values or political beliefs, yet, it was something that I was expected to do in order to play basketball. [But it] really had nothing to do with basketball."

When her boyfriend asked why she was standing for the anthem and then challenged her answers, she couldn't "shake what I felt like was really the truth: that I didn't have to do this, I shouldn't have to do it." Smith-Thompson identified the basketball court as a specific place where she could practice those values. "I could kind of assert a different truth or a different way to engage in democracy," she says, "and if I didn't have the courage to do that, then what does that say about the kind of activist I say I am?" She was twenty-one years old.

And so, to protest the obligation to stand for the anthem, as well as the United States potentially going to war in Iraq, she decided to turn her back during the anthem. For two months she did this without much attention. And then she became the center of a national story.

On February 26, 2003, the *New York Times* wrote a piece about her: "Player's Protest Over the Flag Divides Fans."[13] Manhattanville was playing at home against the Merchant Marine Academy, and Smith-Thompson believes a coach or player from a previous opponent had called ahead to let that school know about her protest. To say it didn't go over well with the Merchant Marines is an understatement, and the result was something you rarely see in a Division III women's basketball game: a sold-out crowd.

Smith-Thompson remembers lots of American flags in the stands, "cadets in uniform lined up along the sideline holding six foot flags," and the taunting. "The whole game they were like, 'Go back to Iraq, you bitch,'" she recalls. "Curses and all kinds of other slurs. And they weren't really just directed at me, either. The slurs were aimed at the entire team." Manhattanville won, 67-51.

In comments she made to the media after the game, Smith-Thompson said: "A lot of people blindly stand up and salute the flag, but I feel that blindly facing the flag hurts more people. There are a lot of inequities in this country, and these are issues that needed to be acknowledged. The rich are getting richer and the poor are getting poorer, and our priorities are elsewhere." When a member of the media asked if her protest ("a half-revolution of the body," as Bill Pennington described it in the *New York Times*) would empower Saddam Hussein, Smith-Thompson replied coolly: "I doubt Saddam Hussein is watching me right now."

The president of Manhattanville supported her, as did her family, her coach, and the Black and Latinx student caucuses on campus. Her teammates were less supportive. Recalling a team meeting about the issue, Smith-Thompson says: "We just ended up having to agree to disagree. Then I was not on great terms with most of my team after that." There were two women on the team who had her back, standing on either side of her in the lineup before the game and holding her hand during the anthem. She received some credible death threats even while she received mail from around the world supporting her.

It was six weeks of her life, she believes, that the news media focused on her, though she admits it is hard to remember the exact time frame. It was a very lonely path to take, as friendships fell off and she felt like a pariah on campus. There was no social media at the time, only her immediate surroundings. And it affected her love of the game. "I was so jaded by the end of that season that I didn't want to do basketball anymore as a professional or other serious endeavor," she says. "A lot of it was really tainted for me."

However, this was the beginning of a journey that led her to become an organizer in the Advocacy Department of the New York Civil Liberties Union. And despite how hard her experience was, she believes that athletes who care about issues of social justice should use their platforms to draw attention to inequities and oppression. "I think athletes certainly occupy a very unique and important place because sports are our biggest public gathering place. The importance of sports is embedded into the culture itself."

But Smith-Thompson cautions that the message can't get lost in the commodification of sport. "How do we retain ownership over our own messaging so you don't have a protest against police violence turn into a stand for something even if it means sacrificing everything?" she asks, nodding to Kaepernick's Nike ad. These are necessary critiques in the current climate of athlete activism.

———

So far we've looked back to find athletes throughout history (some far in the past, some recent) protesting social injustices, but beginning in the early 2010s, and continuing today, we are witnessing a new wave—some might say avalanche—of athlete activism. In the age of social media, with the visibility and ubiquity of police violence, racist brutality, and the organization of movements against those things (such as Black Lives Matter), athletes started to mobilize. In 2012, LeBron James and Dwyane Wade, along with Miami Heat teammates, donned hoodies for a photo they captioned "We Are Trayvon Martin," referring to the seventeen-year-old Black kid who was shot to death by George Zimmerman while walking home from the store in his father's neighborhood in Sanford, Florida.[14]

In November 2014, NFL wide receivers Stedman Bailey, Tavon Austin, Chris Givens, and Kenny Britt and tight end Jared Cook, all of them with the St. Louis Rams, took the field during pregame introductions with their hands raised in the air, honoring eighteen-year-old Michael Brown, who was shot to death by officer Darren Wilson in neighboring Ferguson, Missouri. Later that year, football and basketball players donned "I Can't Breathe" shirts, echoing the final words of Eric Garner, a New York man who was choked to death by a cop in July 2014.[15] Also, in November 2015, University of Missouri football players went on strike in solidarity with Black students on campus, demanding the resignation of the university's president, Tom Wolfe, who had been heavily criticized for his poor response to racist attacks against Mizzou students. It took one day for Wolfe to resign.[16]

And then, of course, Kaepernick started kneeling in August 2016.[17] These high-profile protests received the most press and attention, but many other athletes were protesting under less publicized circumstances.

On November 29, 2014, a junior at Knox College took the basketball court at Fontbonne University in Clayton, Missouri, twenty minutes from Ferguson. After the national anthem played, Ariyana Smith laid down on the ground. And she refused to get up for four and a half minutes; after Darren Wilson shot and killed Michael Brown in Ferguson, it took four and a half hours for police to remove Brown's body from the scene. She then stood, raised her fist, and walked out of the gym. She later told Dave Zirin of *The Nation*, who dubbed her "the first athlete activist of #BlackLivesMatter," that

the point of what I did was to demonstrate why I felt and still feel so stifled [at Knox]. When it comes down to supporting students in the ways we need to be supported, not just when we're basketball players but supporting us when we take off our uniforms, that doesn't happen. Supporting us as academics, supporting us as black people, as survivors of sexual assault. That support isn't happening and marginalized voices are not being heard. So I had to do a physical demonstration.[18]

In the month before Kaepernick's first protest, women in the WNBA made, as Christina Cauterucci of *Slate* described it at the time, "one of the most united, persistent political statements in sports history." On July 9, 2016, following the police shooting and killing of Alton Sterling and Philando Castile (the latter near the city of Minneapolis), and the deadly ambush on police in Dallas, the Minnesota Lynx wore shirts honoring all of them. Then the New York Liberty did something similar the next day. Players for the Indiana Fever and Phoenix Mercury followed suit. The league tried to financially punish the players, who responded by calling out the league for refusing to fight racism. Players refused to talk to the media unless the questions were related to social justice, and they continued to wear shirts before and after games, though not on the court. The league eventually relented, rescinding the fines.[19]

Amira Rose Davis notes that women as athlete activists deserve much more space in our tellings of this history. They too have fought for "inclusion, for opportunities, for pay equity," all of which is active activism. But they are, instead, written and celebrated most often as passive activists. "You'll find that happening a lot with women," Davis says, "because it lets them be silent, smiling symbols, and not fully agents of change."

This is part of a larger pattern within activism generally. The work of women—especially Black women—in social justice movements is often overlooked, forgotten. But that is a false narrative and an unfair one, inside sports and outside. As Smith-Thompson says: "If you're telling a story about protest and resistance in a way that doesn't include women, you're telling the story wrong. It's not that we weren't there. It's that you're not telling it in a way that is including us."

———

No discussion about politics in sports is complete without looking at how nonathletes use sports as sites of protest and, in many cases, sites of propaganda. If we are going to chide athletes for how they use sports as a platform, then we must be willing to chide politicians, owners, and fans, too.

The most obvious place to start is politicians. They love sports.

Politics and sports have been intertwined in the United States for so long that, according to Kenneth Cohen of *Slate*, "Americans began describing elections as 'races,' a turn of phrase that uniquely arose in the United States during the 1810s and 1820s." Lots of politicians throw out the ceremonial first pitch at baseball games, including many presidents, or make the coin toss before a football game. During political campaigns or when trying to build support while in office, they visit local sporting events and sometimes even play a little. One headline, printed the day of the college football championship in January 2020, read: "Facing Iran and Impeachment, Donald Trump Reaches Out to Supporters at LSU-Clemson game." Some argue that George W. Bush's ownership of the Texas Rangers, and specifically his construction of their new stadium in 1993, paved the way for his run to the governor's mansion in Texas, which ultimately led to his successful campaign to be president.[20]

As we saw in chapter 12 on stadium financing, leagues and teams are, metaphorically, happy to get into bed with politicians when seeking subsidies for stadiums. That stadium Bush built in Arlington for the Rangers? Bush received huge subsidies from the city to do so. According to *Pacific Standard*, during the first fifteen years of the twenty-first century, "more than $12 billion in public money [was] spent on privately owned stadiums."[21]

Regular folks use the platform of sports, too, and much like athletes they use it to protest. It's a smart move because of how important sports are to our culture, and any interruption of matches will garner attention (but also anger).

Protests in the stands are often accomplished with a banner. Greenpeace activists unfurled a banner during a soccer match in 2013 in Switzerland, calling on jailed environmental activists in Russia to be released. In October 2014, protesters at a St. Louis Rams home game held a large white sheet reading "RAMS FANS KNOW ON AND OFF THE FIELD BLACK LIVES MATTER." Activists trying to stop a liquified natural gas project also dropped a banner at the Carolina Panthers stadium during a *Monday Night Football* broadcast. Women protesting Iran's banning of women from stadiums sometimes carry banners and hold them up if/when they are able to get into a match. And during the 2018 World Series, members of the TransLatin@ Coalition released a banner that was the large blue, white, and pink transgender flag on top of which was written "TRANS PEOPLE DESERVE TO LIVE."[22]

During the final of the Men's World Cup in 2018 in Russia, the biggest sporting match in the world, members of the Russian protest-art group Pussy Riot ran onto the field during the fifty-second minute. They were arrested, but the group quickly released a statement on Twitter saying, in part, that they wanted political prisoners freed, for the Russian government to stop illegal arrests at protests, to push for political competition, and to stop putting people in jail for no reason. As Masha Gessen wrote in the *New Yorker*: "And so Pussy Riot became the only people to make a meaningful statement about Russian politics during the World Cup. . . . They also created, on one of the biggest stages in the world, an image of unjust and arbitrary authority, the sort with which a hundred and forty-five million Russians live day to day."[23]

Governments love sports, too. They are great outlets for propaganda. The images of Hitler at the 1936 Summer Olympics in Berlin is the most obvious example, as he used the international competition to show off what he believed to be superior Aryan athletes. If we look back at the Cold War, sporting events played a big role. This is, in part, because governments used sports to spread messages around the world via athletes and athletic competitions. "During the 1950s and 1960s," according to Davis, "the State Department sponsored Goodwill Trips abroad as a key effort to bolster global perceptions of the United States during the Cold War. The US government sought to capitalize on Black musicians, artists, and athletes who would offer "living proof . . . of the great progress achieved by the race under the American democratic system."[24] There were also high-profile matchups that were proxies for larger international tensions. The "Miracle on Ice," when the underdog US men's hockey team beat the formidable Soviet Union team during the 1980 Olympics in Lake Placid, New York, was perhaps the most famous of all. It was followed up by the US boycott of the 1980 Summer Olympics in Moscow in protest of the USSR's invasion of Afghanistan. The Soviet Union returned the favor four years later when Los Angeles hosted the Summer Games.[25]

And then there is the United States in the post-9/11 world. Howard Bryant, a senior writer for ESPN and author of *The Heritage: Black Athletes, a Divided America, and the Politics of Patriotism*, says of his own son, who was born in 2004: "It's normal for him to see flags and flyovers and phony induction ceremonies, and to see cops in almost every camera shot. This sort of post 9-11 war on terror authoritarianism is normal to him."[26]

In 2015, it came out in a report commissioned by Senators John McCain and Jeff Flake that "in all, the military services reported $53 million in spending on marketing and advertising contracts with sports teams between 2012 and 2015. More than $10 million of that total was paid to teams in the National Football League (NFL), Major League Baseball (MLB), National Basketball Association (NBA), National Hockey League (NHL) and Major League Soccer (MLS)." NASCAR received $1.56 million in 2015 alone. Additionally, Department of Defense taxpayer dollars went to eighteen NFL teams, ten MLB teams, eight NBA teams, eight soccer teams, and six NHL teams, as well as the Iron Dog snowmobile race, Indiana University, and Purdue University. The DOD claimed this money was "integral to its recruiting efforts," but Flake and McCain, both Republicans, were upset at this paid patriotism. "What we take issue with," wrote Flake, "is the average fan thinking teams are doing this on behalf of the military."[27]

Bryant says that we have to think hard about these overlapping interests because "I want people to think about who we are, where we are, and why we are here." And he means literally "here." "In this space that we're in, where it is normal to have 50 law enforcement appreciation days across the Major League Baseball calendar, yet, people say they don't want sports to be political," Howard says. "But they want you to genuflect toward the police in between getting a hot dog and some cheese fries."

————

In the end, sports fans will always have to reckon with the reality that sports—whether we are watching or playing them—are political. That's that. Wishing it otherwise does not change it. This is brutally clear to Kaepernick, who will most likely never play in the NFL again. But his time in the NFL will not be his legacy.

In late February 2019, as pro-Confederate groups were rallying in Oxford, Mississippi, in protest of the University of Mississippi's decision to distance itself from its Confederate past, eight Ole Miss basketball players kneeled during the national anthem. Devontae Shuler, a sophomore guard on the team, said later: "I felt like I needed to stand up for my rights for righteousness sake. My emotions were just for the students. I didn't want anything to happen with us playing that game while the protest was going on. I felt like I couldn't pass that moment by without making a difference."[28]

During her 2018–2019 senior basketball season, University of Wisconsin forward Marsha Howard sat during the national anthem and prayed. "I want to be there for the [Black Wisconsin students], and let them know that I'm speaking up for us," she told ThinkProgress.[29]

In Cape Town, South Africa, in November 2018, according to the *Jerusalem Post*, "two Grade 9 students at" a Jewish middle school "'took a knee' in solidarity with Palestinians while Hatikva, the Israeli national anthem, was sung during an award ceremony last week, and were disciplined by the school for their protest."[30]

In August 2019, at the Pan American Games, an international competition for amateur athletes in the Americas that often features competitors who go on to compete in the Olympics, two US athletes made news by using their gold-medal platform. Race Imboden, a white fencer, kneeled on the podium, and later explained his decision: "We must call for change," he wrote on Twitter.

This week I am honored to represent Team USA at the Pan Am Games, taking home Gold and Bronze. My pride however has been cut short by the multiple shortcomings of the country I hold so dear to my heart. Racism, Gun Control, mistreatment of immigrants and a president who spreads hate are at the top of a long list. I chose to sacrifice my moment today at the top of the podium to call attention to issues that I believe need to be addressed. I encourage others to please use your platforms for empowerment and change.[31]

A day later, his USA teammate, the hammer-thrower Gwen Berry, a Black woman, raised her fist as the end of the US national anthem played—a throwback to the famous fists of Tommie Smith and John Carlos at the 1968 Mexico Olympics. Afterward, she told *USA Today* that she did this because "somebody has to talk about the things that are too uncomfortable to talk about. Somebody has to stand for all of the injustices that are going on in America and a president who's making it worse. It's too important to not say something."[32]

It's no surprise that when the IOC released a list for "what would constitute a protest, as opposed to expressing views," as discussed in chapter 13 on the Olympics, its "non-exhaustive list" was, in total, "displaying any political messaging, including signs or armbands," "gestures of a political nature, like a hand gesture or kneeling," and "refusing to follow the Ceremonies protocol." Like so much in sports and life, the line dividing political from non-political, or protest from advocacy, is thin and always moving. In response to the IOC's clarification of its policy, Henry Bushnell at Yahoo! Sports had some questions that threw the arbitrariness into relief: "What if an Australian athlete, whose family is devastated by wildfires back home, wears wristbands honoring the victims? Surely he would not be punished . . . but what if that same athlete criticizes politicians for failing to protect the forests, and criticizes world leaders for failing to curb climate change? Does that give his wristbands new meaning? Does that make them 'political'?" Well, does it?[33]

Athletes risk so much when they use their platforms as activists—but they can do so much good.

The Players Coalition, which originally was formed as an advocacy group by the NFL players Malcolm Jenkins and Anquan Boldin, both of whom supported Kaepernick and the reason behind his protest, made a deal with the NFL in November 2017. The league pledged $89 million to social justice organizations over the next seven years; the players would match it. Kaepernick and Eric Reid were not happy, and there was a fracture among players. Despite that, and people's concerns about anything NFL money touches, by early 2019 the Players Coalition had already helped in tangible ways in politics: successfully lobbying legislators and voters, raising the minimum age of children who could enter the juvenile justice system in Massachusetts from seven to twelve, and passing an amendment in Florida that restored the voting rights to over a million former felons. Whether or not Kaepernick likes the direction the Players Coalition is headed, there's no denying it exists because of his own bold actions.[34]

Journalist Chuck Modi has covered police shootings and killings of Black men, and he talked to some of the family members of the dead about what Kaepernick's protest has meant to them. Mike Brown Sr., whose eighteen-year-old son, Mike Brown, was shot to death in Ferguson, Missouri, by Darren Wilson, a white cop, in 2014, setting off months of protests for racial justice in the city, told Modi on the fifth anniversary of his son's death: "The stance that [Kaepernick] did for us, he didn't just do it for me. He did it for all of us. That was definitely big. . . . I really appreciate him standing up for Black and Brown." Another father, Cary Ball Sr., said: "My son, Cary Terrell Ball, Jr., was shot 21 times . . . with 25 bullet wounds in him. Now, for Kaepernick to take a knee, I believe it's a big stand. When he took that knee, he took the knee for my child. . . . He took a stand for justice and humanity." Veda Washington-Abusaleh, whose nephew, Alton Sterling, was killed by Baton Rouge police in July 2016—a death for which the Baton Rouge Police Chief later apologized—told Modi: "I love Kaepernick. I stand in solidarity with him until the day that I die." She said that Kaepernick made her feel supported and less alone.[35]

Despite the fact that these athletes are up against a sports system that is always political, usually conservative, and punishes those who step out of line, they continue to push back.

In February 2018, LeBron James and Kevin Durant talked to ESPN's Cari Champion about a host of things, including politics. James said Trump, the "appointed person," who has the "No. 1 job in America," is "someone who doesn't understand the people, and really don't give a fuck about the people." He went on: "At this time right now, with the president of the United States, it's at a bad time, and while we cannot change what comes out of that man's mouth, we can continue to alert the people that watch us, that listen to us, that this is not the way."[36]

Fox News TV host Laura Ingraham responded to James on her show: "It's always unwise to seek political advice from someone who gets paid $100 million a year to bounce a ball. Keep the political comments to yourselves. . . . Shut up and dribble."[37]

The following year, LeBron James released a documentary he helped produce that was about "the changing role of athletes in our fraught cultural and political environment, through the lens of the NBA." He titled it *Shut Up and Dribble*, making clear he had no intention to remain silent.[38]

CONCLUSION

As we've demonstrated in this book, no two fans experience fandom in the same way, and no two fans cope with the dilemmas of that fandom in the same way. Some fans are able to completely disengage from moral questions of sports; others have given up completely and stopped watching teams they love; and many fans lie somewhere in the middle of this broad spectrum.

The reason for such varied experiences—and varied coping strategies—is rooted in our core identities outside the world of sports. Sports fans are hard-wired in ways that can affect their attitudes and values, feelings and expectations, prejudices and failings, needs and wants—a whole range of emotions and psychological aspects of human behavior. This means that loving sports—and tolerating the business of sports—creates a legitimate psychological conundrum that deserves a book such as this to help us address all of it, from the bad actors to the glorious championship celebrations.

So what can we do from a psychological standpoint to cope with a sports world that creates such a sense of internal conflict within sports fans' psyches? We encourage readers to revisit the introduction, where we discuss the incisive observations provided by Dr. Susan K. Whitbourne (the Massachusetts professor and expert on the psychology of sports) on the link between fandom, family, and identity.

First and foremost, reconciling some of these dilemmas starts by being honest with—and kinder to—ourselves.

If we're *really* being honest about it, then sports fans need to recognize that the athletes we admire and cherish are human beings, and they may have problems of their own. "It doesn't mean you are an idiot or immoral person for wanting your team to win," Whitbourne cautions.

I think you just have to disengage your feelings about a player [or anyone else] who is . . . affiliated with the team and your desire to remain a fan. It's harder for a loyal fan. You have to see the cleansing as some sort of an improvement, and not [as] an admission that you are a bad person for liking this team. Give yourself permission not to feel like you have to defend them against all kinds of evidence to the contrary.

Using fandom to spark some positive change is a good place to start. Recall Tanya Bondurant, the Yankees fan who chose to donate to a domestic violence charity every time Aroldis Chapman recorded a strikeout. "I think that sounds like an excellent coping strategy," Whitbourne observes. "It starts to focus out toward larger issues and actually can do some good."

In addition, despite all of sports' negative aspects, sports can also provide a lot of positive things. Recognizing this dichotomy is key—even if sometimes we allow the positive to obscure the problematic. "You have to remember, too, that for all the really terrible people who do terrible things, there are some people who do amazing things. The good guys and the good women and the people you admire and respect—turn your attention to them," Whitbourne advises.

"You want to bring your attitudes and behaviors and values in concert," she continues. "I mean, everybody wants to. So finding a way to do that, I think, is a very great coping strategy. And if you're actually donating money to charity or to a good cause, so much better."

And yet—even though Whitbourne admits the total compartmentalization of "sticking to sports" might help push aside the uneasy feelings caused by the dilemmas inherent in fandom—it does little to reconcile those conflicting attitudes, behaviors, and values. "Once you start to go down that path, you get pretty far down and then really lose sight of your moral compass," she says. You can only stick your head in the sand for so long before you have to come up for air. Or, in our case, meet a deadline.

As huge sports fans ourselves—we make our livings writing about them, and trust us, we wouldn't do this if we didn't actually love sports—we know firsthand how hard it is to reassess your relationship to the sports you love. It's also devastating to find out that a sport or a team or an athlete that you have poured your heart and time into seems to care very little about you, or the players, or the communities that house and support it. The dilemma facing many sports fans is whether you stick with it, whether you try to change it from the inside, whether you make it into something you *wish* it was today and *hope* that it might some day become. Or do you wash your hands of it? Grieve for your loss? Find something else to fill that spot in the schedule? How and when do you draw a line in the sand? How do you decide when enough is enough?

We have no definitive answer to those questions. We are each left to decide the responses for ourselves.

―――

We'd like to close with some personal insights into our professional selves. For people like us, who are constantly consumed by sports, we find it next to impossible to shut ourselves off from both the good and the bad that comes with covering the athletes we're assigned and the teams we love. It's important to speak candidly: for readers, for ourselves and our families, and for all fans who find themselves loving sports.

Jessica

I have been writing and speaking out about gendered violence in college football for many years, and over that time my intense fandom—which was forged when I was a child and reached its zenith during my college days at Florida State, where I witnessed the football team win the national championship—has waned dramatically in recent years. The hard hits, the unpaid labor, and my up-close experience with the harmful risks the system encourages have made it hard to watch. I have lost my ability to make casual small talk about the sport, no longer plan my falls around the weekends

FSU plays Miami or the University of Florida, and I go long stretches without knowing which teams are ranked or how well my alma mater is (or, as the case has been, is not) doing. But I still cave to the fandom from time to time, rarely missing the College Football Playoffs, joining in on Thanksgiving viewings, and tuning in to the end of an FSU game just to see how it is going.

My ideas about FSU's mascot and related traditions, which we write about in chapter 3 on Native mascots, have also changed—and especially after working on this book. Listening and learning about the contestation of the Seminole mascot has made me toss out depictions of it from my house.

I'm still not sure how to give up the Olympics, my takes on doping are much more nuanced now, and I'm going to continue to watch March Madness while tweeting about how the players deserve to be paid.

—J. L.

Kavitha

Like Jessica, a lot of my sports coverage over the years has centered on domestic violence and sexual assault, as well as the eternal questions of how much, if anything, we learn from each incident.

In the course of writing this book, something cataclysmic happened in the sports world that wholly encapsulated all the conflict and tension we tried to cover here. When Kobe Bryant died, I was hit with this wave of emotions, just this profound sadness, but also a million thoughts about his complicated legacy. I can't overstate how much I loved Kobe growing up; I'm a die-hard Knicks fan, but I loved watching Kobe play. He was poetry on the court, and I related to him personally as the nerdy kid who was good at math but also loved sports. His persona as an outsider—as the player others didn't relate to because he spoke Italian and was more of a thinker—really resonated with me.

In February 2003, when I was fourteen years old, my parents and I went to Los Angeles for my birthday, and my mom and I went to a Lakers game. It was my first time at Staples Center and my first time seeing Kobe play live. (We couldn't afford Lakers-Knicks tickets at Madison Square Garden, but that's a whole other discussion.) I remember that game, and that feeling of witnessing Kobe, to this day.

Just a few months later, Kobe was arrested for sexual assault in Eagle, Colorado. At the time, I made every excuse for him and repeated every line of victim-blaming. It was so internalized; I was so young; but more than anything, I wanted him to be innocent. Fourteen-year-old Kavitha made every mistake that thirty-year-old Kavitha calls out from others.

In the years since, I've learned much, much more about the politics of rape. But in those years, Kobe also really seemed to grow, to change, to become the man and the father we'd hope him to be. It's grating when men profess to be feminists simply because they have daughters, but in Kobe's case it really does seem like being a father made him be a better man. His support for women's sports really did seem genuine, sparked by his support for his daughter, Gianna, a player herself. His second act was shaping up to be remarkable, and one of the many tragedies of his death is that we'll never know just how he got to that place.

And still, I'm torn. As a sexual assault survivor myself, it's particularly difficult for me to reconcile my fandom with instances of violence against women. I genuinely don't know if I believe Kobe transformed himself—that he learned and grew after potentially ruining that woman's life—simply because I so desperately want that to be true. I need that to be true. Because, you see, I still love Kobe Bryant; perhaps I never stopped loving him. Every time I see his photo or a highlight of him doing some ridiculous circus move at the rim, I at once feel the pure joy I had watching him play, profound sadness that he's no longer with us, and guilt over what my continued love for him means for the woman who says he raped her.

I'm grateful for the small strategies I picked up from the people we interviewed, even if sitting down during a game or donating to a domestic violence charity seems like a tiny act of good comparatively. Perhaps my hope in writing this book, and in the journalism Jessica and I practice in our daily lives, is that every word we print attempting to hold players and teams and institutions accountable can be a small step toward ultimately reconciling the dilemmas we face as sports fans. Perhaps this book was as much for us as it was for all of you.

—K. A. D.

Working on *Loving Sports When They Don't Love You Back* has given us hope. There is so far to go in so many ways, but at the same time, sports like tennis are diversifying, LGBTQ+ athletes are carving out a space for themselves, athletes from college superstars to WNBA players to professional baseball players are demanding deserving compensation, and owners and mega event organizers are subject to sustained, organized criticism. This is why we can't all just walk away. Sports are worth saving and changing.

———

One last thing before we go. We want to tell a quick story and leave you with some parting words from a woman we think would get where we are coming from.

In July 2019, on the steps of City Hall in New York City, Megan Rapinoe stood behind a podium. The purple-haired attacking midfielder for the US Women's National Soccer Team and girl-friend of the WNBA's Sue Bird was addressing the crowd there to celebrate the team's fourth World Cup championship, its second in a row. Rapinoe had been at the center of a contentious, high-pro-file debate over patriotism and politics for a few weeks, though the origins for it stretched back years.

In 2016, after the San Francisco 49ers quarterback Colin Kaepernick began to kneel during the national anthem as a form of protest against racial injustice and police violence, Rapinoe soon joined him, becoming the first white athlete to do so. She explained at the time that she felt compelled to do this because "I simply can-not stand for the kind of oppression this country is allowing against its own people. I have chosen to kneel because, in the words of Emma Lazarus, 'Until we are all free, we are none of us free.'"[1]

People were, to say the least, upset with her. When Rapinoe's professional NWSL team visited the Washington Spirit, the owner of the Spirit played the national anthem while the players were still in the locker room. Unlike Kaepernick, Rapinoe sometimes was kneeling while wearing a Team USA uniform before representing her country on the pitch. And so, US Soccer passed a policy forcing players to stand "respectfully" during the anthem.[2]

Rapinoe went back to standing but made a point of leaving her hands at her side and not singing. This made people mad, too.[3]

And then, midway through the World Cup in June 2019, a soccer site called Eight by Eight released a video that had been recorded behind the scenes months earlier during the reveal of the USWNT's kit for the tournament. When the filmmaker asked Rapinoe if she would go to the White House if the team won, Rapinoe, a vocal critic of the Trump administration, replied: "I'm not going to the fucking White House. No, I'm not going to the White House. We're not going to be invited. I doubt it." This wasn't a new position; she had told *Sports Illustrated* something similar in May.[4]

The Eight by Eight clip, though, went viral. Donald Trump responded, as he does, on Twitter, by citing Black unemployment levels, claiming teams love to visit the White House, chastising Rapinoe for disrespecting the flag, and scolding her: "Megan should WIN first before she TALKS! Finish the job!"

She did. Not only did the team win the whole thing (again), but Rapinoe was the tournament's best player (winner of the Golden Ball) and the highest scorer (winner of the Golden Boot). Still, people complained that she was dividing the country and being too political and not patriotic enough. As one *New York Post* columnist described Rapinoe: "Soccer was fun! But now it's as if Rapinoe dropped a Baby Ruth in the swimming pool everyone had been loving."[5]

Then came the ticker-tape parade in New York, followed by Rapinoe—with team members sitting on each side of her—standing at a podium in front of City Hall, addressing fans and the country after everything that had happened over the previous month. She talked for about seven minutes and ended by telling the crowd: "We have to be better. We have to love more, hate less. We gotta listen more and talk less." She said that this was everyone's responsibility. The USWNT, she went on, "does an incredible job of taking that on our shoulders, and understanding that position that we have and the platform that we have within this world. Yes, we play sports. Yes, we play soccer. Yes, we are female athletes but we're so much more than that." And then she turned the spotlight around and shone it onto the crowd—the fans attending in person and everyone else listening at home: "You're so much more than that. You're more than a fan. You're more than someone who just supports sports. You're more than someone who tunes in every four years. You're someone who walks these streets every single day. You interact with your community every single day. How do you make your community better? How do you make the people around you better?"

After telling people to "do what you can," and "be more, be better, be bigger than you've ever been before," she brought it back to her team. "If this team is any representation of what you can be when you do that, please take this as an example. This group is incredible. We took so much on our shoulders to be here today, to celebrate with you today, and we did it with a smile. So do the same for us, please, I ask you."

Sports can lead the way as much as they can impede progress. And so, we are asking sports and everyone involved in them to be more and to be better; like Rapinoe, we are asking that of fans as well. Like the USWNT team, with sports, we have to embrace the messy, yell loudly about its existence, and keep being great as we do it. Perhaps, ultimately, doing that work is what will allow us to continue loving sports until they love us back.

ACKNOWLEDGMENTS

We would like to thank our patient and thoughtful editor, Casey Kittrell, for everything, as well as the entire crew at University of Texas Press for getting this book to print. Jennifer Johnson-Blalock was the agent who got us started, and Liza Dawson got us over the finish line. We appreciate everyone who spoke to us for *Loving Sports*—for your wisdom and your time. We alone, though, accept responsibility for any errors or mistakes in this book.

Jessica
This book began in a coffee shop in Austin when Brian Contine handed me an idea in the selfless, kind way that is a hallmark of his friendship. I wouldn't have gotten through this without Dan Solomon, Shireen Ahmed, Brenda Elsey, Lindsay Gibbs, and Amira Rose Davis, the best friends and colleagues for whom a person could ask. Bless my therapist, seriously. GrassIron Gym, and Amalia Litras in particular, have given me strength both externally and internally. My parents and sister are always in my corner, and that means more to me than I can adequately express here. Aidan is my joy, and his presence in my life grounds me. Aaron, my rock. Thanks for always doing the dishes. Circle and thumbs-up. K, we got through it. I'm so glad.

Kavitha
This book would not have seen the light of day without the tireless effort and endless patience of my coauthor: J, I'll be thanking you for the rest of my life.

To my family: my parents, Mercy and Terry, and my sister and brother-in-law, Preeti (Akka) and Stephen, who have always supported me and instilled in me such unearned confidence that I believe I can do anything—including writing a book. To Tristian Thomas-Allen, the most stabilizing force in my unstable life.

To my mentors: Tim O'Brien, who for some reason believed I could be a sportswriter, and Toby Harshaw, the best editor I'll ever have—look at the monster you've created; S. Mitra Kalita, for always being there for me and my family; and Jane McManus, who has never allowed me to feel imposter syndrome and is the best example I know of women uplifting women.

To my people, who always keep me grounded, yet surrounded by love: my Stuy guys, my media gals, and my O'Flanagan's crew— you all know who you are. But especially: Doug Berns, Ian Murphy, and Peter Velez, who have known me better than anyone since high school; Marlenas McMahon-Purk, the most ride-or-die bitch you'll ever meet; Ruzan Sarwar, who somehow manages to stay close to me even from 10,000 miles away; Karen and Emily Claman, who have always brought music to my life; Jonathan August, my attorney (and my first sports editor); Emily Thomas, Sara Gates, and Meredith Bennett-Smith, who have been up close in every stage of my career with nothing but love and maybe a few bottles of wine; Stephanie Haberman, the only other person I know who will come to the opera house and the ballpark on the same day; Rossa Quinn, my favorite Irishman, my heart; Chris Hart, for always being there for 5 A.M. bourbon and 6 A.M. conversations—there's no one I'd rather argue with; Nicole Salicetti, the best example of hate turning to love; Kristen Busalacchi, who never suffers fools, especially when they try to talk sports to her; and Claudia Bombeck and Kim Simmons, for being my partners in crime at ballparks around the country—nay, the world.

All I can say is: Thank you. I love you. *Sláinte, l'chaim, santé, salut.*

NOTES

Introduction

1. Jenna West, "Megan Rapinoe on IOC's Ban on Political Protests at 2020 Olympics: 'We Will Not Be Silenced,'" *Sports Illustrated*, January 10, 2020, si.com /olympics/2020/01/10/megan-rapinoe-olympic-protests-reaction-tokyo.

2. Susan K. Whitbourne, telephone interview by Kavitha Davidson, January 16, 2020. Unless otherwise noted, related quotations are from this interview.

Chapter 1: Watching Football When We Know (Even a Little) about Brain Trauma

1. A. H. Hosseini and J. Lifshitz, "Brain Injury Forces of Moderate Magnitude Elicit the Fencing Response," *Medicine & Science in Sports & Exercise* 41, no. 9: 1687–1697, 2009.

2. Cindy Boren, "An ugly Hit That Left Texans' Tom Savage Shaking Brings Scrutiny to the NFL's Concussion Protocol Again," *Washington Post*, December 11, 2017, washingtonpost.com/news/early-lead/wp/2017/12/10/hit-that-left-texans -tom-savage-shaking-will-bring-scrutiny-to-the-nfls-concussion-protocol.

3. John McClain (tweet), @McClain_on_NFL, December 10, 2017, twitter. com/McClain_on_NFL/status/939944607575691265.

4. Kristie Rieken, "NFL Changes Concussion Protocol after Tom Savage Incident," Associated Press, December 29, 2017, boston.com/sports/nfl/2017/12/29 /nfl-changes-concussion-protocol-after-tom-savage-incident.

5. Erin Flynn, "What Is the NFL's Concussion Protocol?," *Sports Illustrated*, September 16, 2016, si.com/nfl/nfl-concussion-protocol-policy-history.

6. American Association of Neurological Surgeons (website), "Sports-related Head Injury," aans.org/Patients/Neurosurgical-Conditions-and-Treatments /Sports-related-Head-Injury.

7. Anahad O'Connor, "Really? Cycling Is the Top Sport for Head Injuries," *New York Times*, June 3, 2013, well.blogs.nytimes.com/2013/06/03/really-the -claim-cycling-is-the-top-sport-for-head-injuries.

8. Patrick Hruby, telephone interview by Jessica Luther, January 18, 2018. Unless otherwise noted, related quotations are from this interview.

9. Tom Goldman, "Repeated Head Hits, Not Just Concussions, May Lead to a Type of Chronic Brain Damage," NPR, January 18, 2018, npr.org/sections /health-shots/2018/01/18/578355877/repeated-head-hits-not-concussions -may-be-behind-a-type-of-chronic-brain-damage.

10. Boston University, CTE Center, "Frequently Asked Questions about CTE," bu.edu/cte/about/frequently-asked-questions.

11. Joe Ward, Josh Williams, and Sam Manchester, "110 N.F.L. Brains," *New York Times*, July 25, 2017, nytimes.com/interactive/2017/07/25/sports/football /nfl-cte.html.

12. Alan Schwarz, Walt Bogdanich, and Jacqueline Williams, "N.F.L.'s Flawed Concussion Research and Ties to Tobacco Industry," *New York Times*, March 24, 2016, nytimes.com/2016/03/25/sports/football/nfl-concussion-research-tobacco.html.

13. National Football League (website), "NFL Donates $30 million to National Institutes of Health," September 5, 2012, nfl.com/news/story /0ap1000000058447/article/nfl-donates-30-million-to-national-institutes-of -health.

14. John Branch, "N.F.L. Tried to Influence Concussion Research, Congressional Study Finds," *New York Times*, May 23, 2016, nytimes.com/2016/05/24 /sports/football/nfl-tried-to-influence-concussion-research-congressional -study-finds.html.

15. Juli Doshan, "High School Sports Injury Surveillance System Now in 10th Year," March 10, 2015, nfhs.org/articles/high-school-sports-injury-surveillance -system-now-in-10th-year.

16. The US Consumer Product Safety Commission tracks product-related injuries through a surveillance system that relies on data from hospitals: cpsc. gov/Research—Statistics/NEISS-Injury-Data. The American Association of Neurological Surgeons (aans.org/en/Patients/Neurosurgical-Conditions-and -Treatments/Sports-related-Head-Injury) notes the limits of this surveillance system: "The actual incidence of head injuries may potentially be much higher for two primary reasons. In the 2009 report, the CPSC excluded estimates for product categories that yielded 1,200 injuries or less, those that had very small sample counts and those that were limited to a small geographic area of the country. Additionally, many less severe head injuries are treated at physicians' offices, immediate care centers or are self-treated." And the way the AANS uses the USCPSC's surveillance system is to find the top "20 sports/recreational activities" that produce "head injuries treated in U.S. hospital emergency rooms." It's not a comprehensive look at the symptoms and treatments related to reported head injuries, only a count of the injuries themselves.

17. Dawn Comstock, telephone interview by Jessica Luther, July 10, 2017. Unless otherwise noted, related quotations are from this interview.

18. More girls are participating in football than ever before. Britni de la Cretaz took a critical look at what this means for girls and brain trauma in "More Girls Are Playing Football. Is That Progress?," *New York Times*, February 2, 2018, nytimes.com/2018/02/02/well/family/football-girls-concussions.html.

19. Lindsay Gibbs, "New Female Brain Bank Will Help Close the Gender Gap in Concussion Research," ThinkProgress, December 18, 2017, thinkprogress .org/first-female-brain-bank-concussion-research-7374ece547c2.

20. Amie Just, "Briana Scurry Embraces New Role as Women's Brain Health Advocate," *Washington Post*, June 19, 2016, washingtonpost.com /sports/briana-scurry-embraces-new-role-as-womens-brain-health -advocate/2016/06/19/17aad636-33d4-11e6-8758-d58e76e11b12_story .html?utm_term=.70a984c842f0.

21. "Brandi Chastain, Michelle Akers Launch Landmark CTE Study for Women's Soccer: "We Can't Ignore This Anymore," CBS News, June 27, 2019, cbsnews.com/news/brandi-chastain-michelle-akers-launch-landmark-cte -study-for-womens-soccer.

22. Liz Roscher, "Three Female Olympians Pledge to Donate Their Brains for Concussion Research," Yahoo! Sports, February 6, 2018, sports.yahoo .com/three-female-olympians-pledge-donate-brains-support-concussion -research-173354493.html.

23. Morty Ain, "Ashley Wagner on Injury Recovery and Career Longevity," ESPN, July 5, 2017, espn.com/olympics/story/_/page/espnwbodywagner/figure -skater-ashley-wagner-talks-concussions-costumes-collisions-body-2017.

24. Baxter Holmes, "BMX Star Mat Hoffman Says He's Had 100 Concussions," *Los Angeles Times*, July 2, 2012, articles.latimes.com/2012/jul/02/sports /la-sp-sn-hoffman-concussions-20120702.

25. Cheryl Rosenberg, "'Are we a ticking time bomb?' BMX Riders Face Up to Dangers of CTE," *The Guardian*, May 27, 2016, theguardian.com/sport/2016 /may/27/bmx-racers-cte-head-trauma-dave-mirra.

26. Deana Simonetto, telephone interview by Jessica Luther, December 15, 2017. Unless otherwise noted, related quotations are from this interview.

27. Brett Popplewell, "Inside the Controversial Concussion Lab That Could Save Football," *The Walrus*, August 16, 2017, thewalrus.ca/inside-the-controversial -concussion-lab-that-could-save-football.

28. Ken Belson, "N.F.L. Official Affirms Link Between Playing Football and C.T.E.," *New York Times*, March 14, 2016, nytimes.com/2016/03/15/sports/football /nfl-official-affirms-link-with-cte.html.

29. Ken Belson, "Canadian Football's Big Steps to Reduce Hits, a Contrast to the N.F.L.," *New York Times*, November 24, 2017, nytimes.com/2017/11/24/sports/football /canadian-footballs-big-steps-to-reduce-hits-a-contrast-to-the-nfl.html.

30. Joel Anderson, telephone interview by Jessica Luther, February 19, 2017. Unless otherwise noted, related quotations are from this interview.

31. "Super Bowl Confetti Made Entirely from Shredded Concussion Studies," *The Onion*, February 2, 2014, sports.theonion.com/super-bowl-confetti -made-entirely-from-shredded-concuss-1819591572.

32. Ken Belson and Alan Schwarz, "Concussion Treatment Cited in Suit Against N.F.L.," *New York Times*, July 20, 2011, nytimes.com/2011/07/21/sports /football/retired-players-sue-nfl-over-treatment-of-concussions.html.

33. "NFL, Ex-players Agree to $765M Settlement in Concussions Suit," Associated Press, August 29, 2013, nfl.com/news/story/0ap1000000235494/article /nfl-explayers-agree-to-765m-settlement-in-concussions-suit.

34. Patrick Hruby, "The Rejected NFL Concussion Settlement Appeal Leaves Former Players with CTE High and Dry," Vice Sports, April 19, 2016, vice.com /en_us/article/mgzvaa/the-rejected-nfl-concussion-settlement-appeal-leaves -former-players-with-cte-high-and-dry.

35. Brett Murphy and Gus Garcia-Robert, "NFL Players with Brain Trauma

Receive Notice of Settlements Stripped to Nothing," *USA Today*, October 27, 2018, usatoday.com/story/sports/nfl/2018/10/23/nfl-players-family-members -settlement/1736602002.

36. John Branch, "N.H.L. Commissioner Gary Bettman Continues to Deny C.T.E. Link," *New York Times*, July 26, 2016, nytimes.com/2016/07/27/sports /nhl-commissioner-gary-bettman-denies-cte-link.html. Michael McCann, "The Wins and Losses of the NHL's Tentative Concussion Lawsuit Settlement," *Sports Illustrated*, November 12, 2018, si.com/nhl/2018/11/13/nhl-concussion-law suit-settlement-wins-losses-former-players. John Branch, "The N.F.L. Has Been Consumed by the Concussion Issue. Why Hasn't the N.H.L.?," *New York Times*, May 31, 2019, nytimes.com/2019/05/31/sports/nhl-concussions-hockey -boogaard.html.

37. Nicholas Pollock, "Hockey's Next Head-Injury Reckoning," *Atlantic*, May 6, 2019, theatlantic.com/health/archive/2019/05/kelli-ewen-is-suing-the -nhl-over-dismissal-of-cte/588643.

38. Ken Belson, "Playing Tackle Football Before 12 Is Tied to Brain Problems Later," *New York Times*, September 19, 2017, nytimes.com/2017/09/19/sports /football/tackle-football-brain-youth.html.

39. Brian Murphy, "'I don't know that we need football as a thing.' Families Flee America's Favorite Sport," *News & Observer*, January 29, 2018, newsobserver .com/news/politics-government/politics-columns-blogs/under-the-dome /article197213314.html.

40. Sarah Petz, "High School Football Game Ends after 9 Players Suffer Head Injuries," *CBC News*, October 15, 2017, cbc.ca/news/canada/new-brunswick /football-game-head-injuries-olympiens-titans-1.4355765?cmp=rss.

41. Kimberly Archie, telephone interview by Jessica Luther, December 15, 2016. Unless otherwise noted, related quotations are from this interview.

Chapter 2: Forgiving the Doper You Love

1. Jeremy Schwartz, "Yellow Fever Reigns as Austin Celebrates Lance; to Cheers of 40,000, the Six-Time Tour de France Champ Takes His Hometown Stage," *Austin American-Statesman*, August 14, 2004, A1.

2. Most comprehensive re-telling of Armstrong rise and fall is Juliet Macur's *Cycle of Lies: The Fall of Lance Armstrong* (New York: Harper, 2014).

3. United States Anti-Doping Agency (website), "Statement from USADA CEO Travis T. Tygart Regarding the U.S. Postal Service Pro Cycling Team Doping Conspiracy," October 10, 2012, cyclinginvestigation.usada.org.

4. "Lance Armstrong & Oprah Winfrey: Interview Transcript," *BBC Sport*, January 18, 2013, bbc.com/sport/cycling/21065539.

5. Michael Hall, "The Man Who Fell to Earth," *Texas Monthly*, March 2013, texasmonthly.com/articles/the-man-who-fell-to-earth.

6. Joshua Rothman, "Just What's Wrong with Doping?," *Boston Globe*, July 15, 2012, bostonglobe.com/ideas/2012/07/14/what-really-wrong-with-sports -doping/qO1GZhk7ay36zoh8GMM18N/story.html.

7. Matthew P. Llewellyn and John Gleaves, *The Rise and Fall of Olympic Amateurism*, Kindle ed. (Urbana: University of Illinois Press, August 2016), location

2122, 2134, 2148; Ian Ritchie, "Cops and Robbers? The Roots of Anti-Doping Policies in Olympic Sport," *Origins* 9, no. 6 (March 2016), origins.osu.edu /article/cops-and-robbers-roots-anti-doping-policies-olympic-sport.

8. Thomas Hunt, telephone interview by Jessica Luther, June 13, 2017. Unless otherwise noted, related quotations are from this interview.

9. Norman Fost, "'Doping' Is Pejorative and Misleading," *BMJ: British Medical Journal* 337, no. 7663 (July 26, 2008): 189.

10. Norman Fost, "Stop the Steroid Witch Hunts," *USA Today*, June 20, 2012.

11. Aaron Gordon, telephone interview by Jessica Luther, July 20, 2017. Unless otherwise noted, related quotations are from this interview. Gina Kolata, "The Flutter Over Heart Rate" *New York Times*, April 10, 2008, nytimes.com/2008 /04/10/health/nutrition/10BEST.html.

12. Alex Hutchinson, "When Doping Isn't Cheating," *New York Times*, November 29, 2014, nytimes.com/2014/11/30/opinion/sunday/when-doping-isnt -cheating.html?_r=1. Aaron Gordon, "How Does WADA Decide What Drugs Are Banned?," Vice Sports, July 13, 2017, sports.vice.com/en_us/article/8xavbp/how -does-wada-decide-what-drugs-are-banned.

13. Mayo Clinic (website), "Performance-enhancing Drugs: Know the Risks," mayoclinic.org/healthy-lifestyle/fitness/in-depth/performance-enhancing -drugs/art-20046134.

14. World Anti-Doping Agency (website), "Dangers of Doping: Get the Facts," October 1, 2009, wada-ama.org/en/resources/education-and-prevention /dangers-of-doping-get-the-facts. Emphasis in original.

15. Jack Moore, "A Brief History of Performance Enhancing Drugs," Vice Sports, September 10, 2014, sports.vice.com/en_us/article/xyjkez/a-brief-history -of-performance-enhancing-drugs. SI Staff, "How We Got Here," *Sports Illustrated*, March 11, 2008, si.com/more-sports/2008/03/11/steroid-timeline.

16. Mary Pilon, "Sprinter in 1988 Olympic Scandal Deplores Doping," *New York Times*, September 4, 2013, nytimes.com/2013/09/05/sports/ben-johnson -sprinter-in-1988-scandal-denounces-doping.html.

17. Cork Gaines, "Crazy Stat Shows Just How Common Doping Was in Cycling When Lance Armstrong Was Winning the Tour de France," *Business Insider*, January 2, 2015, businessinsider.com/lance-armstrong-doping-tour-de -france-2015-1. Teddy Cutler, "Cycling in the EPO Era: 65 Percent Juiced . . . and Probably More," Sportingintelligence, December 31, 2014, sportingintelligence .com/2014/12/31/cycling-in-the-epo-era-65-per-cent-dirty-and-probably -more-311201.

18. John Leicester, "Tour Is Once Again Tainted by Drugs Just Before Race Begins," Associated Press, July 1, 2017, registerguard.com/rg/sports/35727439-81 /tour-is-once-again-tainted-by-drugs-just-before-race-begins.html.csp.

19. Kate Kelland, "Doping: EPO Does Little for Cyclists' Race Performance, Study Finds," Reuters, June 30, 2017, reuters.com/article/us-sport-doping -epo-idUSKBN19L1EE.

20. Rebecca R. Ruiz and Michael Schwirtz, "Russian Insider Says State-Run Doping Fueled Olympic Gold," *New York Times*, May 12, 2016, nytimes.com/2016 /05/13/sports/russia-doping-sochi-olympics-2014.html.

21. Tariq Panja, "Russia Banned from Olympics and Global Sports for 4 Years Over Doping," *New York Times*, December 10, 2019, nytimes.com/2019/12/09 /sports/russia-doping-ban.html.

22. Andrew Keh and Tariq Panja, "The Russia Ban That Isn't Really a Ban Stokes Anger," *New York Times*, December 10, 2019, nytimes.com/2019/12/10 /sports/Russia-doping.html.

23. "BALCO Scandal Goes Deep," *San Francisco Chronicle*, December 3, 2004, sfchronicle.com/opinion/editorials/article/BALCO-scandal-goes-deep -2667246.php. Mark Fainaru-Wada, "Graham Admits BALCO Role," *San Francisco Chronicle*, August 23, 2004, sfchronicle.com/sports/article/Graham -admits-BALCO-role-2699809.php. Helene Elliott, "Rio Olympics: Justin Gatlin Defends His Past, Moves Forward in Men's 100," *Los Angeles Times*, August 27, 2016, latimes.com/sports/olympics/la-sp-oly-rio-2016-gatlin-defends -his-past-moves-forward-1471107703-htmlstory.html. Sarah Bridge, "Athlete Jones Stripped of Olympic Medals," *The Guardian*, December 12, 2007, theguardian.com/world/2007/dec/12/usa.athletics.

24. "McGwire Admits Nothing; Sosa and Palmeiro Deny Use," ESPN.com news services, March 18, 2005, espn.com/mlb/news/story?id=2015420.

25. "McGwire Apologizes to La Russa, Selig," ESPN.com news services, January 12, 2010, espn.com/mlb/news/story?id=4816607.

26. Keith Law, telephone interview by Jessica Luther, June 19, 2017, and July 20, 2017. Unless otherwise noted, related quotations are from this interview.

27. Rachel Axon and Nick McCarvel, "Maria Sharapova Receives Two-year Ban for Meldonium Use," *USA Today*, June 8, 2016, usatoday.com/story/sports /tennis/2016/06/08/maria-sharapova-receives-two-year-ban-meldonium -use/85285912.

28. Emmett Knowlton, "Former NFL Player Thinks Performance-Enhancing Drugs Are on the Rise in the NFL," *Business Insider*, November 4, 2015, businessinsider.com/brady-quinn-peds-nfl-injuries-2015-11.

29. Michael S. Schmidt and Duff Wilson, "Ex-N.F.L. Player Pleads Guilty in Balco Case," *New York Times*, January 19, 2008, nytimes.com/2008/01/19/sports /football/19doping.html. "Probe of Supplement Lab Continues," Associated Press, December 11, 2003, espn.com/gen/news/2003/1211/1683995.html. "Romo Tells '60 Minutes' He Used Steroids," Associated Press, October 13, 2005, espn .com/nfl/news/story?id=2190441.

30. Nick Zaccardi, "Olympian Failed Drug Test Due to 'Frequent, Passionate' Kissing," NBC Sports, July 14, 2017, olympics.nbcsports.com/2017/07/14/gil -roberts-kissing-drug-test-doping.

31. Aaron Gordon, "The Five-buck Bump of Cocaine That Destroyed an Olympic Dream," Vice Sports, July 13, 2017, sports.vice.com/en_us/article /padq5y/the-five-buck-bump-of-cocaine-that-destroyed-an-olympic-dream.

32. GLAAD (website), "GLAAD Media Reference Guide—Transgender," glaad.org/reference/transgender. InterACT Youth (website), "Trans? Intersex? Explained!," interactyouth.org/post/100048044990/laverne-cox-is-on-this -weeks-faking-it-in-honor. Ruth Padawer, "The Humiliating Practice of Sex-Testing Female Athletes," *New York Times*, June 28, 2016, nytimes

.com/2016/07/03/magazine/the-humiliating-practice-of-sex-testing-female
-athletes.html?_r=2.

33. For more, see Natasha Singer, "Does Testosterone Build a Better Athlete?," *New York Times*, August 10, 2006, nytimes.com/2006/08/10/fashion
/10Fitness.html.

34. Lindsay Crouse, "When One of the World's Most Visible Athletes Is Told
She Can't Be One," *New York Times*, May 4, 2019, nytimes.com/2019/05/04
/opinion/sunday/caster-semenya-running.html. Katrina Karkazis, "Stop
Talking about Testosterone—There's No Such Thing as a 'True Sex,'" *The Guardian*, March 6, 2019, theguardian.com/commentisfree/2019/mar/06/testosterone
-biological-sex-sports-bodies.

35. Andy Bull, "IAAF Accused of 'Blatant Racism' Over New Testosterone
Level Regulations," *The Guardian*, April 27, 2018, theguardian.com/sport/2018
/apr/27/iaaf-accused-blatant-racism-over-new-testosterone-regulations
-caster-semenya.

36. Marissa Payne, "Move Over, Blood Doping; Cyclists Might Be 'Poop Doping' Soon," *Washington Post*, June 21, 2017, washingtonpost.com/news/early-lead
/wp/2017/06/20/move-over-blood-doping-cyclists-might-be-poop-doping
-soon/?utm_term=.69cd5228de90.

37. For example, see John Horgan, "Could Olympians Be Tweaking Their
Genes?," *Scientific American*, July 26, 2016, blogs.scientificamerican.com
/cross-check/could-olympians-be-tweaking-their-genes.

38. Aaron Gordon, "How Does WADA Decide What Drugs Are Banned?," Vice
Sports, July 13, 2017, sports.vice.com/en_us/article/8xavbp/how-does
-wada-decide-what-drugs-are-banned. Aaron Gordon, "We Asked Veteran
Track & Field Athletes How to Possibly Fix the Doping Problem," Vice Sports,
February 27, 2017, sports.vice.com/en_us/article/pgnz8v/we-asked-veteran
-track-field-athletes-how-to-possibly-fix-the-doping-problem.

39. Jan Todd, personal interview by Jessica Luther, June 20, 2017, University
of Texas. Unless otherwise noted, related quotations are from this interview.

40. Clean Sport Collective (website), cleansport.org.

41. Juliet Macur, "Tour de France Analysis from Its Most Infamous Rider:
Lance Armstrong," *New York Times*, July 18, 2017, nytimes.com/2017/07/18/sports
/cycling/lance-armstrong-tour-de-france-podcast-blog.html.

Chapter 3: Cheering for a Team with a Racist Mascot

1. If you look up "redskin" in the dictionary, it's defined as a slur. And
as such, this is the only time we will write it in this chapter. We will refer to
the team as "the Washington NFL team." If we need to refer to that word in
particular, we use r*dskin(s), as author C. Richard King does in his book by the
same name. He explains that putting the asterisk in the word reminds readers
each time of the word's "unspeakable, problematic nature." C. Richard King,
Redskins: Insult and Brand (Lincoln: University of Nebraska Press, 2016), xii.

2. There are a range of terms to describe Native peoples, including "Indigenous" and "Indian." For this chapter, we use "Native" as an all-encompassing
term while noting that this is not, in fact, all-encompassing.

3. "Not Your Mascot Rally," Facebook Event Page, September 17, 2017, facebook.com/events/514700648863086.

4. Temryss Lane, telephone interview by Jessica Luther, September 20, 2017. Unless otherwise noted, related quotations are from this interview.

5. N7 Ambassadors (website), n7fund.com/ambassadors.

6. Ariel Zambelich and Cassi Alexandra, "In Their Own Words: The 'Water Protectors' of Standing Rock," NPR, December 11, 2016, npr .org/2016/12/11/505147166/in-their-own-words-the-water-protectors-of -standing-rock.

7. "Native mascotry" is a term coined by the activist Jacqueline Keeler.

8. That scholar is Colin Calloway, and in his *First Peoples: A Documentary Survey of American Indian History*, 4th ed. (Boston: Bedford/St. Martin's, 2011), 83–84, he gives more specifics: "The population of Hispaniola was estimated at some 8 million in 1492, but by 1535 the original inhabitants were all but extinct; the Native population of Mexico dropped from an estimated 25 million in 1519 to perhaps 1.3 million by the end of the century; Peru's population dwindled from as high as 9 million to a half million in 1600." Another example of this is from Daniel Richter's *Facing East from Indian Country: A Native History of Early America* (Cambridge: Harvard University Press, 2001), 7: "Exact statistics will never be known, but in 1492 the diverse but interconnected areas east of the Mississippi may have been home to more than 2 million Native people. . . . By 1750 the population balance had shifted decisively, with Europeans and their enslaved African workforce exploding to nearly 1.25 million and the Native population probably shrinking to less than 250,000."

9. Benjamin Madley, "It's Time to Acknowledge the Genocide of California's Indians," *Los Angeles Times*, May 22, 2016, latimes.com/opinion/op-ed/la -oe-madley-california-genocide-20160522-snap-story.html.

10. Spencer Phips, "A Proclamation," 1755, static1.squarespace.com/static /54f8b4cfe4b0b230c7abfe97/t/58de6185f5e231507d67da73/1490968965807 /Phips+Bounty+Proclamation+Broadside.pdf.

11. Baxter Holmes, "A 'Redskin' Is the Scalped Head of a Native American, Sold, Like a Pelt, for Cash," *Esquire*, June 17, 2014, esquire.com/news-politics /news/a29445/true-redskins-meaning. There are challenges to this etymology of the word. King, *Redskins*, 12–17, addresses different possible origins of the term (including Holmes's). All of the possible etymologies, though, have roots in violent colonization and oppression.

12. Baxter Holmes, "Update: Yes, a 'Redskin' Does, in Fact, Mean the Scalped Head of a Native American, Sold, Like a Pelt, for Cash," *Esquire*, June 18, 2014, esquire.com/news-politics/news/a29318/redskin-name-update.

13. *Los Angeles Herald* 27, no. 24, October 24, 1897, reprinted at UC-Riverside's Center for Bibliographical Studies and Research, California Digital Newspaper Collection, cdnc.ucr.edu/cgi-bin/cdnc?a=d&d=LAH18971024.2.212.

14. "Hopi Prisoners on the Rock," National Park Service, nps.gov/alca/learn /historyculture/hopi-prisoners-on-the-rock.htm.

15. Calloway, *First Peoples*, 435.

16. King, *Redskins*, 20, 31.

17. King, 9.

18. Sally Jenkins, "Why Are Jim Thorpe's Olympic Records Still Not Recognized?," *Smithsonian Magazine*, July 2012, smithsonianmag.com/history/why -are-jim-thorpes-olympic-records-still-not-recognized-130986336.

19. Richard Leiby, "The Legend of Lone Star Dietz: Redskins Namesake, Coach—And Possible Impostor?," *Washington Post*, November 6, 2013, washingtonpost.com/lifestyle/style/the-legend-of-lone-star-dietz-redskins -namesake-coach—and-possible-imposter/2013/11/06/a1358a76-466b-11e3 -bf0c-cebf37c6f484_story.html.

20. Bill Mears, "Court Rejects Appeal Over Redskins Trademark," CNN, November 16, 2009, cnn.com/2009/CRIME/11/16/scotus.redskins/index.html.

21. National Congress of American Indians, "Ending the Era of Harmful 'Indian' Mascots," ncai.org/proudtobe.

22. Cleveland American Indian Movement (website), "About Cleveland American Indian Movement," clevelandaim.us/aim.

23. "In Whose Honor?," website, jayrosenstein.com/pages/honorfilm.html.

24. Shannon Ryan, "Illinois Must Finally Remove All Links to Chief Illiniwek," *Chicago Tribune*, August 26, 2017, chicagotribune.com/sports/columnists /ct-illinois-chief-illiniwek-ryan-spt-0827-20170826-column.html.

25. "NCAA American Indian Mascot Ban Will Begin Feb. 1," ESPN, August 12, 2005, espn.com/college-sports/news/story?id=2125735.

26. Amy Wimmer Schwarb, "Where Pride Meets Prejudice," *NCAA Champion Magazine*, Winter 2016, ncaa.org/static/champion/where-pride-meets -prejudice/index.php.

27. Florida State University (website), "Relationship with the Seminole Tribe of Florida," unicomm.fsu.edu/messages/relationship-seminole-tribe-florida.

28. Perry Kostidakis, "SGA Passes Resolution Discouraging Headdresses at Games," *FSView*, May 3, 2016, fsunews.com/story/news/2016/05/03 /fsu-sga-passes-resolution-banning-headdresses-games/83871296.

29. Florida State University, "Relationship with the Seminole Tribe."

30. Chuck Culpepper, "Florida State's Unusual Bond with Seminole Tribe Puts Mascot Debate in a Different Light," *Washington Post*, December 29, 2014, washingtonpost.com/sports/colleges/florida-states-unusual-bond-with -seminole-tribe-puts-mascot-debate-in-a-different-light/2014/12/29/5386841a -8eea-11e4-ba53-a477d66580ed_story.html?utm_term=.d3ebd14c7dca.

31. Florida Department of State (website), "Seminole History," dos .myflorida.com/florida-facts/florida-history/seminole-history.

32. Jacqueline Keeler, telephone interview by Jessica Luther, June 21, 2017. Unless otherwise noted, related quotations are from this interview.

33. Schwarb, "Where Pride Meets Prejudice," 2006.

34. Erik Brady, "Daniel Snyder Says Redskins Will Never Change Name," *USA Today*, May 9, 2013, usatoday.com/story/sports/nfl/redskins/2013/05/09 /washington-redskins-daniel-snyder/2148127.

35. Adrienne Keene, telephone interview by Jessica Luther, July 17, 2017. Unless otherwise noted, related quotations are from this interview.

36. Adrienne Keene, "10 Examples of Indian Mascots 'Honoring' Native

Peoples," *Native Appropriations*, December 8, 2013, nativeappropriations
.com/2013/12/10-examples-of-indian-mascots-honoring-native-peoples.html.

37. Jacqueline Keeler, telephone interview by Jessica Luther, July 17, 2017.

38. Stephanie A. Fryberg, Hazel Rose Markus, Daphna Oyserman, and Joseph M. Stone, "Of Warrior Chiefs and Indian Princesses: The Psychological Consequences of American Indian Mascots," *Basic and Applied Social Psychology* 30, no. 3 (September 2008): 208–218.

39. *Jody Tallbear v. Ernest Moniz*, Case No. 1:17-cv-00025, United States District Court for the District of Columbia, January 5, 2017.

40. Andre B. Rosay, "Violence Against American Indian and Alaska Native Women and Men," Department of Justice's National Institute of Justice, May 2016. The numbers are also very high, though not nearly as high as women, for male Native and Indigenous victims of sexual violence (25 percent have experienced sexual violence; roughly 30 percent of perpetrators are non-Native).

41. adidas (website), "adidas Announces Support for Mascot Name Changes Ahead of White House Tribal Nations Conference," November 5, 2015, news. adidas.com/US/Latest-News/ALL/adidas-Announces-Support-For-Mascot -Name-Changes-Ahead-Of-White-House-Tribal-Nations-Conference/s /7197ec89-d0fe-4557-b737-cd27dc76aba1.

42. John Woodrow Cox, "Adidas Stand Against Native American High School Mascots Praised by Obama, Condemned by Redskins," *Washington Post*, November 5, 2015, washingtonpost.com/news/local/wp/2015/11/05/rgiii-sponsor -adidas-announces-support-for-high-schools-that-want-to-drop-native -american-mascots/?utm_term=.eeeefbf3ebf6. Change the Mascot responded to the Washington NFL team's condemnation: "Change the Mascot Blasts R-dskins Statement on adidas," changethemascot.org/wp-content/uploads /2015/11/Change-the-Mascot-Response-to-Washington-Team-on-adidas.pdf.

43. Nick Martin, "NFL Assures Fans There's No Tolerance for Racial Slurs at Redskins Games," Deadspin, October 5, 2017, deadspin.com/nfl-assures-fans -theres-no-tolerance-for-racial-slurs-i-1819182310.

44. Gene Demby, "Which Outlets Aren't Calling the Redskins 'The Redskins'? A Short History," NPR, August 25, 2014, npr.org/sections/codeswitch /2014/08/25/343202344/which-outlets-arent-calling-the-redskins-the -redskins-a-short-history.

45. Monica Anderson, "Media Take Sides on 'Redskins' Name," Pew Research Center, October 30, 2013, pewresearch.org/fact-tank/2013/10/30/media-take -sides-on-redskins-name.

46. "Washington Post Editorials Will No Longer Use 'Redskins' for the Local NFL Team," *Washington Post*, August 22, 2014, washingtonpost.com/opinions /washington-post-editorials-will-no-longer-use-redskins-for-the-local-nfl -team/2014/08/22/1413db62-2940-11e4-958c-268a320a60ce_story.html?utm _term=.d77fe715a974.

Chapter 4: Embracing Tennis despite Its Inequities

1. "The Greatest of All Time," *Los Angeles Times*, August 29, 2016, latimes.com /projects/la-sp-serena-williams-greatest-all-time.

2. "How Serena Won Wimbledon," IBM, July 9, 2016, ibm.com/blogs/game
-changers/how-serena-won-wimbledon.

3. Steve Tignor, "An Act of Serena," Tennis.com, July 9, 2016, tennis.com
/pro-game/2016/07/act-serena/59449.

4. Melissa Isaacson, "How Serena Williams Has Mastered the Art of the
Comeback," ESPN, June 26, 2015, espn.com/espnw/news-commentary/article
/13142903/how-serena-williams-mastered-art-comeback.

5. Elena Bergeron, "How Serena Williams Became the G.O.A.T.," The Fader,
October 4, 2016, thefader.com/2016/10/04/serena-williams-interview
-cover-story.

6. Serena Williams, "Serena Williams Poses Unretouched for Harper's
BAZAAR," *Harper's Bazaar*, July 9, 2019, harpersbazaar.com/culture/features
/a28209579/serena-williams-us-open-2018-essay.

7. Wimbledon (website), "History," wimbledon.com/en_GB/atoz/history
.html.

8. Ben Rothenberg, "All-White Is the Style, Whether the Players Appreciate
It or Not," *New York Times*, July 4, 2014, nytimes.com/2014/07/05/sports/tennis
/at-wimbledon-white-is-in-style-whether-players-like-it-or-not.html.

9. Wimbledon (website), "Clothing and Equipment," wimbledon.com
/en_GB/atoz/clothing_and_equipment.html.

10. Wimbledon (website), "Prize Money and Finance," wimbledon.com
/en_GB/atoz/prize_money_and_finance.html.

11. Nadja Popovich, "Battle of the Sexes: Charting How Women in Tennis
Achieved Equal Pay," *The Guardian*, September 11, 2015, theguardian.com
/sport/2015/sep/11/how-women-in-tennis-achieved-equal-pay-us-open.

12. Alison Muscatine, "Top Women Players Argue for Equal Pay," *Washington
Post*, April 24, 1991, washingtonpost.com/archive/sports/1991/04/24/top
-women-players-argue-for-equal-pay.

13. "Venus Vs.," Part of ESPN's *Nine for IX* documentary series, directed by Ava
Duvernay, 2013.

14. Venus Williams, "Wimbledon Has Sent Me a Message: I'm Only a
Second Class Champion," *London Times*, June 26, 2006, thetimes.co.uk/article
/wimbledon-has-sent-me-a-message-im-only-a-second-class-champion
-f056h05hmzq.

15. BNP Paribas Open (website), "About," bnpparibasopen.com/en/visit-us.

16. "Indian Wells CEO Issues Apology for Sexist Comments; Serena
Williams Reacts," *Tennis Panorama*, March 20, 2016, tennispanorama.com
/archives/54982.

17. "Novak Djokovic: Men's Tennis Should Fight for More Prize Money Than
Women," Associated Press/*The Guardian*, March 21, 2016, theguardian.com
/sport/2016/mar/21/novak-djokovic-indian-wells-equal-prize-money-tennis.

18. "Novak Djokovic," *Forbes*, July 11, 2016, forbes.com/profile/novak-djokovic
/?list=athletes. ATP World Tour, "Djokovic Passes $100 Million Prize Money
Milestone," June 1, 2016, atpworldtour.com/en/news/djokovic-100-million
-prize-money-milestone.

19. WTA Tennis (website), "Serena Williams," wtatennis.com/players

/player/230234/title/Serena-Williams. Kurt Badenhausen, "Serena Williams Tops Sharapova as the World's Highest-Paid Female Athlete," *Forbes*, June 6, 2016, forbes.com/sites/kurtbadenhausen/2016/06/06/serena-tops-sharapova-as-the-worlds-highest-paid-female-athlete/#7b1c01ec1fda. "Federer Leads *Forbes* List in Endorsements," ATP World Tour, ATP, September 22, 2016, atpworldtour.com/en/news/federer-leads-atp-stars-on-forbes-list-2016.

20. Joe O'Connor, "Game, Set and Sexism in Today's Tennis," *National Post*, September 10, 2011, news.nationalpost.com/full-comment/game-set-and-sexism-in-todays-tennis. "WTA Chief Says Women 'Ready, Willing' for Five Sets," Agence-France Presse/NDTV Sports, September 24, 2013, sports.ndtv.com/tennis/wta-chief-says-women-ready-willing-for-five-sets-1529750. Lindsay Gibbs, "Why Women Don't Play Best-of-five Matches at Grand Slams," ThinkProgress, May 27, 2016, thinkprogress.org/why-women-dont-play-best-of-five-matches-at-grand-slams-6458f5b803df.

21. Lindsay Gibbs, telephone interview by Jessica Luther, March 5, 2017. Unless otherwise noted, related quotations are from this interview. Jesse Lawrence, "BNP Paribas Open Tickets Up 16% with Serena Williams Announcing Her Return," *Forbes*, February 12, 2015, forbes.com/sites/jesselawrence/2015/02/12/bnp-paribas-open-tickets-up-16-with-serena-williams-announcing-her-return/#4fe16fba2ed0.

22. Tom Fordyce, "Equal Pay Is as Much a Myth as It Is a Minefield," BBC Sport, March 21, 2016, bbc.com/sport/tennis/35863208.

23. Ben Rothenberg, "Roger Federer, $731,000; Serena Williams, $495,000: The Pay Gap in Tennis," *New York Times*, April 13, 2016, nytimes.com/2016/04/13/sports/tennis/equal-pay-gender-gap-grand-slam-majors-wta-atp.html.

24. Brittney C. Cooper, "Refereeing Serena: Racism, Anger, and U.S. (Women's) Tennis," Crunk Feminist Collective, September 12, 2011, crunkfeministcollective.com/2011/09/12/refereeing-serena-racism-anger-and-u-s-womens-tennis.

25. Sharapova technically won their last match but they didn't actually play; Serena withdrew from the 2018 French Open an hour before they were to meet, citing an injury. See Serena Williams vs. Maria Sharapova, Tennis.com, tennis.com/players/405/serena-williams/vs/462/maria-sharapova. Kurt Badenhausen, "Serena Williams vs. Maria Sharapova: By the Numbers," *Forbes*, July 9, 2015, forbes.com/sites/kurtbadenhausen/2015/07/09/serena-williams-vs-maria-sharapova-by-the-numbers/#7816eb02183d.

26. Claudia Rankine, "The Meaning of Serena Williams," *New York Times*, August 25, 2015, nytimes.com/2015/08/30/magazine/the-meaning-of-serena-williams.html.

27. Jenée Desmond-Harris, "Serena Williams Is Constantly the Target of Disgusting Racist and Sexist Attacks," Vox, September 7, 2016, vox.com/2015/3/11/8189679/serena-williams-indian-wells-racism. Mark Hodgkinson, "Serena 'Shocked' by More Racist Abuse," *The Telegraph*, March 28, 2007, telegraph.co.uk/sport/tennis/wtatour/2309944/Serena-shocked-by-more-racist-abuse.html. Jessica Luther, "Serena Williams Is Not a Costume," December 11, 2012, jessicawluther.com/2012/12/11/serena-williams-is-not-a-costume.

"Shamil Tarpischev Fined, Banned Year," ESPN.com, October 18, 2014, espn
.com/tennis/story/_/id/11718876/russian-tennis-federation-president-shamil
-tarpischev-sanctioned-serena-venus-williams-gender-comments. Matt Bonesteel and Kelyn Soong, "Serena Williams Calls Ilie Nastase's Comments
'Racist' and 'Sexist,'" *Washington Post*, April 24, 2017, washingtonpost.com/news
/early-lead/wp/2017/04/22/ilie-nastase-booted-from-fed-cup-after-nasty
-comments-leave-johanna-konta-in-tears/?tid=a_inl&utm_term
=.a765aed56805. Yolanda Sangweni, "Serena Williams Responds to Caroline
Wozniacki's 'Racist' Impersonation," *Essence*, December 23, 2012, essence.com
/news/serena-williams-responds-caroline-wozniackis-racist-impersonation.
    28. "Williams's Dad Alleges Racism," *Washington Post*, March 27, 2001,
washingtonpost.com/archive/sports/2001/03/27/williamss-dad-alleges
-racism/63720e58-1ae9-48e7-8577-da4d4b55dd39/?utm_term=.dea80222a6ae.
Doug Smith, "Williams' Father Says Booing Racially Motivated," *USA Today*,
March 28, 2001, usatoday30.usatoday.com/sports/tennis/stories/2001-03-26
-williams.htm.
    29. Serena Williams, "I'm Going Back to Indian Wells," *Time*, February 4,
2015, time.com/3694659/serena-williams-indian-wells. Dave Zirin, "Serena
Williams, Indian Wells and Rewriting the Future," *The Nation*, February 6, 2015,
thenation.com/article/serena-williams-indian-wells-and-rewriting-future.
Equal Justice Initiative (website), "About EJI," eji.org/about-eji.
    30. Paul Oberjuerge, "No Changing the Williams Sisters' Minds," *New York
Times*, March 19, 2009, nytimes.com/2009/03/20/sports/tennis/20tennis.html.
Bill Dwyre, "Serena Williams Will End 14-Year Boycott and Return to Indian
Wells," *Los Angeles Times*, February 4, 2015, latimes.com/sports/la-sp-serena
-williams-20150205-column.html.
    31. Lindsay Gibbs, telephone interview by Jessica Luther, March 5, 2017.
Unless otherwise noted, related quotations are from this interview.
    32. Carl Bialik, "Tennis Has an Income Inequality Problem," FiveThirty-
Eight, December 30, 2014, fivethirtyeight.com/features/tennis-has-an
-income-inequality-problem.
    33. Chris Oddo, "Prize Money Rises for Slams; Not So Much Elsewhere," *USA
Today*, August 28, 2013, usatoday.com/story/sports/tennis/2013/08/28/us-open
-2013-prize-money-distribution-debate/2718233. Lindsay Gibbs, "The Real
Problems Behind Tennis' Match-Fixing Scandal," ThinkProgress, January 20,
2016, thinkprogress.org/the-real-problems-behind-tennis-match-fixing
-scandal-1bb5183d4dc9.
    34. Tom Perrotta, "Why the USTA Benched America's Best Junior," *Wall Street
Journal*, September 8, 2012, wsj.com/articles/SB100008723963900444273704577
635530959121916.
    35. Courtney Nguyen, "Taylor Townsend Dispute: USTA Cuts Funding until
No. 1 Junior Loses Weight," *Sports Illustrated*, September 7, 2012, si.com/tennis
/beyond-baseline/2012/09/07/taylor-townsend-usta-controversy.
    36. David Waldstein, "Naomi Osaka Asks: What Would Serena Do? Then She
Defeats Her," *New York Times*, March 21, 2018, nytimes.com/2018/03/21/sports
/naomi-osaka-serena-williams.html.

37. "Naomi Osaka Captures US Open; Serena Williams Fined, Penalized Game for Calling Chair Umpire 'a Thief,'" ESPN News Service, September 9, 2018, espn.com/tennis/story/_/id/24617080/naomi-osaka-wins-controversial-2018-us-open-serena-williams.

38. Serena Williams, "Serena Williams Poses Unretouched for Harper's BAZAAR," *Harper's Bazaar*, July 9, 2019, harpersbazaar.com/culture/features/a28209579/serena-williams-us-open-2018-essay. Soraya Nadia McDonald, "The One and Only Naomi Osaka," The Undefeated, March 8, 2019, theundefeated.com/features/the-one-and-only-naomi-osaka.

39. Soraya McDonald, telephone interview by Jessica Luther, December 8, 2019. Unless otherwise noted, related quotations are from this interview.

40. Serena Williams, "What My Life-Threatening Experience Taught Me about Giving Birth," CNN, February 20, 2018, cnn.com/2018/02/20/opinions/protect-mother-pregnancy-williams-opinion/index.html.

Chapter 5: Coping When the Sports You Love Are Anti-LGBTQ+

1. Wade Davis, telephone interview by Jessica Luther, March 2, 2018. Unless otherwise noted, related quotations are from this interview.

2. You Can Play (website), youcanplayproject.org/pages/our-cause. Wade Davis (website), wadeadavis.com.

3. Eric Anderson, *In the Game: Gay Athletes and the Cult of Masculinity* (Albany: SUNY Press, 2005), 7.

4. "Falcons' Julio Jones Reflects on Journey to NFL," NBC Sports, October 24, 2017, youtube.com/watch?v=oeuXXV_IidE.

5. Amanda Goad, "A Proud History: LGBT Athletes in American Pro Sports," ACLU, May 1, 2013, aclu.org/blog/lgbt-rights/proud-history-lgbt-athletes-american-pro-sports. Heather Hogan, "22 Lesbian, Bisexual and Trans Women Athletes Who Changed the Game," AutoStraddle, October 31, 2017, autostraddle.com/22-lesbian-bisexual-and-trans-women-athletes-who-changed-the-game-399393. Cyd Zeigler, "Outsports' 100 Most Important Moments in LGBT-sports History," Outsports, July 5, 2011, outsports.com/2011/7/5/4051478/outsports-100-most-important-moments-in-lgbt-sports-history.

6. James Ellingworth, "FIFA Charges Mexico after Fans Chant Anti-Gay Slur," Associated Press, June 18, 2018, apnews.com/5dcade8a3b0141858d83 9812f39b061c. Terrance F. Ross, "Rajon Rondo's Homophobic Slur Shows How Prejudice Runs Deep," *The Guardian*, December 15, 2015, theguardian.com/sport/2015/dec/15/rajon-rondo-gay-slur-nba. Kim McCauley, "What on Earth Is U.S. Soccer Doing with Jaelene Hinkle?," SBNation, July 25, 2018, sbnation.com/soccer/2018/7/25/17609060/jaelene-hinkle-uswnt-roster-tournament-of-nations-roster-homophobic-700-club-interview. Katie Barnes, "They Are the Champions: In the Face of Fear and Anger, Two Young Transgender Athletes Fight to Compete in the Sports They Love," *ESPN The Magazine* and espnW, June 18, 2018, espn.com/espnw/feature/23592317/how-two-transgender-athletes-fighting-compete-sports-love.

7. Kristin Russo, "An Athlete Makes the Case for Gender Not to Matter in Sports," *Time*, October 7, 2015, time.com/4063096/how-important-is-gender.

8. Megan Ryan, "Minnesota United Player Collin Martin Comes Out Publicly That He's Gay," *Star Tribune*, June 30, 2018, startribune.com/minnesota-united -player-collin-martin-comes-out-publicly-that-he-s-gay/486944251. Dawn Ennis, "Out Gay Pro Soccer Player Collin Martin Signs with San Diego Loyal SC," Outsports, February 7, 2020, outsports.com/2020/2/7/21127634/mls-usl-soccer -collin-martin-san-diego-loyal-sc-minnesota-hartford.

9. Billy Witz, "Milestone for Gay Athletes as Rogers Plays for Galaxy," *New York Times*, May 27, 2013, nytimes.com/2013/05/28/sports/soccer/milestone -for-gay-athletes-as-robbie-rogers-plays-for-galaxy.html.

10. Jason Collins, "Why NBA Center Jason Collins Is Coming Out Now," *Sports Illustrated*, April 29, 2013, si.com/more-sports/2013/04/29/jason-collins-gay -nba-player.

11. Jason Collins, "Parting Shot: Jason Collins Announces NBA Retirement in His Own Words," *Sports Illustrated*, November 19, 2014, si.com/nba/2014/11/19 /jason-collins-retirement-nba.

12. John Branch, "N.F.L. Prospect Michael Sam Proudly Says What Teammates Knew: He's Gay," *New York Times*, February 9, 2014, nytimes. com/2014/02/10/sports/michael-sam-college-football-star-says-he-is-gay -ahead-of-nfl-draft.html.

13. Jarrett Bell, "What Took So Long for Michael Sam to Be Drafted?," *USA Today*, May 10, 2014, usatoday.com/story/sports/nfl/columnist/bell/2014/05/10 /michael-sam-nfl-draft-rams/8950709.

14. Cyd Zeigler, *Fair Play: How LGBT Athletes Are Claiming Their Rightful Place in Sports* (New York: Akashic Books, 2016), 121.

15. Jared Dubin, "Michael Sam, First Openly Gay Player, Retires for Mental Health Reasons," CBS Sports, August 14, 2015, cbssports.com/nfl/news/michael -sam-first-openly-gay-player-retires-for-mental-health-reasons.

16. Peter Moskovitz, "The Faggy Magic of Adam Rippon," Splinter News, February 2, 2018, splinternews.com/the-faggy-magic-of-adam-rippon -1823028967.

17. Curtis M. Wong, "Adam Rippon Responds to Being Called America's First 'Respected Faggot,'" *HuffPost*, March 11, 2018, huffingtonpost.com/entry /adam-rippon-build-series_us_5aa3f180e4b07047bec6d67d.

18. Michelle Smith, "Inside the W: Love & Basketball for Dupree, Bonner," WNBA.com, June 24, 2018, wnba.com/news/inside-the-w-love-basketball-for -dupree-bonner.

19. Jemele Hill, "Rapinoe on Body Issue Cover: 'Visibility is important,'" ESPN, June 24, 2018, espn.com/wnba/story/_/page/espnwbodybirdrapinoe/wnba -sue-bird-uswnt-megan-rapinoe-debate-better-athlete-body-issue-2018.

20. Katie Barnes, telephone interview by Jessica Luther, February 28, 2018. Wade Davis, telephone interview by Jessica Luther, March 2, 2018. Unless otherwise noted, related quotations are from these interviews.

21. Katie Barnes, "Having Short Hair or Playing with Action Figures Is No Indication of Gender," espnW, June 9, 2017, espn.com/espnw/voices/article /19587919/having-short-hair-playing-action-figures-no-indication-gender.

22. "Penn State's Portland Makes 'Difficult' Decision to Quit," Associated

Press, March 25, 2007, espn.com/ncw/news/story?id=2808075. There is a documentary about Harris, Portland, and discrimination in sport based on sexual orientation titled *Training Rules*. On the website for the film, it reads: "Although Jen's story of harassment and dismissal repeats itself with remarkable consistency among other basketball players at her school, this is a tale told not just at Penn State, but also at universities and colleges across the country. Rene Portland may be a blatant example of homophobia in women's sports, but she is NOT the only coach who discriminates based on sexual orientation. Penn State is NOT the only university that disregards its own code of ethics in order to preserve its cash flow." See trainingrules.com/training-rules.html.

23. Christine Hopkins, "'I know who I am': Brittney Griner's Radical Existence," Swish Hoops, June 29, 2018, swishappeal.com/2018/6/29/17508976/wnba-2018-book-review-in-my-skin-i-know-who-i-am-brittney-griners-radical-existence-pride-lgbtq.

24. Pat Griffin, "No Lesbians Allowed on the Team: Déjà Vu All Over Again," Outsports, December 15, 2014, outsports.com/2014/12/15/7398423/pepperdine-lesbian-basketball-rene-portland.

25. Human Rights Campaign, "HRC Highlights LGBTQ Visibility in NCAA Women's Basketball," March 31, 2017, hrc.org/blog/hrc-highlights-lgbtq-visibility-in-ncaa-womens-basketball.

26. Shannon Ryan, "Lesbian College Coaches Still Face Difficult Atmosphere to Come Out," *Chicago Tribune*, January 17, 2017, chicagotribune.com/sports/college/ct-lesbian-college-coaches-challenges-spt-0118-20170117-story.html.

27. John Altavilla, "Sun Coach Curt Miller Aims for Honesty with Team and Family," *New York Times*, August 22, 2018, nytimes.com/2018/08/22/sports/connecticut-sun-curt-miller-wnba.html.

28. Ryan Russell (as told to Kevin Arnovitz), "No Distractions: An NFL Veteran Opens Up on His Sexuality," ESPN, August 29, 2019, espn.com/nfl/story/_/id/27484719/no-distractions-nfl-veteran-opens-sexuality.

29. Britni de la Cretaz, "How Ryan Russell Is Combating Bisexual Stigma, for the NFL and Fans Alike," MTV News, September 5, 2019, mtv.com/news/3138176/ryan-russell-bisexual-stigma-nfl-fans.

30. Christina Kahrl, "Chris Mosier Becomes First Known Transgender Athlete in World Duathlon Championship," ESPN, June 23, 2016, espn.com/sports/endurance/story/_/id/15976460/chris-mosier-becomes-first-known-transgender-athlete-compete-world-duathlon-championship. Dawn Ennis, "Chris Mosier: 'I'm competing in the Olympic Trials!,'" Outsports, December 20, 2019, outsports.com/2019/12/18/21028737/chris-mosier-transgender-tokyo-olympic-trials-2020-race-walk.

31. GLAAD (website), "Glossary of Terms," glaad.org/reference/transgender.

32. Chris Mosier, telephone interview by Jessica Luther, June 16, 2017. Unless otherwise noted, related quotations are from this interview.

33. Parker Marie Molloy, "Heroes, Martyrs, and Myths: The Battle for the Rights of Transgender Athletes," Vice Sports, November 6, 2014, sports.vice.com/en_us/article/bmea9w/heroes-martyrs-and-myths-the-battle-for-the-rights-of-transgender-athletes.

34. Andrew, "The Opposite of Fair Play: Part II," The Victory Press, October 24, 2017, victorypress.org/2017/10/24/the-opposite-of-fair-play-part-ii.

35. Jennifer Doyle, "Capturing Semenya," The Sport Spectacle, August 16, 2016, thesportspectacle.com/2016/08/16/capturing-semenya.

36. Cyd Zeigler, "Meet Some Trans Athletes Who Work Hard, Train Like Mad and (Almost) Never Win," Outsports, December 3, 2019, outsports.com/2019/12/3/20990763/trans-women-athlete-sports-winning-losing-transgender.

37. Dave Phillips, "North Carolina Bans Local Anti-Discrimination Policies," *New York Times*, March 23, 2016, nytimes.com/2016/03/24/us/north-carolina-to-limit-bathroom-use-by-birth-gender.html. Marc Tracy, "N.C.A.A. Ends Boycott of North Carolina after So-Called Bathroom Bill Is Repealed," *New York Times*, April 4, 2017, nytimes.com/2017/04/04/sports/ncaa-hb2-north-carolina-boycott-bathroom-bill.html.

38. Barnes, "They Are the Champions."

39. Katie Barnes, "When Basketball Became a Stranger," espnW, June 9, 2016, espn.com/espnw/voices/article/16021466/when-basketball-became-stranger.

40. GLAAD (website), "Glossary of Terms," glaad.org/reference/transgender.

41. Layshia Clarendon, "How LGB Too Often Leaves Off the T," *Esquire*, June 24, 2016, esquire.com/news-politics/a45824/layshia-clarendon-gender-binaries.

42. Jon Shadel, "This Gender Neutral Athlete Wants to End Sex Segregation in Sports," VICE, November 10, 2016, vice.com/en_us/article/mvk33x/this-gender-neutral-athlete-wants-to-end-sex-segregation-in-sports. Heather Dockray, "How the Olympics Can Embrace Non-Binary Athletes in 2020 and Beyond," Mashable, February 26, 2018, mashable.com/2018/02/26/olympics-non-binary-genderqueer-athletes/#H.ZIyCitbSqE.

43. For example, see Doriane Lambelet Coleman, "A Victory for Female Athletes Everywhere," Quilette, May 3, 2019, quillette.com/2019/05/03/a-victory-for-female-athletes-everywhere. "IAAF World Athletics Championships: The Battle Against Doping Continues," DW.com, September 26, 2019, dw.com/en/iaaf-world-athletics-championships-the-battle-against-doping-continues/a-50599017. Camilla Tominey, "Transgender Athletes in Women's Sport Are as Unfair as East German Drugs Cheats, Says Sharron Davies," *The Telegraph*, July 11, 2019, telegraph.co.uk/news/2019/07/11/transgender-athletes-womens-sport-unfair-east-german-drugs-cheats.

44. National Gay Flag Football League (website), ngffl.com/Home/tabid/56/Default.aspx.

45. North American Gay Amateur Athletic Alliance (website), nagaaasoftball.org.

46. International Gay Rodeo Association (website), igra.com/index.htm.

47. Homoclimbtastic (website), homoclimbtastic.com.

48. Federation of Gay Games (website), gaygames.org.

49. Federation of Gay Games (website), "FAQ," gaygames.org/FAQs.

50. Christine Linnell, "7 Historical Facts about the Gay Games," *The Advocate*,

August 3, 2018, advocate.com/sports/2018/8/03/7-fascinating-facts-about -gay-games#media-gallery-media-0.

51. Human Rights Campaign (website), "Play to Win," hrc.org/resources /play-to-win-improving-the-lives-of-lgbtq-youth-in-sports. Lindsay Gibbs, "Staggering Number of LGBTQ Teens Are Excluded from School Sports, New Study Finds," ThinkProgress, June 29, 2018, thinkprogress.org/lgbtq-sports -youth-exclusion-64773aa45997.

Chapter 6: Watching Women's Basketball When People Tell You You're the Only One

1. WNBA (website), "History," wnba.com/history.

2. Matt Bonesteel, "Brittney Griner Throws Down First Dunk in WNBA Play-off History," *Washington Post*, August 24, 2014, washingtonpost.com/news /early-lead/wp/2014/08/25/brittney-griner-throws-down-first-dunk-in-wnba -playoff-history.

3. Natalie Weiner, "How Viral Dunkers Can Revolutionize Women's Basketball," Bleacher Report, September 29, 2017, bleacherreport.com /articles/2735856-how-viral-dunkers-can-revolutionize-womens-basketball.

4. Phil Thompson, "Elena Delle Donne Doubles Down on Defense of Lower Rim Height," *Chicago Tribune*, March 31, 2016, chicagotribune.com/sports/ct -elena-delle-donne-diana-taurasi-wnba-lower-rim-20160330-story.html.

5. Kate Fagan, "Why Lowering the Rims Is a Flawed Strategy for Women's Basketball," ESPN, March 29, 2016, espn.com/espnw/voices/story /_/id/15090920/fagan-why-lower-rims-women-basketball-flawed.

6. Imani McGee-Stafford, telephone interview by Jessica Luther, December 17, 2019. Unless otherwise noted, related quotations are from this interview.

7. Howard Megdal, telephone interview by Kavitha Davidson, February 6, 2019. Unless otherwise noted, related quotations are from this interview.

8. Layshia Clarendon, "Layshia Clarendon: 'It's not about dunking. It's about the system,'" ESPN, April 1, 2016, espn.com/espnw/voices/story /_/id/15112298/layshia-clarendon-says-lower-rims-not-answer.

9. Hannah Withiam, "The Athletic's Expanded WNBA Coverage Will Include On-the-ground Reporting of All 12 Teams," The Athletic, May 20, 2019, theathletic.com/984508/2019/05/20/the-athletics-expanded-wnba-coverage -will-include-on-the-ground-reporting-of-all-12-teams. Maitreyi Anantha-raman, "How the WNBA Became a Hot Newsroom Beat," *Columbia Journalism Review*, May 22, 2019, cjr.org/united_states_project/wnba-basketball.php. Ben Strauss, "The WNBA Has Craved Mainstream Attention. This Season, It Might Be Turning a Corner," *Washington Post*, August 9, 2019, washingtonpost.com /sports/2019/08/09/wnba-has-craved-mainstream-attention-this-season-it -might-be-turning-corner.

10. Jerry Barca, "Why Are WNBA TV Ratings Rising?," *Forbes*, July 9, 2018, forbes.com/sites/jerrybarca/2018/07/09/why-are-wnba-tv-ratings-rising /#6f2203016f83.

11. Bill Plaschke, "I Regret Marginalizing Pat Summitt's Greatness," *Los Angeles Times*, June 28, 2016, latimes.com/sports/nba/la-sp-pat-summitt-plaschke -20160628-snap-story.html.

12. Nate Taylor, "Griner and Other Rookies Rejuvenate W.N.B.A.," *New York Times*, Sept. 18, 2013, nytimes.com/2013/09/19/sports/basketball/griner -and-other-rookies-rejuvenate-wnba.html. Douglas A. McIntyre, "Ten Brands That Will Disappear in 2014," 24/7 Wall St., May 23, 2013, 247wallst.com/special -report/2013/05/23/ten-brands-that-will-disappear-in-2014.

13. "ESPN, WNBA Extend Agreement," espnW, March 28, 2013, espn.com /wnba/story/_/id/9108870/wnba-espn-wnba-extend-agreement-2022.

14. John Lombardo, "With 20th Season Ahead, League Sees Attendance, Ratings Drop," *Sports Business Journal*, September 21, 2015, sportsbusinessdaily.com /Journal/Issues/2015/09/21/Leagues-and-Governing-Bodies/WNBA.aspx.

15. Jenn Hatfield, "WNBA Attendance Declines in 2018: What Does That Mean for the League?," Her Hoop States, August 29, 2018, medium.com/her-hoop-stats/wnba-attendance-declines-in-2018-what-does-that-mean-for-the -league-4b88e59583f1. Tara Chozet, "ESPN Tips Off WNBA Postseason with First Round Doubleheader Tonight," ESPN, August 21, 2018, espnpressroom.com/us /press-releases/2018/08/espn-tips-off-wnba-postseason-with-first-round -doubleheader-tonight.

16. CBS Sports, "WNBA and CBS Sports Agree to Multi-Year Television Partnership," April 22, 2019, viacomcbspressexpress.com/cbs-sports/releases /view?id=52524.

17. Claire Breen, "For the First Time, the WNBA Will Be Featured in NBA 2K. Here's a Behind-the-scenes Look at the New Game," The Lily, August 8, 2019, thelily.com/for-the-first-time-the-wnba-will-be-featured-in-nba-2k-heres -a-behind-the-scenes-look-at-the-new-game. Ben Strauss, "The WNBA Has Craved Mainstream Attention. This Season, It Might Be Turning a Corner," *Washington Post*, August 9, 2019, washingtonpost.com/sports/2019/08/09/wnba -has-craved-mainstream-attention-this-season-it-might-be-turning-corner.

18. Kelly Whiteside, "Not a Single W.N.B.A. Star Has a Shoe Line to Call Her Own," *New York Times*, August 25, 2017, nytimes.com/2017/08/25/sports /basketball/wnba-shoe-deals.html.

19. Jessica Dickler, "This WNBA Superstar Earns Just 20% of an NBA Player's Salary," CNBC, October 3, 2017, cnbc.com/2017/10/03/this-wnba-superstar -earns-just-20-percent-of-an-nba-players-salary.html.

20. Madeline Kenney, "Breanna Stewart's Injury Highlights Larger Issue with WNBA's Business Model," *Chicago Sun Times*, April 19, 2019, chicago. suntimes.com/chicago-sky-and-wnba/2019/4/19/18619396/breanna-stewart -s-injury-highlights-larger-issue-with-wnba-s-business-model.

21. Mirin Fader, "Inside the WNBA's Fight for Higher Pay," Bleacher Report, October 29, 2018, bleacherreport.com/articles/2802759-inside-the-wnbas -fight-for-higher-pay.

22. Nneka Ogwumike, "Bet on Women," *The Players' Tribune*, November 1, 2018, theplayerstribune.com/en-us/articles/nneka-ogwumike-wnba-cba -bet-on-women.

23. Howard Megdal, "W.N.B.A. Makes 'Big Bet on Women' with a New Contract," *New York Times*, January 14, 2020, nytimes.com/2020/01/14/sports /basketball/wnba-contract-collective-bargaining-agreement.html.

24. Shea Serrano, "How to Fall in Love with a Team in the NCAA Tournament," The Ringer, March 24, 2018, theringer.com/college-basketball /2018/3/24/17153752/oregon-womens-basketball-ncaa-tournament-sabrina -ionescu. Sam Gordon, "Best-selling Author, Twitter Personality Shea Serrano All-in with the Aces," *Las Vegas Review-Journal*, July 6, 2018, reviewjournal.com /sports/basketball/aces-wnba/best-selling-author-twitter-personality-shea -serrano-all-in-with-the-aces.

25. Calvin Wetzel, "Making Sense of How to Watch the WNBA on Your TV," Her Hoop Stats, June 21, 2019, medium.com/her-hoop-stats/making-sense-of -how-to-watch-the-wnba-on-tv-fddd5ea3142b.

Chapter 7: Consuming Sports Media . . . Even If You Don't Look Like the People on TV

1. "Cisgender" refers to people who are not transgender. According to GLAAD, "transgender" (which is an adjective, never used as a noun), is defined thus: "An umbrella term for people whose gender identity and/or gender expression differs from what is typically associated with the sex they were assigned at birth. People under the transgender umbrella may describe themselves using one or more of a wide variety of terms—including transgender. Some of those terms are defined below. Use the descriptive term preferred by the person. Many transgender people are prescribed hormones by their doctors to bring their bodies into alignment with their gender identity. Some undergo surgery as well. But not all transgender people can or will take those steps, and a transgender identity is not dependent upon physical appearance or medical procedures." See GLAAD (website), glaad.org/reference /transgender.

2. Women's Media Center (website), "Divided 2017: The Media Gender Gap," March 22, 2017, womensmediacenter.com/reports/divided-2017.

3. Sports Media Racial & Gender Report Card (APSE) (website), tidesport .org/associated-press-sports-editors.

4. Richard Lapchick, "The 2018 Associated Press Sports Editors Racial and Gender Report Card," ESPN, May 3, 2018, espn.com/espn/story/_/id/23382605 /espn-leads-way-hiring-practices-sports-media.

5. UNESCO, "UNESCO Calls for Fairer Media Coverage of Sportswomen," February 9, 2018, en.unesco.org/news/unesco-calls-fairer-media-cove rage-sportswomen.

6. Women's Media Center (website), "Writing Rape: How U.S. Media Cover Campus Rape and Sexual Assault," December 15, 2015, womensmediacenter. com/reports/writing-rape-how-u-s-media-cover-campus-rape-and-sexual -assault.

7. David J. Halberstam, "ESPN's Suzy Kolber, a Pro's Pro and NFL Fixture, Talks Life, Her Career and Joe Namath: 'He's a good person,'" *Sports Broadcast Journal*, November 7, 2018, sportsbroadcastjournal.com/espns-suzy-kolber-a -pros-pro-and-nfl-fixture-talks-life-her-career-and-joe-namath-hes-a-good -person. Barry Petchesky, "Let's Talk about Sex, Ines Sainz, and the Sideline," Deadspin, September 13, 2010, deadspin.com/5636603/lets-talk-about-sex-ines -sainz-and-the-sideline. "We Need to Talk about Sexism at the World Cup,"

FARE Network, June 26, 2018, farenet.org/news/women-in-football-term-slug/fare-blog-we-need-to-talk-about-sexism-at-the-world-cup-2018.

8. Emma Baccellieri, "The Everlasting Legacy of Melissa Ludtke, Who Dared to Join the Boys Club of the Baseball Press," *Sports Illustrated*, September 28, 2018, si.com/mlb/2018/09/28/melissa-ludtke-lawsuit-anniversary. Jaclyn Hendricks, "Female Reporters Barred from NFL Locker Room," *New York Post*, October 5, 2015, nypost.com/2015/10/05/female-reporters-barred-from-nfl-locker-room.

9. Rhiannon Walker, statement via email, December 13, 2018. Ben Baby, statement via email, December 8, 2018.

10. Dexter Rogers, "The White World of Sports Journalism," Colorlines, January 3, 2011, colorlines.com/articles/white-world-sports-journalism. Jesse Washington, "A New Chapter for Black Olympic Swimming," The Undefeated, August 12, 2016, theundefeated.com/features/a-new-chapter-for-black-olympic-swimming-simone-manuel-lia-neal. Jesse Washington (tweet), @jessewashington, August 11, 2016, twitter.com/jessewashington/status/763943451628965890. Hugh Woozencroft, "Why BBC Sport Can't Escape Sports Journalism's Problem," BBC, December 14, 2018, bbc.com/sport/46571432.

11. John Carvalho, "Sports Media Is Still Racist Against Black Athletes," Vice Sports, October 3, 2014, sports.vice.com/en_us/article/4x987d/sports-media-is-still-racist-against-black-athletes.

12. Bill Simmons, "The Dr. V Story: A Letter from the Editor," Grantland, January 20, 2014, grantland.com/features/the-dr-v-story-a-letter-from-the-editor. Christina Kahrl, "What Grantland Got Wrong," January 20, 2014, grantland.com/features/what-grantland-got-wrong. GLAAD has a short media reference guide for sports reporters writing on LGBTQ+ people in sports: glaad.org/reference/sports.

13. Richard Deitsch, "LGBTQ Media Members Discuss Their Experiences, Future, Ryan O'Callaghan and More," *Sports Illustrated*, June 25, 2017, si.com/tech-media/2017/06/25/media-roundtable-sports-lgbtq-ryan-ocallaghan. Kate Schmidt, "Christina Kahrl: The Sportswriter Who Happens to Be Trans," *Chicago Reader*, December 7, 2016, people.chicagoreader.com/who/christina-kahrl/profile.

14. Jessica has written for all of these outlets, except for Grantland. Kavitha wrote for *ESPN The Magazine*. Laura Wagner, David Roth, and Kelsey McKinney, "Inside The Maven's Plan to Turn *Sports Illustrated* into a Rickety Content Mill," Deadspin, October 4, 2019, deadspin.com/inside-themavens-plan-to-turn-sports-illustrated-into-a-1838756286. Louisa Thomas, "The Ham-Handed, Money-Driven Mangling of Sports Illustrated and Deadspin," New Yorker, November 3, 2019, newyorker.com/culture/cultural-comment/the-ham-handed-money-driven-mangling-of-sports-illustrated-and-deadspin. Daniel Roberts, "Sports Illustrated Will Reduce Print Output to Monthly," Yahoo! Finance, November 13, 2019, finance.yahoo.com/news/exclusive-sports-illustrated-will-reduce-print-output-to-monthly-214408997.html. Bryan Curtis, "The Mavening of Sportswriting," The Ringer, October 31, 2019, theringer

.com/2019/10/31/20942249/deadspin-g-o-media-fired-quit-sports-illustrated
-maven-sports-media.

15. Kavitha was on staff at espnW and is on staff at The Athletic. Jessica has written for Bleacher Report and SBNation.

16. Shireen Ahmed and Shakeia Taylor, "Women of Color in Media: Progress Required," The Shadow League, June 5, 2018, theshadowleague.com/women
-of-color-in-media-progress-required.

17. Jen Ramos, telephone interview by Jessica Luther, December 3, 2018. Unless otherwise noted, related quotations are from this interview.

18. Lindsay Gibbs, "Meet Jen Ramos, the First Openly Non-Binary Executive in Pro Sports," ThinkProgress, Feb. 27, 2017, thinkprogress.org/meet-jen
-ramos-the-first-openly-non-binary-executive-in-pro-sports-11553c02878a.

19. Disclosure: Luther is one of her cohosts on "Burn It All Down." Shireen Ahmed, statement via email, August, 1, 2017. shireenahmed.com/about1.

20. Joel Anderson, telephone interview by Jessica Luther, July 17, 2017. Unless otherwise noted, related quotations are from this interview. Kara Bloomgarden-Smoke, "Sportswriter Joel Anderson Is Going to BuzzFeed," *The Observer*, July 17, 2013, observer.com/2013/07/sportswriter-joel-anderson-is
-going-to-buzzfeed.

21. Stefanie Loh, statement via email, December 7, 2018. Mohammed Kloub, "Behind the Byline: Assistant Sports Editor Stefanie Loh on the Inherent Drama of Sports Journalism," *Seattle Times*, August 1, 2018, seattletimes.com
/seattle-news/behind-the-byline-assistant-sports-editor-stefanie-loh-on
-the-inherent-drama-of-sports-journalism.

22. Mirin Fader, statement via email, December 7, 2018. mirinfader.com
/about.

23. Emily Kaplan, statement via email, August 8, 2017. Andrew Bucholtz, "Following Massive Hockey Cuts, ESPN Hires the MMQB'S Emily Kaplan to Cover NHL," Awful Announcing, June 22, 2017, awfulannouncing.com/espn
/following-massive-hockey-cuts-espn-hires-emily-kaplan-to-cover-nhl.html.

24. DeVon Pouncey statement via email, December 7, 2018.

25. Christine Brennan, telephone interview by Jessica Luther, July 27, 2017. christinebrennan.com. Unless otherwise noted, related quotations are from this interview.

26. Rhiannon Walker, statement via email, December 13, 2018. theathletic
.com/author/rhiannon-walker.

27. Patrick Claybon, statement via email, December 6, 2018. nfl.com
/nflnetwork/onairtalent/patrick-claybon.

28. Reem Abulleil, statement via email, August 12, 2017. sport360.com
/author/17561/reem-abulleil.

29. Keme Nzerem, telephone interview by Jessica Luther, December 10, 2018. knightayton.co.uk/male-presenters/keme-nzerem. Unless otherwise noted, related quotations are from this interview.

30. Harrods is a major department store in London.

31. Juliet Macur, statement via email, December 15, 2018. Kristi Berner,

"Keeping Score: Juliet Macur '92," Barnard College, June 2, 2014, barnard.edu /news/keeping-score.

32. Ishmael Johnson, statement via email, December 6, 2018. sjmcnews .wordpress.com/2018/07/11/alumnus-spotlight-ishmael-johnson.

33. Meg Linehan, statement via email, December 13, 2018. theathletic.com /author/megan-linehan.

34. Morgan Campbell, telephone interview by Jessica Luther, December 3, 2018, thestar.com/authors.campbell_morgan.html. Unless otherwise noted, related quotations are from this interview.

35. Zito Madu, statement via email, December 3, 2018.

36. Tamyrn Spruill, statement via email, December 10, 2018. tamrynspruill .com.

37. Keri Potts statement via email, December 7, 2018. A Fight Back Woman (website), "About," afightbackwoman.com/about-2. John Ourand, "ESPN's Potts an Important Voice on Tough Topics," *Sports Business Journal*, January 15, 2018, sportsbusinessdaily.com/Journal/Issues/2018/01/15/Media/MeToo.aspx.

38. Karim Zidan, statement via email, December 4, 2018.

Chapter 8: Rooting for Your Team When the Star Is Accused of Domestic Violence

1. Kristie Ackert, "Jose Reyes Returning to Mets as Team Signs Shortstop after His Domestic Violence Suspension," *New York Daily News*, June 26, 2016, nydailynews.com/sports/baseball/mets/reyes-returning-mets-signs-deal -domestic-violence-ban-article-1.2687846.

2. Chelsea Davis, "Rockies 'Concerned' after Learning Shortstop Jose Reyes Arrested on Maui for Assaulting Wife," Hawaii News Now, November 5, 2015, hawaiinewsnow.com/story/30476680/mlb-all-star-arrested-on-maui-for -allegedly-assaulting-his-wife.

3. Paul Hagen, "MLB, MLBPA Reveal Domestic Violence Policy," MLB.com, August 21, 2015, mlb.com/news/mlb-mlbpa-agree-on-domestic-violence -policy/c-144508842.

4. Anthony DiComo, "Tears to Cheers: Flores Hits Dramatic Walk-Off Blast," MLB.com, August 1, 2015, mlb.com/mets/news/wilmer-flores-hits-dramatic -walk-off-home-run/c-140172256.

5. Tim Brown and Jeff Passan, "Police Report: Aroldis Chapman Allegedly Fired Gunshots, 'Choked' Girlfriend in Domestic Incident," Yahoo! Sports, December 7, 2015, is available on the Wayback Machine, web.archive.org /web/20151209062948/sports.yahoo.com/news/aroldis-chapman-s-girlfriend -alleged-he—choked—her—according-to-police-report-023629095.html. The original URL for this citation (sports.yahoo.com/news/aroldis-chapman-s -girlfriend-alleged-he-choked-her-according-to-police-report-023629095 .html) no longer links to the article.

6. Paul Hagen and Bryan Hoch, "Chapman Gets 30-Game Suspension from MLB," MLB.com, March 1, 2016, mlb.com/news/yankees-aroldis-chapman -suspended-30-games-c165860226.

7. "Greg Hardy Found Guilty of Assault," Associated Press, July 15, 2014,

espn.com/nfl/story/_/id/11220817/greg-hardy-carolina-panthers-guilty
-2-counts-domestic-violence.

8. DallasCowboys.com Report, "Jerry Jones Mentions Hardy's Character, Rush Ability in Official Statement," March 18, 2015, is available on the Wayback Machine, web.archive.org/web/20180129131942/dallascowboys.com/news/2015 /03/18/jerry-jones-mentions-hardy%E2%80%99s-character-rush-ability -official-statement. The original URL for this citation (dallascowboys.com /news/2015/03/18/jerry-jones-mentions-hardy%E2%80%99s-character-rush -ability-official-statement) no longer links to the article.

9. Dale Hansen, telephone interview by Kavitha Davidson, April 22, 2018. Unless otherwise noted, related quotations are from this interview.

10. Stephanie Apstein, "Astros Staffer's Outburst at Female Reporters Illustrates MLB's Forgive-and-Forget Attitude Toward Domestic Violence," *Sports Illustrated*, October 21, 2019, si.com/mlb/2019/10/22/houston-astros-roberto -osuna-suspension.

11. Dan Solomon, "Why Is Astros Management Making It So Hard to Root for the Team Right Now?," *Texas Monthly*, October 23, 2019, texasmonthly.com /the-culture/houston-astros-management-brandon-taubman-roberto-osuna.

12. David Folkenflik, "Astros Executive's Rant at Reporters Draws Firestorm on Eve of Series," NPR, October 22, 2019, npr.org/2019/10/22/772368868/astros -executives-rant-at-reporters-draws-firestorm-on-eve-of-series.

13. Tonya Bondurant, "Donating $1 to Domestic Violence Charity for Every Strikeout by the Yankees' Closer This Season," SBNation, December 8, 2016, pinstripealley.com/platform/amp/2016/12/8/13881710/yankees-domestic -violence-charity-donation. Ben Strauss and Des Bieler, "In Wake of Sports Illustrated Story: Astros and MLB Go into Damage-control Mode," *Washington Post*, October 22, 2019, washingtonpost.com/sports/2019/10/22/astros -respond-sports-illustrated-report-alleging-executives-clubhouse-blowup.

Chapter 9: Loving Your Team When You Hate the Owner

1. Jeff Zillgitt, "Adam Silver Gives Donald Sterling Lifetime Ban from NBA," *USA Today*, April 29, 2014, usatoday.com/story/news/usanow/2014/04/29 /donald-sterling-fine-penalty-racism-audio-commissioner-adam-silver-los -angeles-suspension/8460575.

2. Alex Crawford, telephone interview by Kavitha Davidson, August 22, 2018. Unless otherwise noted, related quotations are from this interview.

3. Bruce Newman, "Can the NBA Save Itself?," *Sports Illustrated*, November 1, 1982, si.com/vault/1982/11/01/625090/can-the-nba-save-itself.

4. George Dohrmann, "Recently Banned Donald Sterling Has Long History of Clashing with NBA," *Sports Illustrated*, May 30, 2014, si.com/nba/2014/05/30 /donald-sterling-history.

5. Dohrmann.

6. Nathan Fenno, "Elgin Baylor Lawsuit among Donald Sterling's Past Racial Issues," *Los Angeles Times*, April 26, 2014, latimes.com/sports/sportsnow/la-sp-sn -elgin-baylor-donald-sterling-20140426-story.html.

7. Peter Keating, "Champagne and Caviar, Paying for Sex, Millions in Profits

. . . Donald Sterling Loves It All," ESPN, July 10, 2012, espn.com/espn/magazine /archives/news/story?page=magazine-20090601-article25.

8. Ben Leibowtiz, "Baron Davis Recalled Donald Sterling's Cursing Him Out and 'Delusional' Demeanor," Bleacher Report, April 28, 2014, bleacherreport .com/articles/2044371-baron-davis-recalls-donald-sterlings-cursing-him -out-and-delusional-demeanor.

9. Matt Verderame, "Ray Rice Comments on Greg Hardy Situation," Aol .com, November 8, 2015, aol.com/article/2015/11/08/ray-rice-comments-on -greg-hardy-situation/21260958.

10. Doug Berns, personal interview by Kavitha Davidson, August 23, 2018, New York, NY. Unless otherwise noted, related quotations are from this interview.

11. Seth Rosenthal, "There Is Going to Be a Knicks Protest This Month," SBNation, March 5, 2014, postingandtoasting.com/2014/3/5/5474572/there-is -going-to-be-a-knicks-protest-this-month. "KF4L Rally Page," Facebook, facebook.com/kf4lrally.

12. Ben Golliver, "Best from Dolan, Jackson at Presser: 'I am by no means an expert in basketball,'" *Sports Illustrated*, March 18, 2014, si.com/nba /point-forward/2014/03/18/phil-jackson-press-conference-james-dolan -new-york-knicks.

13. Angel Diaz, "Knicks Fans Should Boycott the Team until James Dolan Sells," Complex, February 10, 2017, complex.com/sports/2017/02/new-york -knicks-boycott-charles-oakley-james-dolan.

14. Katie Honan and Murray Weiss, "Knicks Legend Charles Oakley Arrested at Madison Square Garden," DNA Info, February 9, 2017, dnainfo.com/new -york/20170208/midtown/charles-oakley-knicks-arrested-madison-square -garden-james-dolan.

15. Sopan Deb, "The Knicks Are Trying Something New: A Rebrand," *New York Times*, February 9, 2020, nytimes.com/2020/02/09/sports/basketball/the -knicks-are-trying-something-new-a-rebrand.html.

16. Malika Andrews, "Knicks Disavow Coaching Comments by Team Rep," ESPN.com, February 11, 2020, espn.com/nba/story/_/id/28681765/knicks -disavow-coaching-comments-team-rep. See the team's statement via Twitter: New York Knicks Public Relations (tweet), "Statements from the New York Knicks and Steve Stoute," @NY_KnicksPR, February 11, 2020, twitter.com /ny_knickspr/status/1227363272938131456?s=21; for context, see "Knicks Issue Statement after Brand Consultant Steve Stoute Hints at Coaching Overhaul," SNY.tv, February 11, 2020, sny.tv/knicks/news/knicks-brand-consultant-steve -stoute-hints-that-coaching-overhaul-could-be-coming/312725702.

17. Kevin Lauriat, telephone interview by Kavitha Davidson, August 24, 2018. Unless otherwise noted, related quotations are from this interview.

18. Joseph Durso, "Doubleday and President of Mets to Buy Ball Club from Publisher," *New York Times*, September 28, 1986, nytimes.com/1986/09/26 /sports/doubleday-and-president-of-mets-to-buy-ball-club-from-publisher .html.

19. Joel Sherman, "Jeff: Amazin's Don't Have Son Poisoning—Younger Wilpon Defends Family's Commitment to Winning, Assures Rebound," *New York Post*,

September 19, 2004, nypost.com/2004/09/19/jeff-amazins-dont-have-son
-poisoning-younger-wilpon-defends-familys-commitment-to-winning
-assures-rebound.

20. Serge F. Kovaleski and David Waldstein, "Madoff Had Wide Role in Mets'
Finances," *New York Times*, February 1, 2011, nytimes.com/2011/02/02/sports
/baseball/02mets.html?_r=0.

21. Josh Kosman, "New Loan Could End Mets Money Problems," *New York
Post*, January 30, 2014, nypost.com/2014/01/30/new-loan-could-end-mets
-money-problems.

22. Mike Vaccaro, "Get the Fred Out! Stay Away from Shea until Wilpon Sells
Mets," *New York Post*, May 2, 2014, nypost.com/2004/05/02/get-the-fred-out
-stay-away-from-shea-until-wilpon-sells-mets.

23. Ian O'Connor, "Hey, Bud Selig: Take our Mets, please!," ESPN, May 24,
2011, espn.com/new-york/mlb/columns/story?columnist=oconnor_ian&id
=6584339.

24. Richard Sandomir, "Mets Resolve Suit with Executive They Fired When
She Was Pregnant and Unmarried," *New York Times*, March 13, 2015, nytimes.
com/2015/03/14/sports/baseball/mets-settle-case-with-executive-who-cited
-discrimination-over-pregnancy.html. Adam Rubin, "Fired Mets Executive
Sues Team," ESPN, September 10, 2014, espn.com/new-york/mlb/story/_/id
/11503974/leigh-castergine-former-new-york-mets-executive-files-lawsuit
-team.

25. David Waldstein, "Wilpon Says He Is Sorry for Remarks," *New York Times*,
May 24, 2011, nytimes.com/2011/05/25/sports/baseball/wilpon-apologizes
-to-mets-for-comments.html.

26. David Waldstein, "For Dodgers Star Justin Turner, the Mets' Rejection
Still Motivates," *New York Times*, August 6, 2017, nytimes.com/2017/08/06/sports
/baseball/los-angeles-dodgers-star-justin-turner.html.

27. Kevin Lauriat, email interview by Kavitha Davidson, January 17, 2020.
Unless otherwise noted, related quotations are from this interview.

28. Kevin Draper and James Wagner, "A 'Disappointed' Steve Cohen
Walks Away from Mets Purchase," *New York Times*, February 6, 2020, nytimes
.com/2020/02/06/sports/baseball/steve-cohen-mets.html.

29. Kevin Lauriat, email interview with Kavitha Davidson, February 6,
2020. Unless otherwise noted, related quotations are from this interview.

30. Michael Klopman, telephone interview by Kavitha Davidson, August 23,
2018. Unless otherwise noted, related quotations are from this interview.

31. Leonard Shapiro and Mark Maske, "Snyder Approved as New Owner of
Redskins," *Washington Post*, May 26, 1999, washingtonpost.com/wp-srv/sports
/redskins/daily/may99/26/skinsbid26.htm.

32. Dave McKenna, "The Cranky Redskins Fan's Guide to Dan Snyder,"
Washington City Paper, November 19, 2010, washingtoncitypaper.com/new
s/article/13039846/the-cranky-redskins-fans-guide-to-dan-snyder. James V.
Grimaldi, "Washington Redskins React to Fans' Tough Luck with Tough Love,"
Washington Post, September 3, 2009, washingtonpost.com/wp-dyn/content
/article/2009/09/02/AR2009090203887.html.

33. Juliet Macur, "Washington Redskins Cheerleaders Describe Topless Photo Shoot and Uneasy Night Out," *New York Times*, May 2, 2018, nytimes .com/2018/05/02/sports/redskins-cheerleaders-nfl.html.

34. Dan Steinberg, "Redskins Owner Daniel Snyder Donated $1 Million to Trump's Inaugural Festivities," *Washington Post*, April 19, 2017, washingtonpost .com/news/dc-sports-bog/wp/2017/04/19/redskins-owner-daniel-snyder -donated-1-million-to-trumps-inaugural-festivities.

Chapter 10: How I Learned to Stop Worrying and Love Baseball's Free Market

1. Baseball Almanac (website), "Town Ball: The Rules of the Massachusetts Game," baseball-almanac.com/ruletown.shtml.

2. Debbie Schaefer-Jacobs, "Civil War Baseball," National Museum of American History, August 2, 2012, americanhistory.si.edu/blog/2012/08 /civil-war-baseball.html.

3. Steven M. Gelber, "'Their Hands Are All Out Playing': Business and Amateur Baseball, 1845–1917," *Journal of Sport History* 11, no. 1 (Spring 1984): 8.

4. Craig Brown, "Collusion and the No-Risk Free Agents of 1988," The Hardball Times, February 29, 2008, fangraphs.com/tht/collusion-and-the-no-risk -free-agents-of-1988.

5. Cliff Corcoran, "The Strike: Who Was Right, Who Was Wrong and How It Helped Baseball," *Sports Illustrated*, August 12, 2014, si.com/mlb/2014/08/12/1994 -strike-bud-selig-orel-hershiser.

6. Sean Gregory, "How Sotomayor 'Saved' Baseball," *Time*, Tuesday, May 26, 2009, content.time.com/time/nation/article/0,8599,1900974,00.html.

7. Baseball Prospectus, "CBA History," baseballprospectus.com /compensation/cots/league-info/cba-history.

8. Major League Baseball Players Association, 2017–2021 Basic Agreement, d39ba378-ae47-4003-86d3-147e4fa6e51b.filesusr.com/ugd/b0a4c2_958836906 27349e0a5203f61b93715b5.pdf.

9. For a list of 1994 MLB team payrolls, see *USA Today*, usatoday.com/sports /mlb/salaries/1994/team/all.

10. Spotrac (website), MLB Team Payroll Tracker, spotrac.com/mlb /payroll/2019.

11. Michael Haupert, "MLB's Annual Salary Leaders since 1874," Society for American Baseball Research, sabr.org/research/mlbs-annual-salary-leaders -1874-2012.

12. Haupert.

13. "The Business of Baseball," *Forbes*, April 10, 2019, forbes.com/mlb -valuations/list/#tab:overall.

14. Maury Brown, "MLB Sees Record $10.7 Billion in Revenues for 2019," *Forbes*, December 21, 2019, forbes.com/sites/maurybrown/2019/12/21/mlb -sees-record-107-billion-in-revenues-for-2019/#238efc8a5d78.

15. Ronald W. Cox and Daniel Skidmore-Hess, *Free Agency and Competitive Balance in Baseball* (Jefferson, NC: McFarland & Company, 2005).

16. "GM Cashman Says Yankees Losing Money," ESPN, August 22, 2006, espn.com/mlb/news/story?id=2557770.

17. Richard Sandomir, "Yankees' Yes Network Stake Not for Sale," *New York Times*, August 3, 2007, nytimes.com/2007/08/03/sports/baseball/03yes.html.

18. Baseball Prospectus, 2015 Kansas City Royals: Complete List of Player Salaries by Year (Default 2015), baseballprospectus.com/compensation /?team=KCA.

19. Spotrac, Oakland Athletics 2015 Payroll, spotrac.com/mlb/oakland -athletics/payroll/2015.

20. Nielsen, "Local Television Market Universe Estimates," September 28, 2019, nielsen.com/wp-content/uploads/sites/3/2019/09/2019-20-dma-ranker .pdf.

21. Baseball Prospectus, Yankees Payrolls, baseballprospectus.com /compensation/cots/al-east/new-york-yankees.

22. Baseball Prospectus, Mets Payrolls, baseballprospectus.com /compensation/cots/national-league/new-york-mets.

23. Howard Megdal, "New Sandy Alderson Book Offers Revealing View of Madoff-Impacted Mets," POLITICO, March 12, 2015, politico.com/media /story/2015/03/new-sandy-alderson-book-offers-revealing-view-of-madoff -impacted-mets-003561.

24. Josh Kosman, "New Loan Could End Mets Money Problems," *New York Post*, January 30, 2014, nypost.com/2014/01/30/new-loan-could-end-mets -money-problems.

25. Rodney Fort and James Quirk, "Cross-Subsidization, Incentives, and Outcomes in Professional Team Sports Leagues," *Journal of Economic Literature* 33, no. 3 (September 1995): 1174.

26. Corcoran, "The Strike."

Chapter 11: Doubling Down on Your March Madness Bracket Even If the Athletes Don't Make a Dime

1. Jane Porter, "5 Steps to Turn a Dorm-Room Startup into a Real-World Success," Inc.com, March 17, 2014, inc.com/jane-porter/from-college-startup -to-breakout-success-advice-from-modcloth-and-insomnia-cookies.html. "Dawn of Def Jam: Watch Rick Rubin Return to His NYU Dorm Room," *Rolling Stone*, October 16, 2014, rollingstone.com/music/music-news/dawn-of-def -jam-watch-rick-rubin-return-to-his-nyu-dorm-room-181208.

2. Andy Schwarz, telephone interview by Kavitha Davidson, March 28, 2018. Unless otherwise noted, related quotations are from this interview.

3. Ramogi Huma, telephone interview by Kavitha Davidson, March 30, 2018. Unless otherwise noted, related quotations are from this interview.

4. Jon Solomon, "Should College Players Be Paid? NCAA Files Vigorous Defense of Amateurism Through Leaders' Words," Al.com, December 13, 2013, al.com/sports/2013/12/ncaa_stages_vigorous_defense_o.html.

5. NCAA (tweet), @NCAA, twitter.com/NCAA/status/980124563353886720.

6. Jeff John Roberts, "Tech Workers Will Get an Average of $5,770 Under Final Anti-Poaching Settlement," *Fortune*, September 3, 2015, fortune .com/2015/09/03/koh-anti-poach-order.

7. Anthony Depalma, "Ivy Universities Deny Price-Fixing but Agree to Avoid

It in the Future," *New York Times*, May 23, 1991, nytimes.com/1991/05/23/us/ivy
-universities-deny-price-fixing-but-agree-to-avoid-it-in-the-future.html.

8. *Edward O'Bannon v. National Collegiate Athletic*, United States Court of Appeals for the Ninth Circuit, September 30, 2015, scotusblog.com/wp-content/uploads/2016/04/ncaa-op-below.pdf.

9. Michael McCann, "Breaking Down Implications of NLRB Ruling on Northwestern Players Union," *Sports Illustrated*, August 17, 2015, si.com/college/2015/08/17/northwestern-football-players-union-nlrb-ruling-analysis.

10. Memo GC 17-01, National Labor Relations Board, Office of the General Counsel Memorandum, to All Regional Directors, etc., from Richard F. Griffin Jr., General Counsel, January 31, 2017, re: General Counsel's Report on the Statutory Rights of University Faculty and Students in the Unfair Labor Practice Context, apps.nlrb.gov/link/document.aspx/09031d4582342bfc. National Labor Relations Board (website), "Interfering with Employee Rights," nlrb.gov/rights-we-protect/whats-law/employers/interfering-employee-rights-section-7-8a1.

11. Alexia Fernández Campbell, "Free Labor from College Athletes May Soon Come to an End," Vox, October 3, 2019, vox.com/identities/2019/10/3/20896738/california-fair-pay-to-play-act-college-athletes. Dan Murphy, "What California Bill Means for NCAA Image and Likeness Debate," ESPN, October 1, 2019, espn.com/college-football/story/_/id/27585301/what-california-bill-means-ncaa-image-likeness-debate. Ben Pickman, "NCAA Votes to Start Process Permitting Athletes to Benefit from Likeness," *Sports Illustrated*, October 29, 2019, si.com/college/2019/10/29/ncaa-student-athlete-likeness-permitted-vote.

12. Patrick Hruby, "Does Racial Resentment Fuel Opposition to Paying College Athletes?," Vice, March 7, 2017, vice.com/en_us/article/bmqdyq/does-racial-resentment-fuel-opposition-to-paying-college-athletes.

13. Kevin Wallsten, Tatishe M. Nteta, Lauren A. McCarthy, and Melinda R. Tarsi, "Prejudice or Principled Conservatism? Racial Resentment and White Opinion toward Paying College Athletes," *Political Research Quarterly* 70, no. 1, 209–222. Kevin Wallsten, Tatishe M. Nteta, and Lauren A. McCarthy, "Racial Prejudice Is Driving Opposition to Paying College Athletes. Here's the Evidence," *Washington Post*, December 30, 2015, washingtonpost.com/news/monkey-cage/wp/2015/12/30/race-affects-opinions-about-whether-college-athletes-should-be-paid-heres-how.

14. "Len Elmore's Closing Arguments on Paying College Athletes," The Shadow League, March 23, 2017, theshadowleague.com/len-elmore-s-closing-arguments-on-paying-college-athletes.

15. National Women's Law Center (website), "Title IX and Men's Sports: A False Conflict," August 2015, nwlc-ciw49tixgw5lbab.stackpathdns.com/wp-content/uploads/2015/08/title_ix_and_mens_sports_8.11.15.pdf.

16. Paul M. Barrett, "In Fake Classes Scandal, UNC Fails Its Athletes—and Whistle-blower," Bloomberg.com, February 27, 2014, bloomberg.com/news/articles/2014-02-27/in-fake-classes-scandal-unc-fails-its-athletes-whistle-blower.

17. Joe Nocera, "NCAA Proves Once Again It Doesn't Care about Classes,"

Bloomberg.com, October 13, 2017, bloomberg.com/opinion/articles/2017-10-13
/ncaa-proves-once-again-it-doesn-t-care-about-classes.

18. Dan Kane, "Deborah Crowder Says in Affidavit That UNC Paper Classes Were Legitimate," *News & Observer*, March 9, 2017, newsobserver.com/news/local/education/unc-scandal/article137575478.html.

19. Pat Forde and Pete Thamel, "Exclusive: Federal Documents Detail Sweeping Potential NCAA Violations Involving High-Profile Players, Schools," Yahoo! Sports, February 23, 2018, sports.yahoo.com/exclusive-federal-documents-detail-sweeping-potential-ncaa-violations-involving-high-profile-players-schools-103338484.html.

Chapter 12: Living with the New Stadium You Didn't Want to Pay For

1. Neil deMause, telephone interview by Kavitha Davidson, January 4, 2018. Unless otherwise noted, related quotations are from this interview.

2. Ted Gayer, Austin J. Drukker, and Alexander K. Gold, "Tax-Exempt Municipal Bonds and the Financing of Professional Sports Stadiums," Brookings Institution, September 2016, brookings.edu/wp-content/uploads/2016/09/gayerdrukkergold_stadiumsubsidies_090816.pdf.

3. Steven D. Zavodnick Jr., "If You (Pay To) Build It, They Will Come: Rethinking Publicly-financed Professional Sports Stadiums after the Atlanta Braves Deal with Cobb County," *Georgia Law Review* 53, no. 1 (2018): 407–441, georgialawreview.org/api/v1/articles/7517-if-you-pay-to-build-it-they-will-come-rethinking-publicly-financed-professional-sports-stadiums-after-the-atlanta-braves-deal-with-cobb-county.pdf.

4. "When Sports Teams Fleece Taxpayers," *The Week*, October 29, 2018, theweek.com/articles/803881/when-sports-teams-fleece-taxpayers.

5. Brad Humphreys, telephone interview by Kavitha Davidson, January 3, 2018. Unless otherwise noted, related quotations are from this interview.

6. Victor Matheson, telephone interview by Kavitha Davidson, January 3, 2018. Unless otherwise noted, related quotations are from this interview.

7. David Berri, telephone interview by Kavitha Davidson, January 3, 2018. Unless otherwise noted, related quotations are from this interview.

8. Adam Nagourney, "Messinger Opposes Helping Yankees Move to Manhattan," *New York Times*, October 17, 1997, nytimes.com/1997/10/17/nyregion/messinger-opposes-helping-yankees-move-to-manhattan.html.

9. Ed Lucas, "How Yankees Almost Ended Up in the Meadowlands," *Jersey Journal*, September 2, 2016, nj.com/hudson/2016/09/how_yankees_almost_ended_up_in_the_meadowlands_luc.html.

10. Allen Barra, "Yankee Stay Home," *New York* magazine, October 12, 1998, nymag.com/nymetro/news/sports/features/2860.

11. Vito Stellino, "Seahawks Defy League, Head for L.A.," *Baltimore Sun*, February 2, 1996, articles.baltimoresun.com/1996-02-02/sports/1996033039_1_seahawks-plan-to-move-slade-gorton.

12. Mark Maske and Leonard Shapiro, "Saints Could End Up in L.A.," *Washington Post*, October 27, 2005, washingtonpost.com/wp-dyn/content/article/2005/10/26/AR2005102602322.html.

13. Sam Mamudi and Matthew Futterman, "NFL's Jacksonville Jaguars Sold," *Wall Street Journal*, November 30, 2011, wsj.com/articles/SB10001424052970204449804577068521537649462.

14. John Harper, "Vikings' Gary Anderson Missed Field Goal in 1999 Opened the Way for the Falcons to Advance to Super Bowl," *New York Daily News*, January 16, 2016, nydailynews.com/sports/football/dan-falcons-heartreeves-gang-stuns-minny-article-1.835247.

15. Michael Khoo, "Metrodome Renovation Plan Gets Lukewarm Reception . . . Again," Minnesota Public Radio, December 18, 2001, news.minnesota.publicradio.org/features/200112/18_khoom_stadium.

16. Brandt Williams, "NFL Owners Approve Vikings Sale to Wilf," Minnesota Public Radio, May 25, 2005, news.minnesota.publicradio.org/features/2005/05/25_williamsb_vikingsale.

17. Kevin Duchschere, Rochelle Olson, and Steve Brandt, "Minneapolis Kicks Off $1 Billion Stadium 'Game Changer,'" *Star Tribune*, May 9, 2011, startribune.com/minneapolis-kicks-off-1-billion-stadium-game-changer/121518294.

18. Rochelle Olson, "Prospect of a Convention Center Shocks Vikings Stadium Watchers," *Star Tribune*, September 4, 2011, startribune.com/prospect-of-a-convention-center-shocks-stadium-watchers/129195898.

19. Baird Helgeson, "Vikings Told Arden Hills Not Workable," *Star Tribune*, January 9, 2012, startribune.com/vikings-told-arden-hills-site-not-workable-for-stadium/136884318.

20. David Bailey, "Minnesota Vikings Reach Tentative Minnesota Stadium Deal," Reuters, March 1, 2012, reuters.com/article/us-nfl-vikings-stadium/minnesota-vikings-reach-tentative-minnesota-stadium-deal-idUSTRE8201NR20120301.

21. Mike Kaszuba, "House Panel Vote Leaves Vikings Stadium Plan in Peril," *Star Tribune*, April 17, 2012, startribune.com/house-panel-vote-leaves-vikings-stadium-plan-in-peril/147631965.

22. "Goodell Meets with Minnesota Leaders to Push Vikings Stadium Vote," Reuters, April 20, 2012, chicagotribune.com/sports/ct-xpm-2012-04-20-sns-rt-fbn-dolphins-newssx994f3a1-20120420-story.html.

23. Steve Wyche, "Vikings to L.A.? Minnesota Stadium Situation Gets Serious," NFL.com, April 20, 2012, nfl.com/news/story/09000d5d8287ac31/article/vikings-to-la-minnesota-stadium-situation-gets-serious.

24. Vincent Bonsignore, "Bonsignore: LA Played a Role in Vikings' Staying in Minnesota," *Los Angeles Daily News*, November 8, 2015, dailynews.com/2015/11/08/bonsignore-la-played-a-role-in-vikings-staying-in-minnesota.

25. Vincent Bonsignore, "Private Plane Belonging to Minnesota Vikings Owner Zygi Wilf Spotted at Southern California Airport," *Los Angeles Daily News*, April 19, 2012, dailynews.com/2012/04/19/private-plane-belonging-to-minnesota-vikings-owner-zygi-wilf-spotted-at-southern-california-airport.

26. KSTP-TV-sponsored poll, "Where Should Vikings Play? Little Consensus in Minnesota," SurveyUSA, February 3, 2012, surveyusa.com/client/PollReport.aspx?g=5a67e54f-5eb1-4515-9662-b080012b50f8.

27. Noreen S. Ahmed-Ullah, "Soldier Field Loses Landmark Status," *Chicago*

Tribune, April 22, 2006, articles.chicagotribune.com/2006-04-22/news
/0604220145_1_historic-landmark-designation-soldier-field-blair-kamin.

28. Hal Dardick and David Mendell, "Stadium Has Lost Landmark Look,
U.S. Says," *Chicago Tribune*, July 21, 2004, chicagotribune.com/news
/chi-0407210322jul21-story.html.

29. Bennett, James T., *They Play, You Pay: Why Taxpayers Build Ballparks, Stadiums,
and Arenas for Billionaire Owners and Millionaire Players* (New York: Springer Science
+Business Media, 2012), 91.

30. "Urban Conversations: U.S. Mayors and Innovative Leadership," *Gotham
Gazette*, May 2, 2005, gothamgazette.com/open-government/2755-urban
-conversations-us-mayors-and-innovative-leadership.

31. Dennis Coates and Brad R. Humphreys, "Do Economists Reach a
Conclusion on Subsidies for Sports Franchises, Stadiums, and Mega-Events?,"
International Association of Sports Economists, Working Paper Series, Paper
No. 08-18, August 2008, college.holycross.edu/RePEc/spe/CoatesHumphreys
_LitReview.pdf.

32. Oren Yaniv, "Sneak Preview of New Yankee Stadium," *New York Daily
News*, February 8, 2008, nydailynews.com/sports/baseball/yankees/sneak
-preview-new-yankee-stadium-article-1.308158.

33. Elaine S. Povich, "Is Obama Proposal the End of Taxpayer-Subsidized
Sports Stadiums?," *USA Today*, March 16, 2015, usatoday.com/story/news
/politics/2015/03/16/stateline-obama-proposal-taxpayer-subsidized-sports
-stadiums/24845355.

34. Michael Oanian, "Is Baseball Really Broke?," *Forbes*, April 3, 2002,
forbes.com/2002/04/01/0401baseball.html#528c716b628d.

35. "Election Day: Arlington Passes Cowboys Stadium Financing," *SportsBusi-
ness Daily*, no. 37, November 3, 2004, is available on the Wayback Machine, web.
archive.org/web/20170212160437/sportsbusinessdaily.com/Daily/Issues
/2004/11/Issue-37/Facilities-Venues/Election-Day-Arlington-Passes-Cowboys
-Stadium-Financing.aspx.

The original URL for this citation (sportsbusinessdaily.com/Daily
/Issues/2004/11/Issue-37/Facilities-Venues/Election-Day-Arlington-Passes
-Cowboys-Stadium-Financing.aspx) no longer links to the article.

36. David Conn, "FC United of Manchester: The Success Story That Proves
What Fans Can Achieve," *The Guardian*, May 26, 2015, theguardian.com/football
/blog/2015/may/26/fc-united-manchester-benfica-united-fans.

Chapter 13: Enjoying the Olympics Despite the Harm to Your Community

1. Andy Bull, "Revealed: The Biggest Threat to the Future of the Olympic
Games," *The Guardian*, July 27, 2016, theguardian.com/sport/2016/jul/27/biggest
-threat-future-olympic-games-rio-2016-ioc-thomas-bach-hosts.

2. Jonathan Cohn and Robin Jacks, "The Boston Olympics Con Job," *The
Nation*, March 24, 2015, thenation.com/article/boston-olympics-con-job.

3. Rick Maese, "A New Olympics Reality: Fewer Cities Want to Host the
Games," *Washington Post*, May 8, 2017, washingtonpost.com/sports
/olympics/a-new-olympics-reality-fewer-cities-want-to-host-the

-games/2017/05/08/2411f720-33f5-11e7-b4ee-434b6d506b37_story.html.

4. Nick Zaccardi, "IOC Pushes Plan to Award 2024, 2028 Olympics to LA, Paris," NBC Sports, June 9, 2017, olympics.nbcsports.com/2017/06/09/los -angeles-paris-olympics-2024-2028. Jason Slotkin, "Dual Olympic Bids Approved for Paris and Los Angeles," NPR, September 13, 2017, npr.org/sections /thetwo-way/2017/09/13/550750891/dual-olympic-bids-approved-for-paris -and-los-angeles.

5. NOlympics LA (website), "Platform," nolympicsla.com/platform.

6. Graham Dunbar, "IOC to Change Process of Olympic Bidding," Associated Press, July 1, 2019, summitdaily.com/sports/ioc-to-change-process-of-olympic -bid-races-host-elections.

7. Nancy Armour, "Skyrocketing Costs Put Future Olympics at Risk," *USA Today*, May 23, 2017, usatoday.com/story/sports/columnist/nancy-armour /2017/05/23/ioc-international-olympic-committee-rio-skyrocketing-costs /102076808.

8. Travis Waldron (tweet), @Travis_Waldron, May 25, 2017, twitter.com /Travis_Waldron/status/867932522025537536.

9. Bruce Douglas, "World Cup leaves Brazil with Bus Depots and Empty Stadiums," BBC Sport, March 29, 2015, bbc.com/sport/football/32073525. Kenneth Rapoza, "Bringing FIFA to Brazil Equal to Roughly 61% of Education Budget," *Forbes*, June 11, 2014, forbes.com/sites/kenrapoza/2014/06/11/bringing-fifa -to-brazil-equal-to-roughly-61-of-education-budget/#2fca8cdb36d6.

10. Michael Powell, "In the Brazilian Rain Forest, 'a White Elephant, a Big One,'" *New York Times*, August 16, 2016, nytimes.com/2016/08/17/sports /manaus-brazil-amazon-rain-forest-stadium.html?_r=0.

11. "FIFA Returns $100M to Brazil; World Cup Cost $15 Billion," Associated Press/*USA Today*, January 20, 2015, usatoday.com/story/sports /soccer/2015/01/20/fifa-returns-100m-to-brazil-world-cup-cost-15 -billion/22050583.

12. Andrew Zimbalist, "Get Ready for a Massive World Cup Hangover, Brazil," *Time*, June 27, 2014, time.com/2930699/world-cup-brazil-spending.

13. Tony Manfred, "FIFA Made an Insane Amount of Money Off of Brazil's $15 Billion World Cup," *Business Insider*, March 20, 2015, businessinsider.com /fifa-brazil-world-cup-revenue-2015-3. "FIFA Returns $100M to Brazil; World Cup Cost $15 Billion," Associated Press/*USA Today*, January 20, 2015, usatoday .com/story/sports/soccer/2015/01/20/fifa-returns-100m-to-brazil-world-cup -cost-15-billion/22050583.

14. "AP Analysis: Rio de Janeiro Olympics Cost $13.1 Billion," Associated Press/*USA Today*, June 14, 2017, usatoday.com/story/sports/olympics/2017/06/14 /ap-analysis-rio-de-janeiro-olympics-cost-13-1-billion/102860310.

15. "In Rio, an Olympic Ghost Town," Associated Press, February 11, 2017, timesunion.com/sports/article/In-Rio-an-Olympic-ghost-town-10926075.php.

16. Tariq Panja, "Rio Olympics Can't Pay Debts, Offer Used Air-Con Units Instead," Bloomberg.com, April 6, 2017, bloomberg.com/news/articles /2017-04-06/rio-olympics-can-t-pay-debts-offers-used-air-con-units -instead.

17. Nick Butler, "Rio State Governor at Time of Olympic Bid Sentenced to 14 Years in Prison," Inside the Games, June 13, 2017, insidethegames.biz /articles/1051492/rio-state-governor-at-time-of-olympic-bid-sentenced-to -14-years-in-prison.

18. "Scathing Report on 2016 Rio Olympics: Venues 'White Elephants,'" Associated Press, May 22, 2017, usatoday.com/story/sports/olympics/2017/05/22 /scathing-report-on-rio-olympics-venues-white-elephants/102041926.

19. Andrew Zimbalist, ed., *Rio 2016: Olympic Myths, Hard Realities* (Washington, DC: Brookings Institution Press, 2017), 229, 231.

20. Jules Boykoff, telephone interview by Jessica Luther, February 5, 2017. Unless otherwise noted, related quotations are from this interview.

21. Paul Farhi, "Did the Winter Olympics in Sochi Really Cost $50 Billion? A Closer Look at That Figure," *Washington Post*, February 10, 2014, washingtonpost .com/lifestyle/style/did-the-winter-olympics-in-sochi-really-cost-50-billion -a-closer-look-at-that-figure/2014/02/10/a29e37b4-9260-11e3-b46a -5a3d0d2130da_story.html.

22. David Wharton, "2020 Tokyo Olympics Could Cost Japan More Than $26 Billion," *Los Angeles Times*, December 20 2019, latimes.com/sports/olympics/story /2019-12-20/2020-tokyo-olympics-could-cost-japan-more-than-26-billion.

23. Branch, John, "Who Is Polluting Rio's Bay?," *New York Times*, July 27, 2016, nytimes.com/interactive/2016/07/28/magazine/rio-sarapu-guanabara-bay -pollution.html.

24. Lulu Garcia-Navarro, "Far from Olympics, Violence Rises in Rio's Poorest Neighborhoods," August 15, 2016, npr.org/sections/thetorch/2016 /08/15/490099241/far-from-olympics-violence-rises-in-rios -poorest -neighborhoods.

25. Amnesty International, "Brazil: Spike in Killings by Rio Police as Country Faces UN Review," May 4, 2017, amnesty.org/en/latest/news/2017/05 /brazil-spike-in-killings-by-rio-police-as-country-faces-un-review.

26. Lindsay Beck, "Beijing to Evict 1.5 Million for Olympics: Group," Reuters, June 5, 2007, reuters.com/article/us-olympics-beijing-housing -idUSPEK12263220070605.

27. Jules Boykoff and Dave Zirin, "These Women Have Lost Their Homes to the Olympics in Tokyo—Twice," The Nation, July 23, 2019, thenation.com /article/tokyo-olympics-displacement.

28. Aaron Gordon, "The Rio Games Were an Unjustifiable Human Disaster, and So Are the Olympics," Vice Sports, August 22, 2016, vice.com/en_us/article /gvayg4/the-rio-games-were-an-unjustifiable-human-disaster-and-so-are -the-olympics.

29. Nicole Auerbach, "Athletes' Bus Gets Lost, Arrives at Swimming Venue Late," *USA Today*, August 12, 2016, usatoday.com/story/sports/olympics /rio-2016/2016/08/12/lost-bus-delays-womens-freestyle-semifinals/88654488.

30. World Anti-Doping Agency, "Report of the Independent Observers: Games of the XXXI Olympiad, Rio de Janerio 2016," October 26, 2016, wada-ama.org/sites/default/files/resources/files/rio2016_io_team _report_26102016.pdf.

31. Jules Boykoff, "Here We Go Again," Jacobin, February, 9, 2017, jacobinmag.com/2017/02/olympics-south-korea-corruption-environment.

32. Human Rights Watch, "Russia/FIFA: Workers Exploited on World Cup 2018 Stadiums," June 14, 2017, hrw.org/news/2017/06/14/russia/fifa-workers -exploited-world-cup-2018-stadiums.

33. Amnesty International, "Qatar World Cup of Shame," amnesty.org/en /latest/campaigns/2016/03/qatar-world-cup-of-shame.

34. FIFA, "FIFA Womens' World Cup France 2019: Global Broadcast and Audience Report," img.fifa.com/image/upload/rvgxekduqpeo1ptbgcng.pdf. Scott Roxborough, "Rio Olympics Worldwide Audience to Top 3.5 Billion, IOC Estimates," *Hollywood Reporter*, August 18, 2016, hollywoodreporter.com/news /rio-olympics-worldwide-audience-top-920526.

35. US Department of State, Bureau of Educational and Cultural Affairs (website), "Global Sports Mentoring Program," eca.state.gov/programs-initiatives /sports-diplomacy/global-sports-mentoring-program. See also, generally, globalsportsmentoring.org.

36. Evan Davis, "Moya Dodd Has a Radical Idea for FIFA Reform: Include Women," Vice Sports, February 10, 2016, sports.vice.com/en_us/article /moya-dodd-has-a-radical-idea-for-fifa-reform-include-women.

37. Moya Dodd, telephone interview by Jessica Luther, February 22, 2017. Unless otherwise noted, related quotations are from this interview.

38. Katja Iversen, "Why You Should Think Twice about Ignoring Women's Sports," *New York Times*, July 9, 2015, nytlive.nytimes.com/womenintheworld /2015/07/09/why-you-should-think-twice-about-ignoring-womens-sports. Xanthe Ackerman and Christina Asquith, "Soccer Is Still Out of Reach for Half the World's Women," *Time*, July 8, 2015, time.com/3949377/world-cup -women-global-equality.

39. Eamonn Tiernan, "Australian Women's Rugby Sevens Program Gets Huge Funding Increase after Rio Gold," *Canberra Times*, June 9, 2017, canberratimes.com.au/sport/act-sport/australian-womens-rugby-sevens -program-gets-huge-funding-increase-after-rio-gold-20170609-gwo266.html.

40. International Olympic Committee (website), "Olympic Charter," June 26, 2019 (at page 90), stillmed.olympic.org/media/Document%20Library /OlympicOrg/General/EN-Olympic-Charter.pdf. See also Olympic.org, "Rule 50 Guidelines Developed by the IOC Athletes' Commission," January 2020, olympic.org/-/media/Document%20Library/OlympicOrg/News/2020/01/Rule -50-Guidelines-Tokyo-2020.pdf.

41. Laurence Halsted, telephone interview by Jessica Luther, September 15, 2017. Unless otherwise noted, related quotations are from this interview. Laurence Halsted, "Olympic Athletes Must Exercise Their Right to Speak Beyond Their Sport," *The Guardian*, May 19, 2016, theguardian.com/sport/blog/2016 /may/19/olympic-athletes-speak-out-politics-social-issues-laurence-halsted -fencer-rio-games.

Chapter 14: Embracing That Athletes—and Sports—Are Political

1. Jennifer Lee Chan (tweet), @jenniferleechan, August 26, 2016, twitter
.com/jenniferleechan/status/769354272735531009.

2. Steve Wyche, "Colin Kaepernick Explains Why He Sat During National
Anthem," NFL.com, August 27, 2016, nfl.com/news/story/0ap3000000691077
/article/colin-kaepernick-explains-why-he-sat-during-national-anthem.

3. Mark Sandritter, "A Timeline of Colin Kaepernick's National Anthem
Protest and the Athletes Who Joined Him," SBNation, September 25, 2017,
sbnation.com/2016/9/11/12869726/colin-kaepernick-national-anthem
-protest-seahawks-brandon-marshall-nfl. Lindsay Gibbs, "One Man Started
a Movement: Tracking the Kaepernick Effect," ThinkProgress, September 26,
2017, thinkprogress.org/kaepernick-effect-database-b2f50ca7277f.

4. Sean Sullivan, "Trump Slams Colin Kaepernick: 'Maybe he should find a
country that works better for him,'" *Washington Post*, August 29, 2016,
washingtonpost.com/news/post-politics/wp/2016/08/29/trump-slams
-colin-kaepernick-maybe-he-should-find-a-country-that-works-better-for
-him/?utm_term=.8b4bf44e37c3. Bryan Armen Graham, "Donald Trump Blasts
NFL Anthem Protesters: 'Get that son of a bitch off the field,'" *The Guardian*, September 23, 2017, theguardian.com/sport/2017/sep/22/donald-trump-nfl
-national-anthem-protests.

5. Ahiza Garcia, "Colin Kaepernick's Jersey Is Top Seller after Protest," CNN,
September 6, 2016, money.cnn.com/2016/09/06/news/companies
/colin-kaepernick-jersey-nfl/index.html. Cindy Boren, "Colin Kaepernick
Protest Has 49ers Fans Burning Their Jerseys," *Washington Post*, August 28, 2016,
washingtonpost.com/news/early-lead/wp/2016/08/28/colin-kaepernick
-protest-has-49ers-fans-burning-their-jerseys/?utm_term=.270841d0cd0d.
Jesse Washington, "The NFL Is Being Squeezed by Boycotts from Both Sides
Over Anthem Protests," The Undefeated, September 13, 2017, theundefeated
.com/features/nfl-boycotts-from-both-sides-over-anthem-protests. MMQB,
"The Fans Who Say They're Walking Away from the NFL," *Sports Illustrated*, September 27, 2017, si.com/nfl/2017/09/26/themmqb-nfl-fans-stopped-watch
ing-colin-kaepernick-anthem-protests-donald-trump-nfl-ratings. Jenna West,
"South Florida Police Asked Not to Buy Dolphins Tickets after Players Protest
During Anthem," *Sports Illustrated*, August 11, 2018, si.com/nfl/2018/08/11
/south-florida-police-tickets-players-protest-anthem-dolphins.

6. David Fucillo, "Here Is a List of Every Organization to Which Colin
Kaepernick Donated Money," SBNation, January 31, 2018, ninersnation.
com/2018/1/31/16956016/colin-kaepernick-donations-full-list-of-organizations
-one-million-dollars. Know Your Rights Camp (website), "About,"
knowyourrightscamp.com/about. Bomani Jones, "Kaepernick Sacrificed His
Career—What More Do People Want?," The Undefeated, February 20, 2019,
theundefeated.com/features/kaepernick-sacrificed-his-career-what-more
-do-people-want. Alex Abad-Santos, "Nike's Colin Kaepernick Ad Sparked
a Boycott—And Earned $6 Billion for Nike," Vox, September 24, 2018,
vox.com/2018/9/24/17895704/nike-colin-kaepernick-boycott-6-billion.

7. Michael Serazio and Emily Thorson, "Sports Were Already Politicized. And

Sports Culture Is Deeply Conservative," *Washington Post*, October 2, 2017, washingtonpost.com/news/posteverything/wp/2017/10/02/sports-were -already-politicized-and-sports-culture-is-deeply-conservative.

8. Amira Rose Davis, telephone interview by Jessica Luther, December 17, 2018. Unless otherwise noted, related quotations are from this interview.

9. "A Letter from Jackie Robinson: Civil Rights Advocate," National Archives, archives.gov/exhibits/featured-documents/jackie-robinson. Robert Lipsyte, "Muhammad Ali Dies at 74: Titan of Boxing and the 20th Century," *New York Times*, June 4, 2016, nytimes.com/2016/06/04/sports/muhammad-ali-dies .html. DeNeen L. Brown, "'A cry for freedom': The Black Power Salute That Rocked the World 50 Years Ago," *Washington Post*, October 16, 2018, washingtonpost.com/history/2018/10/16/a-cry-freedom-black-power-salute -that-rocked-world-years-ago. "Billie Jean King: Biography," billiejeanking. com/biography. "Venus Vs.," part of ESPN's *Nine for IX* documentary series, directed by Ava Duvernay, 2013.

10. Amira Rose Davis, telephone interview by Jessica Luther, December 17, 2018. Unless otherwise noted, related quotations are from this interview. For more, see Dave Zirin, "Uncovering the Hidden Resistance History of Black Women Athletes," *The Nation*, May 21, 2018, thenation.com/article/uncovering -the-hidden-resistance-history-of-black-women-athletes. Amira Rose Davis, "Sixty Years Ago She Refused to Stand for the Anthem," *Zora*, September 26, 2019, zora.medium.com/sixty-years-ago-she-refused-to-stand-for-the -anthem-cf443b4e75c7.

11. Damola Durosomo, "The Dashiki: The History of a Radical Garment," OkayAfrica, May 28, 2017, okayafrica.com/history-politics-dashiki. Ira Berkow, "The Case of Hodges vs. the N.B.A.," *New York Times*, December 25, 1996, nytimes.com/1996/12/25/sports/the-case-of-hodges-vs-the-nba.html. Ben Joravsky, "Did the NBA Blacklist Former Chicago Bulls Player Craig Hodges Because of His Political Beliefs?," *Chicago Reader*, December 14, 2016, chicagoreader.com/chicago/craig-hodges-bulls-blacklisted-nba-long-shot -book-politics/Content?oid=24671704.

12. Toni Smith-Thompson, telephone interview by Jessica Luther, December 6, 2018. Unless otherwise noted, related quotations are from this interview.

13. Bill Pennington, "Player's Protest Over the Flag Divides Fans," *New York Times*, February 26, 2003, nytimes.com/2003/02/26/sports/college-basketball -player-s-protest-over-the-flag-divides-fans.html.

14. Jemele Hill, "The Heat's Hoodies as Change Agent," ESPN.com, March 26, 2012, espn.com/espn/commentary/story/_/page/hill-120326/lebron-james -other-athletes-protest-trayvon-martin-shooting-show-change-agent-power -sports.

15. Chris Strauss, "Rams Players Come Out with Hands Up in Pregame Intros," *USA Today*, November 30, 2014, ftw.usatoday.com/2014/11/rams-hands -up-pregame. Chris Strauss and Nate Scott, "LeBron James, Kyrie Irving and Nets Players Wear 'I Can't Breathe' Shirts Before Cavs Game," *USA Today*, December 8, 2014, ftw.usatoday.com/2014/12/kyrie-irving-i-cant-breathe-t -shirt-before-cavaliers-eric-garner-lebron-james. Ben Candea, "Pro Athletes

Don 'I Can't Breathe' Shirts in Support of Eric Garner Protesters," ABC News, December 8, 2014, abcnews.go.com/Sports/pro-athletes-don-breathe-shirts -support-eric-garner/story?id=27437509.

16. Kate Briquelet, "How Mizzou Football Sacked President Over Racism on Campus," *Daily Beast*, November 10, 2015, thedailybeast.com/how-mizzou -football-sacked-president-over-racism-on-campus.

17. Jeremy Bembry, "Athletes Passing on Visiting the White House Is Nothing New," The Undefeated, Feb. 6, 2018, theundefeated.com/features/athletes -passing-on-visiting-the-white-house-is-nothing-new-philadelphia-eagles. Jon Terbush, "18 Athletes Who Refused to Visit the White House," *The Week*, August 21, 2013, theweek.com/articles/460872/18-athletes-who-refused-visit -white-house.

18. Dave Zirin, "Interview with Ariyana Smith: The First Athlete Activist of #BlackLivesMatter," *The Nation*, December 19, 2014, thenation.com/article /interview-ariyana-smith-first-athlete-activist-blacklivesmatter.

19. Christina Cauterucci, "The WNBA's Black Lives Matter Protest Has Set a New Standard for Sports Activism," *Slate*, July 25, 2016, slate.com/human -interest/2016/07/the-wnbas-black-lives-matter-protest-has-set-new -standard-for-sports-activism.html.

20. Kenneth Cohen, "The Forgotten Origins of Politics in Sports," *Slate*, January 2, 2018, slate.com/news-and-politics/2018/01/americans-have-mixed -sports-and-politics-for-longer-than-you-think.html. Noah Weiland, "Trump Declines First Pitch on Opening Day, Throwing Ritual a Curveball," *New York Times*, April 3, 2017, nytimes.com/2017/04/03/us/politics/first-pitch-baseball -trump-nationals.html. Clay Skipper and Jay Willis, "The Oral History of President Barack Obama Playing Pickup Basketball," *GQ*, January 19, 2017, gq.com /story/obama-basketball-oral-history. David Jackson, "Facing Iran and Impeachment, Donald Trump Reaches Out to Supporters at LSU-Clemson Game," *USA Today*, January 13, 2020, usatoday.com/story/news/politics/2020/01/13 /facing-iran-and-impeachment-donald-trump-attend-lsu-clemson -game/2832629001. Nicholas D. Kristoff, "The 2000 Campaign: Breaking into Baseball; Road to Politics Ran Through a Texas Ballpark," *New York Times*, September 24, 2000, nytimes.com/2000/09/24/us/2000-campaign-breaking -into-baseball-road-politics-ran-through-texas-ballpark.html.

21. Chris Heller, "The Impossible Fight Against America's Stadiums," *Pacific Standard*, September 2, 2015, psmag.com/economics/the-shady-money -behind-americas-sports-stadiums.

22. "Football Protest Stokes Row with Russia," Spiegel Online, October 2, 2013, spiegel.de/international/europe/greenpeace-activists-protest-with -banner-at-champions-league-game-a-925730.html. "Ferguson Protesters Hold Up Banner at Monday Night Football Game Between 49ers, Rams," Associated Press, October 13, 2014, sanfrancisco.cbslocal.com/2014/10/13 /ferguson-protesters-hold-banner-briefly-at-monday-night-football-game -between-san-francisco-49ers-saint-louis-rams-michael-brown-fatal -officer-involved-shooting-darren-wilson-police. Alex Johnson, "'Monday Night Football' Protest: Anti-Fracking Banner Unfurled in Stadium," NBC News,

November 2, 2015, nbcnews.com/news/us-news/monday-night-football -protest-anti-fracking-banner-unfurled-stadium-n456261. Amie Ferris-Rotman, "'Let us be free': Iranian Women Mount Protest Over Stadium Ban at World Cup Match," *Washington Post*, June 15, 2018, washingtonpost.com/world /europe/let-us-be-free-iranian-women-mount-protest-over-stadium-ban-at -world-cup-match/2018/06/15/9755ddle-6fdb-11e8-b4d8-eaf78d4c544c_story .html?utm_term=.d86a6e136b66. Cindy Boren, "Transgender Rights Activists Unfurl Giant Banner During World Series: 'Trans people deserve to live,'" *Washington Post*, October 29, 2018, washingtonpost.com/sports/2018/10/29 /transgender-rights-activists-unfurl-giant-banner-during-world-series -trans-people-deserve-live/?utm_term=.bfc06c91a2c7.

23. Masha Gessen, "World Cup 2018: The Moral Clarity of Pussy Riot's Protest," *New Yorker*, July 15, 2018, newyorker.com/sports/replay/world-cup-2018 -the-moral-clarity-of-pussy-riots-protest.

24. Amira Rose Davis, "Black Athletes, Anthem Protests, and the Spectacle of Patriotism," *Black Perspectives*, June 7, 2018, aaihs.org/black-athletes-anthem -protests-and-the-spectacle-of-patriotism.

25. Emma Ockerman, "What Happened When Hitler Hosted the Olympics 80 Years Ago," *Time*, August 1, 2016, time.com/4432857/hitler-hosted -olympics-1936. Olympic.org, "Snapped: The Moment That Proved Miracles Do Happen," February 22, 2019, olympic.org/news/snapped-the-moment -that-proved-miracles-do-happen. Andrew Glass, "President Carter Orders an Olympic Boycott, March 21, 1980," POLITICO, March 21, 2017, politico.com /story/2017/03/president-carter-orders-an-olympic-boycott -march-21-1980-236185. Dusko Doder, "Soviets Withdraw from Los Angeles Olympics," *Washington Post*, May 9, 1984, washingtonpost.com/archive/politics /1984/05/09/soviets-withdraw-from-los-angeles-olympics/027363e6-4d89 -4dd9-b0d7-89a05a567f11/?utm_term=.fd110cfc3511.

26. Howard Bryant, telephone interview by Jessica Luther, December 19, 2018. Unless otherwise noted, related quotations are from this interview.

27. Cindy Boren, "Report: At Least 50 Teams Were Paid by Department of Defense for Patriotic Displays," *Washington Post*, November 4, 2015, washingtonpost .com/news/early-lead/wp/2015/11/04/report-at-least-50-teams-were-paid-by -department-of-defense-for-patriotic-displays/?utm_term=.3b65f8473b89.

28. Billy Witz, "Kneeling During the Anthem at Ole Miss: 'I Needed to Stand Up for My Rights,'" *New York Times*, February 27, 2019, nytimes.com/2019/02/27 /sports/ole-miss-kneeling.html. Jacob Bogage, "Mississippi Basketball Players Kneel in Protest During Anthem as Confederate Groups Rally in Oxford," *Washington Post*, February 23, 2019, washingtonpost.com/sports/2019/02/23 /mississippi-basketball-players-kneel-during-national-anthem-confederate -groups-rally-oxford/?utm_term=.c9922102c38a.

29. Lindsay Gibbs, "Wisconsin Basketball Star Has No Plans to Stop Protesting Racism During the National Anthem," ThinkProgress, February 2, 2019, thinkprogress.org/marsha-howard-protest-racism-anthem-8b882ba0c7db.

30. Jeremy Sharon, "Jewish Students 'Take a Knee' During Hatikva in Support of Palestinians," *Jerusalem Post*, November 14, 2018, jpost.com/Diaspora

/Jewish-students-take-a-knee-during-Hatikva-in-support-of-Palestinans
-571921.

31. Race Imboden (tweet), @Race_Imboden, August 9, 2019, twitter.com
/Race_Imboden/status/1159988039902466049.

32. Nancy Armour, "US Fencer, Hammer Thrower Show Principles with
Podium Protests at Pan American Games," *USA Today*, August 10, 2019, usatoday
.com/story/sports/columnist/nancy-armour/2019/08/10/pan-american-games
-us-fencer-race-imboden-kneels-national-anthem/1976426001.

33. Olympic.org (website), "Rule 50 Guidelines Developed by the IOC Athletes' Commission," January 2020, olympic.org/-/media/Document%20Library
/OlympicOrg/News/2020/01/Rule-50-Guidelines-Tokyo-2020.pdf. Henry Bushnell, "The IOC's Own History Makes Its New Olympic Protest Policy Problematic," Yahoo! Sports, January 10, 2020, sports.yahoo.com/how-a-2016-olympic
-controversy-exposes-the-io-cs-new-protest-policy-as-problematic
-232814904.html.

34. Howard Bryant, "A Protest Divided," *ESPN The Magazine*, February 5, 2018,
espn.com/espn/feature/story/_/page/enterpriseCoalition180126/colin
-kaepernick-movement-endures-supporters-more-fragmented-ever. Ronda
Racha Penrice, "The Players Coalition Continues Its Social Justice Work as the
NFL Season Ends," NBC News, February 4, 2019, nbcnews.com/news/nbcblk
/players-coalition-continues-its-social-justice-work-nfl-season-ends-n966006.

35. Chuck Modi (tweet), @ChuckModi1, August 11, 2019, twitter.com
/ChuckModi1/status/1160615613410217986, twitter.com/ChuckModi1
/status/1160613531819171842 and twitter.com/ChuckModi1/status
/1160606535116087298.

36. Des Bieler, "LeBron James and Kevin Durant Discuss How Trump
Doesn't 'Give a F— about the People,'" *Washington Post*, February 16, 2018,
washingtonpost.com/news/early-lead/wp/2018/02/16/lebron-james-and
-kevin-durant-discuss-how-trump-doesnt-give-a-f-about-the-people
/?utm_term=.b70fb643a1ad.

37. Emily Sullivan, "Laura Ingraham Told LeBron James to Shut Up and
Dribble; He Went to the Hoop," NPR, February 19, 2018, npr.org/sections
/thetwo-way/2018/02/19/587097707/laura-ingraham-told-lebron-james
-to-shutup-and-dribble-he-went-to-the-hoop.

38. "Shut Up and Dribble," Showtime, sho.com/shut-up-and-dribble.

Conclusion

1. Megan Rapinoe, "Why I Am Kneeling," *The Players' Tribune*, October 6, 2016,
theplayerstribune.com/en-us/articles/megan-rapinoe-why-i-am-kneeling.

2. Steven Goff, "Megan Rapinoe Doesn't Get Chance to Kneel for National
Anthem. It Was Played with Teams in Locker Room," *Washington Post*, September
7, 2016, washingtonpost.com/news/soccer-insider/wp/2016/09/07/megan
-rapinoe-doesnt-get-chance-to-kneel-for-national-anthem-it-was-played
-with-teams-in-locker-room/?utm_term=.9f3c4c691069. Kim McCauley, "U.S.
Soccer Institutes Policy Requiring Players to 'Stand Respectfully During the
Playing of National Anthems,'" SBNation, March 4, 2017, sbnation.com/soccer

/2017/3/4/14815760/us-soccer-national-anthem-policy-megan-rapinoe
-protest.

3. Lee Moran, "Here's Why Megan Rapinoe Is Protesting During the National Anthem at the World Cup," *HuffPost*, June 18, 2019, huffpost.com/entry /megan-rapinoe-world-cup-anthem-protest_n_5d0895f2e4b0886dd15e3d2b.

4. Eight by Eight (tweet), @8by8mag, June 25, 2019, twitter.com/8by8mag /status/1143595809910530048. Jenny Vrentas, "Megan Rapinoe Will Be Heard," *Sports Illustrated*, May 29, 2019, si.com/soccer/2019/05/29/megan-rapinoe-usa -womens-world-cup-uswnt-voice.

5. Kyle Smith, "Megan Rapinoe Wrongly Thinks She's a Preacher—Not a Player," *New York Post*, July 13, 2019, nypost.com/2019/07/13/megan-rapinoe -wrongly-thinks-shes-a-preacher-not-a-player.

INDEX